Aviation Leadership

This book identifies the responsibilities of management in the regulatory territories of the FAA (USA), the EASA (European Union) and the GCAA (UAE), identifying the daily challenges of leadership in ensuring their company is meeting the regulatory obligations of compliance, safety and security that will satisfy the regulator while also meeting the fiducial responsibilities of running an economically viable and efficient lean company that will satisfy the shareholders.

Detailing each responsibility of the Accountable Manager, the author breaks them down to understandable and achievable elements where methods, systems and techniques can be applied to ensure the role holder is knowledgeable of accountabilities and is confident that they are not only compliant with the civil aviation regulations but also running an efficient and effective operation. This includes the defining of an Accountable Manager "tool kit" as well as possible software "dashboards" that focus the Accountable Manager on the important analytics, such as the information and data available, as well as making the maximum use of their expert post holder team.

This book will be of interest to leadership of all aviation-related companies, such as airlines, charter operators, private and executive operators, flying schools, aircraft and component maintenance facilities, aircraft manufacturers, engine manufacturers, component manufacturers, regulators, legal companies, leasing companies, banks and finance houses, departments of transport, etc; any relevant organisation regulated and licensed by civil aviation authority. It can also be used by students within a wide range of aviation courses at colleges, universities and training academies.

Mark J. Pierotti has a PhD in Aircraft Engineering from City University, an MBA from Edinburgh Business School and is a Fellow of the Royal Aeronautical Society. He also holds an aircraft maintenance license and a private pilot's license. He has held senior executive positions in airlines and aviation companies having been both a Post Holder and an Accountable Manager. Dr Pierotti is also an adjunct Professor at USW, UWS and ADU lecturing in aviation and leadership subjects.

Managing Aviation Operations
Series Editor: Peter J. Bruce
Associate Editor: John M. C. King

The purpose of this series is to provide a comprehensive set of materials dealing with the key components of airline and airport operations. To date, this innovative approach has not been evident among aviation topics and certainly not applied to operational areas of airlines or airports. While more recent works have begun, in brief, to consider the various characteristics of operational areas, the Managing Aviation Operations series will expand coverage with far greater breadth and depth of content.

Airlines and airports are devoid of specific topic knowledge in ready-made, easy-to-read, creditable resources. Tapping into industry expertise to drive a range of key niche products will resource the industry in a way not yet seen in this domain. Therefore, the objective is to deliver a collection of specialised, internationally sourced and expertly written books to serve as readily accessible guides and references primarily for professionals within the industry. The focus of the series editors will be to ensure product quality, user readability and appeal, and transparent consistency across the range.

Managing Airline Networks
Design, Integration and Innovative Technologies
Markus Franke

Airline Governance
The Right Direction
Victor Hughes

Airline Operations Control
Peter J. Bruce and Chris Mulholland

Aviation Leadership
The Accountable Manager
Mark J. Pierotti

For more information about this series, please visit: www.routledge.com/Aviation-Fundamentals/book-series/MAO

Aviation Leadership
The Accountable Manager

Mark J. Pierotti

LONDON AND NEW YORK

First published 2022
by Routledge
2 Park Square, Milton Park, Abingdon, Oxon OX14 4RN

and by Routledge
605 Third Avenue, New York, NY 10158

Routledge is an imprint of the Taylor & Francis Group, an informa business

© 2022 Mark J. Pierotti

The right of Mark J. Pierotti to be identified as author of this work has been asserted in accordance with sections 77 and 78 of the Copyright, Designs and Patents Act 1988.

All rights reserved. No part of this book may be reprinted or reproduced or utilised in any form or by any electronic, mechanical, or other means, now known or hereafter invented, including photocopying and recording, or in any information storage or retrieval system, without permission in writing from the publishers.

Trademark notice: Product or corporate names may be trademarks or registered trademarks, and are used only for identification and explanation without intent to infringe.

British Library Cataloguing-in-Publication Data
A catalogue record for this book is available from the British Library

Library of Congress Cataloging-in-Publication Data
Names: Pierotti, Mark J., author.
Title: Aviation leadership : the accountable manager / Mark J. Pierotti.
Description: Milton Park, Abingdon, Oxon ; New York, NY : Routledge, 2022. | Includes bibliographical references and index.
Identifiers: LCCN 2021030461 (print) | LCCN 2021030462 (ebook) | ISBN 9780367556846 (hardback) | ISBN 9780367556822 (paperback) | ISBN 9781003094685 (ebook)
Subjects: LCSH: Aircraft industry–Management.
Classification: LCC HD9711.A2 P54 2022 (print) | LCC HD9711.A2 (ebook) | DDC 387.7/068–dc23
LC record available at https://lccn.loc.gov/2021030461
LC ebook record available at https://lccn.loc.gov/2021030462

ISBN: 978-0-367-55684-6 (hbk)
ISBN: 978-0-367-55682-2 (pbk)
ISBN: 978-1-003-09468-5 (ebk)

DOI: 10.4324/9781003094685

Typeset in Bembo
by Newgen Publishing UK

Aviation has filled my life with adventure and learning, but my family has more so.

This book is for my children Marco, Luke, Iona, Kristian, Hannah and my wonder wife Sacira.

Contents

List of figures x
List of tables xi
About the author xii
Acknowledgements xiii

Introduction 1

1 An introduction to civil aviation, the regulations and air law 3
   The Chicago Convention and the International Civil Aviation Organization 3
   The Articles, Annexes and Standards and Recommended Procedures of the Chicago Convention 5
   The National and Civil Aviation Authorities 8
   US Federal Aviation Regulations, EASA Regulations and the UAE Civil Aviation Regulations 13
   Safety management and the civil aviation regulations 20

2 An introduction to the Accountable Manager 24
   Civil aviation regulatory responsibilities 26
   The quality management system 36
   The safety management system 40
   Occupational and environmental safety and health programme 45
   The Accountable Manager and their relationship with the NAA 46
   Fiduciary corporate responsibilities 53
   Corporate leadership 54
   Financial leadership 56
   Reporting to the board 59

3 Leadership of the Post Holders 66
An introduction to the Nominated Persons, Nominated Post Holders and Management Personnel 66
The relationship between the Accountable Manager and the Post Holders 73

4 Organisational structures in a civil aviation company 79
A correct organisational structure and why 79
A wrong organisational structure and why 82
The job description of the Accountable Manager 84

5 Ethical leadership and the Accountable Manager 90
The passengers 90
The employees 90
The environment 91

6 A tool kit and SOPs for the Accountable Manager 96
Civil aviation regulatory accountability 96
Fiduciary accountability 97
The Accountable Manager's tool kit 97
A preparation guide for the NAA Accountable Manager interview 97
A timetable of meetings for the Accountable Manager 99
A dashboard of information for the Accountable Manager 107

7 How to select an effective Accountable Manager 113

8 Female Accountable Managers and the added challenges 118
Workplace climate/culture 120
Mentors and role models 120
Male resistance 121
Leadership traits 123
Fulfilment 123

9 A lawyer's review of the Accountable Managers responsibilities 127
Introduction 127
Legal framework 128
A manager's corporate responsibility 129
Airline or operator liability 131
Regulatory considerations 132
Operational matters 134
Instances of Accountable Manager issues 135
Conclusion 138

10 Case studies of Accountable Manager challenges   140
Case study 1: Funding safety training or a marketing campaign 140
Case study 2: Conducting commercial operations on a private category aircraft 141
Case study 3: Adjusting pilot duty time to allow for the arrival of a VIP 143
Case study 4: Imposing on the PH Continuing Airworthiness not to report an AD overrun 144
Case study 5: Maximising airline crew utilisation without affecting the safety or compromising compliance 145
Case study 6: The CEO attempts to impose a Post Holder appointment on the Accountable Manager 145
Case study 7: When a board member imposes a pilot's selection on the Accountable Manager 146
Case study 8: When the CAA told the new AM that the PH Quality was just not competent enough 147
Case study 9: A board instructed the CEO/AM to incentivise maximum utilisation by minimum turnaround time, with a company target turnaround time of 30 minutes 148
Case study 10: A CEO/AM of an MRO reduces certifying LAE head count to cut salary costs 150
Case study 11: Serving plastic bottles of water on board 151

Summary	153
Glossary	156
Index	171

Figures

1.1	The structure of the ICAO Annexes and their responsibilities	10
1.2	A cascading structure of the Chicago Convention Annexes to NAA civil aviation regulations	15
1.3	The EASA basic regulation structure	18
1.4	The structure of GCAA CARs	21
2.1	Canadian TC Accountable Executive compliance statement	31
2.2	EASA AM and NP organisational structure	34
2.3	FAA AE and Management Personnel organisational structure	34
2.4	GCAA AM and NPH organisational structure	35
2.5	An EASA or GCAA company quality policy statement signed by the Accountable Manager	38
2.6	An FAA company safety policy statement signed by the Accountable Executive	43
2.7	An EASA or GCAA company safety policy statement signed by the Accountable Manager	44
2.8	A company safety and health policy statement signed by the CEO and Accountable Manager	47
2.9	The triangle of authority when the CEO is the Accountable Manager	60
2.10	The triangle of authority when the CEO is not the Accountable Manager	60
4.1	Organisation structure 1 for an EASA EU 965/2012 AOC	80
4.2	Organisation structure 2 for an EASA EU 965/2012 AOC	81
4.3	Organisation structure 3: A wrong structure for an EASA EU 965/ 2012 AOC	83
4.4	Organisation structure 4: A wrong structure for an EASA EU 965/ 2012 AOC	85
6.1	An operations dashboard for the Accountable Manager	108
6.2	A technical dashboard for the Accountable Manager	109
6.3	A safety dashboard for the Accountable Manager	110
6.4	A quality/compliance dashboard for the Accountable Manager	110
6.5	A commercial/financial dashboard for the Accountable Manager	111
7.1	An Accountable Manager/executive selection flow chart	115
7.2	An Accountable Manager/executive selection question list	116

Tables

1.1	Important and relevant FAA FAR Parts	16
1.2	Examples of aircraft types that hold an FAA Type Certificate	17
1.3	Important and relevant EASA Parts and CSs	19
1.4	Important and relevant GCAA CAR Parts	22
2.1	Objectives of the CEO vs the CFO	59
3.1	EASA, GCAA, FAA Nominated Persons, Post Holders and management positions	72
4.1	A job description for the Accountable Manager	86
6.1	A preparation guide for the Accountable Manager NAA interview	100
6.2	A timetable of regulatory meetings for the Accountable Manager	102
6.3	A timetable of fiduciary meetings for the Accountable Manager	106

About the author

Dr Mark J. Pierotti MBA, PhD, FRAeS, IEng, as a Scottish Italian 18-year-old, started in the aviation industry in 1986 as a student trainee aircraft engineer with British Airways in London and Glasgow. After completing his initial training, he went on to work with Garuda Airlines in Indonesia, Shannon Aerospace in Ireland, Emirates Airlines, followed by The Presidential Flight of Abu Dhabi, AJA Private Jets and Abu Dhabi Aviation in the UAE. Dr Pierotti is a qualified aircraft engineer with both an aircraft maintenance license and a PhD in Aircraft Engineering from the City University of London, and also holds an MBA from Edinburgh Business School. He is a qualified aviation auditor, Post Holder and Accountable Manager and also a qualified sports private pilot, flying many light sports and general aviation aircraft all over the world.

Dr Pierotti's knowledge of aviation engineering, aviation operations and aviation management is extensive and wide-reaching, and he has achieved the top executive position of Accountable Manager and COO of a large jet ETOPs AOC and AMO, as well as Accountable Manager and MD for a CAMO and aviation training and consultancy company, for which he received a Fellowship of the Royal Aeronautical Society, FRAeS and two industry leadership award nominations. He has written and implemented feasibility studies, business plans as well as restructuring plans for civil aviation companies to help them become leaner, more efficient and closer to profitability. He has bought and sold many aircraft from airliners to private jets and helicopters.

Dr Pierotti is also a Global Scot, a Scottish industrial ambassador, lecturer and professor of Aviation, aircraft engineering and management at ADU, USW and UWS.

It is Dr Pierotti's ambition to assist all aviation leaders and Accountable Managers in better understanding the responsibilities of aviation leadership and to assist them to oversee and facilitating safer, more compliant and sustainable civil aviation companies that continuously improve.

Acknowledgements

Special thanks for the contributors to this book:

- Dr Laurie Earl, Aviation Lecturer for Chapter 8
- Anthony Frances, Aviation Lawyer for Chapter 9

Special thanks to my dear friends in aviation:

- Lee Roberts, Accountable Manager
- Capt. Dave Prior, Safety Manager & Civil Aviation Regulator & Inspector
- Capt. Francois, Lassale Post Holder Safety
- Capt. Michel Theriault, Post Holder Safety
- Derrick Murray, Post Holder Quality & Compliance
- Justin Goatcher, Accountable Manager & Post Holder Airworthiness
- Capt. Darko Vucic, Civil Aviation Regulator & Inspector
- Roger Hobson, Post Holder Airworthiness
- Travis Tauro, Aviation Intern

Introduction

Aviation is one of the most regulated industries in the world. Leaders of aviation companies face daily challenges in meeting the civil aviation regulations and meeting the board and shareholders' requirements of revenue and profit.

The leader responsible for complete compliance with the civil aviation regulations and leading a safe operation is legally called the Accountable Manager (AM). The AM's co accountable leaders for each aspect of the company's operation are legally called Post Holders (PH) or Nominated Persons (NP). Both positions, AMs and PHs, have clear legal and regulatory responsibilities of compliance, as well as those of safety, security and airworthiness for the operation of the company. These responsibilities are applicable whether it is an airline, a flight training school, a maintenance, repair and overhaul organisation, or indeed any regulated or licensed civil aviation company.

The AM is very often also the CEO. This means a CEO who is also the AM has both regulatory and fiduciary accountabilities where he or she is answerable to the civil aviation authority and to the board of shareholders.

This book will clearly identify the responsibilities and, more importantly, the accountabilities of the leadership in the regulatory territories of the FAA (USA), the EASA (the European Union) and the GCAA (the United Arab Emirates). We shall then identify the leadership challenges in ensuring that the company is meeting the regulatory obligations of compliance, safety and security, to satisfy the regulator, while also meeting the fiducial responsibilities of running an economically viable, sustainable and efficient, lean company that will satisfy the shareholders.

At times the responsibilities, regulatory and fiducial, appear at first to be at odds with each other and even sometimes appear to be conflicting with each other. This book will help the AM navigate those times and, whether they are a seasoned aviation professional or a newcomer to the industry, they will have a document to refer to, to assist them in their decision-making and clarify their understanding of what they are accountable for, and to whom.

It is also the intention of this book to supply a tool kit of techniques, processes and methods that will assist the AM in ensuring he or she meets their obligations in the most efficient and effective way, supported by their highly qualified Post Holder staff to advise and guide them in leadership decision-making. The book

DOI: 10.4324/9781003094685-1

also shares case studies and real-life AM challenges and details how they successfully, or otherwise, lead the company through those decision-making times.

Accountable Managers can be recruited from within the industry as seasoned professionals that have served their time as Post Holders, pilots, engineers or as aviation executives, but they can also be recruited from outside of the industry, from other sectors, and are attractive to the shareholders for their leadership and commercial success in other fields. When they are from outside of the aviation industry, this means the highly regulated aviation environment and the serious accountable responsibilities that come with civil aviation leadership will be new to them. This book intends to help them prepare and understand the seriousness of the position and its accountable responsibilities.

It is essential that the AM understands his or her accountable responsibilities and knows how to meet these responsibilities in using the Post Holders to comply with the regulations and run an efficient, effective, safe and secure operation. This book will give details about the responsibilities of the AM, taking each responsibility and breaking it down into understandable and achievable elements where methods, systems and techniques can be applied to ensure that the AM has full knowledge of what they are accountable for and are confident enough about not only being compliant with the civil aviation regulations, but also running an efficient and effective operation. The book includes the identification of an Accountable Manager "Tool Kit", as well as suggesting software "dashboards" that will assist the AM in focusing on the important analytics that are needed at their fingertips to assist them in decision-making.

The book starts by introducing the origins of the modern-day civil aviation regulations, why they exist and how they are administered internationally. This is important to know, as an AM needs to set a culture of compliance and safety and such knowledge is essential to this. We will highlight the particularly important regulations and review them to ensure the reader understands the principles of the civil aviation regulations that govern the modern civil aviation industry and that are intrinsic to good leadership of a civil aviation company.

1 An introduction to civil aviation, the regulations and air law

It is important that an established or a new or a soon to be Accountable Manager understands the existence and the development of civil aviation standards and the reasoning behind the regulations that they, as the Accountable Manager, are accountable for.

In this section of the book we shall examine the approach that the political world took to ensure a supported, safe and secure civil aviation industry is established. This includes the formulation and the establishment of internationally accepted procedures and standards for civil aviation operations and aircraft airworthiness specifications. Also, this section of the book shall review the organisation and treaties established to support this standardisation. After this chapter, the Accountable Manager shall have a very detailed understanding of why and how civil aviation is regulated today.

The Chicago Convention and the International Civil Aviation Organization

World War II was coming to an end. As a result of the conflicts in Europe and the Pacific and the need for faster and better aircraft, great advances were made in aeronautics over the five years of the war. Aeronautical science was better understood by aviation scientists. New metals and materials were developed by metallurgists, new aircraft designs were developed by aeronautical engineers and new, more capable engines were developed by mechanical power plant engineers.

Prior to the war, and even more so after the war, entrepreneurs and businessmen saw the aviation industry as a fast developing, potentially very profitable, new industry that would enable businesses to go not only intercity or international but also intercontinental. The pre-war achievements of KLM and Imperial Airways in Europe, Pan American Airways and American Airways in the USA and Aeroflot in Russia, all proved the concept that air transport services could be a profitable and sustainable growth business. Aircraft proved to greatly satisfy the need for freight and cargo to be transported fast and far. The movement of people from city to city and country to country was made much more efficient by the larger, longer-range aircraft. At the end of the war,

DOI: 10.4324/9781003094685-2

the aeronautics companies that were focused on developing and building war machines could now get back to the business of developing and building civil aircraft for the new growing civil aviation industry. The scientists and the engineers that were forced to focus their skills on the war effort could now redeploy to the great civil aviation companies that existed prior to the war. The returning aircraft mechanics and pilots from the theatres of Europe and the Pacific were ready to apply their trade in civilian life.

It was 1 November 1944 where the Convention on International Civil Aviation took place at the Stevens Hotel in Chicago, Illinois, USA, later to be known as the Chicago Conference or Chicago Convention. The US Government took the initiative and invited 55 representatives (53 states and two representatives of territories) to come to the US for this post-war convention on international civil aviation. Fifty-two international states were present, including the USA, interested in establishing civil aviation standards for international operations.

On 7 December, the document was signed by all 52 attending states plus the USA hosting state (The Chicago Conference, 1944). On 5 March 1947, the signed Articles of the Convention were ratified by the 26th state; this was the trigger to place the treaty into effect and, hence on 4 April that year, the treaty was validated and put into effect. As a record of the Convention, the host country's Department of State drafted the "Final Act", a document including the "Proceedings of the International Civil Aviation Conference", a written account of all the meetings, the working groups, the agreements and the treaties that were deliberated on and the "Articles" (The Chicago Conference, 1944), the legal items that each state signed contracting to adhere to. These documents became a very important record for the Conference. That same year in October, as a result of the International Civil Aviation Conference, the International Civil Aviation Organization (ICAO) was formed and became a part of the United Nations as a specialised agency of the United Nations Economic and Social Council. Dr Albert Jean François Roper, a decorated French aviator and dedicated civil aviation advocate, was nominated as the first Secretary-General. In the beginning, Dr Roper was the director general (DG) of the Provisional International Civil Aviation Organization (PICAO) prior to the final ratification by the 26th state of the Chicago Convention, then, subsequently, he became Secretary-General of ICAO on 27 May 1947. Dr. Roper was invited by the Canadian Government to assist it in preparing for the launch meeting of the PICAO to be convened in Canada, Montreal on 15 August 1945. Montreal then became the headquarters for ICAO, along with all the other UN departments.

ICAO was essentially established to define standards for civil aviation. A standard, as defined by the first ICAO Assembly, is:

> "... any specification for physical characteristics, configuration, material, performance, personnel, or procedures, the uniform application of which is recognized as necessary for the safety or regularity of international air navigation and to which member states will conform."

Standards may thus include specifications for such matters as the length of runways, the materials to be used in aircraft construction and the qualifications to be required of a pilot flying an international route. A recommendation is any such specification, the uniform application of which is recognised as "*desirable* in the interest of safety, regularity, or efficiency of international air navigation and to which member states will *endeavour to conform*".

(The Chicago Conference, 1944)

The Convention identified 96 Articles that were documented as "principles and arrangements" and signed upon by all the present states. The objectives of these Articles were to develop international civil aviation in a safe and orderly manner, to quote the Convention:

> ... the undersigned governments having agreed on certain principles and arrangements in order that international civil aviation may be developed in a safe and orderly manner and that international air transport services may be established on the basis of equality of opportunity and operated soundly and Economical.
>
> (The Chicago Conference, 1944)

The Articles, Annexes and Standards and Recommended Procedures of the Chicago Convention

It is important that an Accountable Manager understands the origins and intentions of civil aviation regulations and is aware of the Annexes and Standards and Recommended Procedures (SARPs) (International Civil Aviation Organisation, 2021).

There were two main documents that were developed as a record of the Chicago Convention: first, the "Proceedings of the International Civil Aviation Conference" (The Chicago Conference, 1944), which detailed and recorded the minutes of all meetings, working committees, and sub-committees that took place. The second was the Record of Articles of the Conference, both documents together being referred to as the "Final Act of the International Civil Aviation Conference of 1944" (The Chicago Conference, 1944). The Articles were detailed and developed after extensive negotiation, discussion and then legally drafted during the period of the Conference. At the Convention, 96 Articles, separated into 22 Chapters were identified and signed by every member state. The proceedings and the Articles of the Convention then became the basis for establishing the international agreements on civil aviation and the formation of the ICAO. From that day, each member state was referred to as a contracting state to the Chicago Convention and as a member state of ICAO.

Some important ICAO Articles are:

> Article 1: Every state has complete and exclusive sovereignty over airspace above its territory.

Article 3 bis: Every other state must refrain from resorting to the use of weapons against civil aircraft in flight.

Article 5: The aircraft of states, other than scheduled international air services, have the right to make flights across the state's territories and to make stops without obtaining prior permission. However, the state may require the aircraft to make a landing.

Article 6: (Scheduled air services) No scheduled international air service may be operated over or into the territory of a contracting state, except with the special permission or other authorisation of that state.

Article 10: (Landing at customs airports) The state can require landing to be at a designated customs airport, and similarly, a departure from the territory can be required to be from a designated customs airport.

Article 12: Each state shall keep its own rules of the air as uniform as possible with those established under the Convention. The duty to ensure compliance with these rules rests with the contracting state.

Article 13: (Entry and clearance regulations) A state's laws and regulations regarding the admission and departure of passengers, crew or cargo from aircraft shall be complied with on arrival, upon departure and whilst within the territory of that state.

Article 16: The authorities of each state shall have the right to search the aircraft of other states on landing or prior to departure, without unreasonable delay.

Article 24: Aircraft flying to, from or across, the territory of a state shall be admitted temporarily free of duty. Fuel, oil, spare parts, regular equipment and aircraft stores retained on board are also exempted from customs duty, inspection fees or similar charges.

Article 29: Before an international flight, the pilot in command must ensure that the aircraft is airworthy, duly registered and that the relevant certificates are on board the aircraft. The required documents are:

- Certificate of registration
- Certificate of airworthiness
- Passenger names, place of boarding and destination
- Crew licenses
- Journey logbook
- Radio license
- Cargo manifest

Article 30: The aircraft of a state flying in or over the territory of another state shall only carry radios licensed and used in accordance with the regulations of the state in which the aircraft is registered. The radios may only be used by members of the flight crew suitably licensed by the state in which the aircraft is registered.

Article 32: The pilot and crew of every aircraft engaged in international aviation must have certificates of competency and licenses issued or validated by the state in which the aircraft is registered.

Article 33: (Recognition of certificates and licenses) Certificates of airworthiness, certificates of competency and licenses issued or validated by the state in which the aircraft is registered, shall be recognised as valid by other states. The requirements for the issuing of those certificates or airworthiness, certificates of competency or licensees must be equal to or above the minimum standards established by the Convention.

Article 40: No aircraft or personnel with endorsed licenses or certificates will engage in international navigation except with the permission of the state or states whose territory is entered. Any license holder who does not satisfy international standards relating to license or certificate shall have attached to or endorsed on that license information regarding the particulars in which they do not satisfy those standards.

In accordance with Appendix V of the Proceedings and Art 37 of the Convention on International Civil Aviation, technical standards and practices shall be developed and published, these standards are called Standards and Recommended Practices, SARPs, and shall be developed to ensure, "the highest practicable degree of uniformity in regulations, standards, procedures and organization in relation to aircraft, personnel, airways, and auxiliary services in all matters in which such uniformity will facilitate and improve air navigation". The SARPs are developed and published by ICAO in the form of Annexes to the Chicago Convention (International Civil Aviation Organisation, 2021). By joining the ICAO and signing the Convention, that state agrees to accept the standards and to apply those standards as far as practicable in their respective state.

Today there exist 19 Annexes in total. Adding or revising an Annex to the SARPs is defined by Art 90 of the Chicago Convention, where a process has to be followed by member States of the ICAO. The last Annex added was Annex 19, Safety management, on 14 November 2013.

Annex 1: Personal licensing
Annex 2: Rules of the air
Annex 3: Meteorological services for international air navigation
Annex 4: Aeronautical charts
Annex 5: Units of measurement used in air
Annex 6: Operation of aircraft (three parts)
Annex 7: Aircraft nationality and registration marks
Annex 8: Airworthiness of aircraft
Annex 9: Facilitation
Annex 10: Aeronautical telecommunications (five parts)
Annex 11: Air traffic services
Annex 12: Search and rescue
Annex 13: Aircraft accident and incident investigation
Annex 14: Aerodromes (four parts)
Annex 15: Aeronautical Information services

Annex 16: Environmental protection (two parts)
Annex 17: Security and safeguarding
Annex 18: Transport of dangerous goods
Annex 19: Safety management

A member state must attempt to apply all Annexes in their civil aviation regulations.

All Annexes are important in their own right, but some Annexes have greater effects on the introduction and operation of civil aircraft today and should be studied carefully. These are Annex 6, Operations of aircraft, Annex 8, Airworthiness of aircraft, and the most recently added Annex, Annex 19, Safety management.

Annex 6: Operation of aircraft (International Civil Aviation Organisation, 2021)

This deals with the certification of operators of aircraft and the required standards they must operate to.

Annex 8: Airworthiness of aircraft (International Civil Aviation Organisation, 2021)

This considers two types of airworthiness:

- Initial airworthiness: This process is called "Type Certification (TC)". This is a process between the original equipment manufacturer (OEM) and the National Aviation Authority (NAA) of the manufacturing country with the involvement of any subsequent operating NAA who wishes to get involved.
- Continuing airworthiness of civil aircraft, components and equipment once in service with operators and airlines, and maintenance engineering. This process is called "Certification of Airworthiness (CofA) and Airworthiness Review Certification (ARC)".

Annex 19: Safety management (International Civil Aviation Organisation, 2021)

This Annex was added in 2013 and is the last Annex to be added to date. It instills the great importance of safety management in civil aviation and the concept that safety must be an integral part of a company's procedures and processes and its culture.

The National and Civil Aviation Authorities

It is important that an Accountable Manager understands the origins of the National Aviation Authorities (NAAs), their structure and their reason for existing. The Accountable Manager is accountable to the NAA, and is expected to understand the function and role of the NAA.

Article 12 of the Chicago Convention of 1944 states:

> Each contracting State undertakes to adopt measures to insure that every aircraft flying over or manoeuvring within its territory and that every aircraft carrying its nationality mark, wherever such aircraft may be, shall comply with the rules and regulations relating to the flight and manoeuvre of aircraft there in force. Each contracting State undertakes to keep its own regulations in these respects uniform, to the greatest possible extent, with those established from time to time under this Convention. Over the high seas, the rules in force shall be those established under this Convention. Each contracting State undertakes to insure the prosecution of all persons violating the regulations applicable.
>
> (The Chicago Conference, 1944)

This means every signatory and contracting state to the Chicago Convention has signed a legal obligation under international law in order to establish national legislation in their country that enforces and ratifies the principles of the Articles of the Chicago Convention and also implements the SARPs and Annexes and oversees their application and conformity. This is done by all registered aircraft carrying their national mark and all aircraft flying into their territory.

Article 37 of the Chicago Convention of 1944 states:

> Each contracting State undertakes to collaborate in securing the highest practicable degree of uniformity in regulations, standards, procedures, and organization in relation to aircraft, personnel, airways, and auxiliary services in all matters in which such uniformity will facilitate and improve air navigation.
>
> (The Chicago Conference, 1944)

This means each contracting signatory state shall use its best efforts to ensure uniformity and harmony of civil aviation regulations and SARPs with other contracting states.

To ensure that a contracting state to the Chicago Convention, a member of ICAO, complies with the Convention, the Articles, Annexes and the SARPs, civil aviation legislation must be implemented and ratified in that state. To ensure that legislation is cascaded into civil aviation regulations and applied to the civil aviation activities in that country, an NAA, or also referred to as a Civil Aviation Authority (CAA), must be formed to keep a national register of aircraft, and to regulate, execute, deliberate, oversee and administer the civil aviation law of that state. The NAA must be sufficiently staffed with qualified people to administer the civil aviation activities in that state. This means if the state has in its territory a company operating large passenger aircraft, the NAA should have civil aviation operations inspectors, regulators and a system for the oversight of the regulated activities as detailed in the Chicago Convention. If the state has an aircraft maintenance facility, the NAA should have qualified maintenance inspectors, regulators and a system for the oversight of the regulated activities as detailed in the Chicago Convention. If the state has an aircraft design and manufacturing facility, the NAA must have qualified inspectors, regulators in aircraft design and manufacturing, and a system for oversight of the regulated activities as detailed in the Chicago Convention (Figure 1.1).

With every contracted signatory state of the Chicago Convention having to establish an NAA or CAA that has the regulatory responsibility of the drafting, implementation and oversight of the Convention's Annexes and SARPs, some of the more advanced aviation states developed their civil aviation industry faster than others. This meant, in some contracting states, there is a need for a more capable NAA with a more complete civil aviation authority and more complete civil aviation regulations. Each of the Annexes of the Chicago Convention shall be a responsibility of the NAA to ensure implementation and oversight is in place. Note that Annex 13 is very often not part of the responsibility of the NAA as it is seen as a possible conflict of interest because the responsibility for an accident may well be the lack of compliance with the SARPs or the lack of regulations and oversight. This is why many contracting states have the Annex 13 responsibility under a non-NAA department, such as in the USA, the National Transport Safety Board (NTSB), not the FAA, and in the UK, the Aircraft Accident Investigation Branch (AAIB), not the CAA, both reporting directly to the Department of Transport of the State Government. It is also important to state that the latest Annex, Annex 19 is embedded into each and every Annex. This will be explored further later in the book.

Some of the more complete NAAs that needed to advance quicker due to the expansion of the civil aviation industry in its territory are:

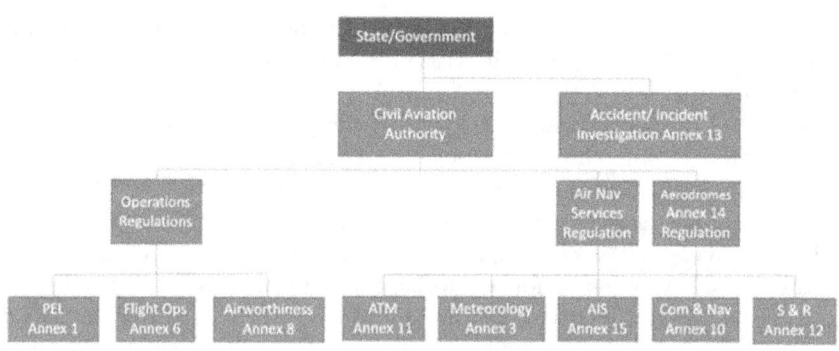

Figure 1.1 The structure of the ICAO Annexes and their responsibilities (International Civil Aviation Organisation, 2021).

- UK: The Civil Aviation Authority (CAA).
  - Ratified and legalised by the Civil Aviation Act (UK Government, 2021).
- USA: The Federal Aviation Administration (FAA).
  - Ratified and legalised by the Federal Aviation Act (US Government, 2021).
- France: The Direction Generali de l`Aviation Civile (DGAC).
  - Ratified and legalised by the Code de transport (French Government, 2021).
- Canada: The Transport Canada (TC).
  - Ratified and legalised by the Aeronautics Act.
- Russia: The Federal Air Transport Agency (Rosaviatsiya) (FAVT).
  - Ratified and legalised by the Air Code (Russian Government, 2019).

The civil aviation industry in the advanced aviation territories was fast expanding, and many great civil aviation companies were developing capabilities and growing. All this activity, listed below, had a need for standards and practices that were regulated and overseen for compliance with the Annexes and SARPs of the Chicago Convention.

- International airline operations
- Domestic airline operations
- Private aircraft operations
- Aircraft design and manufacturer
- Aircraft engine design and manufacture
- Aircraft parts and components design and manufacturer
- Aircraft, engine and component maintenance, repair and overhaul facilities
- Air training organisation for pilots
- Air training academies for maintenance technicians

This meant the advancement of these NAAs as they had extensive civil aviation activities taking place in their territories and hence required regulating and oversight in accordance with the Annexes and SARPs of the Chicago Convention. Other contracting states had smaller civil aviation industries, perhaps only an airport. These countries developed civil aviation regulations and oversight capabilities at a slower pace, as per their industry requirements. The more capable NAAs developed their civil aviation regulations in accordance with the Annexes and SARPs as per Art 37 in as uniformed way as possible, but inevitably regional interpretations of the Annexes and SARPs were developed, so, to some extent, slight differences started to exist between contracting states. The interpretation and establishment of each state of civil aviation law and regulations were subjected to ICAO compliance and audit to meeting the intent of the Chicago Convention Annexes and SARPs.

Two very important and very interesting applications of the Annexes and SARPs of the Chicago Convention in modern times are the United Arab Emirates, UAE, and the European Union, EU:

- The United Arab Emirates, General Civil Aviation Authority (GCAA).
  - Ratified and legalised by the Civil Aviation Law (UAE Government, 1991).
  - Became a member of ICAO and signatory state of the Chicago Convention 1972.
  - Established the GCAA in 1996 then developed the Civil Aviation Regulations (UAE Government, 1996) in accordance with the Annexes and SARPs of the Chicago Convention (International Civil Aviation Organisation, 2021).
- European Union, European Aviation Safety Agency (EASA).
  - Ratified and legalised by EU Regulations 1592/2002 (EU Government, 2002).
  - Did not become a member of ICAO but did ratify the Chicago Convention in 2002.
  - Established EASA in 2002 (EU Government, 2002) then developed the EU Regulations on civil aviation in accordance with the Annexes and SARPs of the Chicago Convention (International Civil Aviation Organisation, 2021).

While the UK, USA, France and Canada are very important members of ICAO and original signatory states of the Chicago Convention constantly involved in developing ICAO and leading the application of the Chicago Convention principles over the years since its formation in 1944, in 1972 the United Arab Emirates joined ICAO and in 1996 formed the General Civil Aviation Authority (GCAA). The GCAA is very interesting as it is a good example of a young country that not only adopted the Chicago Convention Annexes and SARPs quickly and effectively in their legal system to support a very important civil aviation industry, but also embraced the principles of the Chicago Convention and, as a result, facilitated the incredible growth of a new, safe and secure civil aviation industry with the development of world-leading airlines, training organisations and maintenance facilities.

Another very interesting case occurred in 2002, when the European Union passed EU Regulation EC1592/2002 (EU Government, 2002) that legally established the European Aviation Safety Agency (EASA). As a legal entity, the EU could issue and ratify laws that must be followed by all member countries. The EASA took on the role of regulating and overseeing all civil aviation activities taking place within the territory of every member state of the EU. Each of the EU member states had to ratify the EU law and apply the EASA regulations into their civil aviation industry. Each NAA of each EU state then had the responsibility of regulating and overseeing the civil aviation activities in their territory to ensure compliance with EASA regulation. This meant that the EASA was responsible for ensuring the Chicago Convention Articles and Annexes were incorporated into law, and each NAA within the EU was responsible for ensuring that the EASA civil aviation regulations were followed in their national territory. So, while the UK CAA and the French DGCA still existed after 2002, they were now responsible for ensuring that EASA civil aviation regulations were followed in their countries. This was possible because the EU had the authority to issue laws. Though there are 28 EU States, but there are 32 countries that have ratified the EASA and the EU Basic Regulations on civil aviation. Further, 13 countries followed the EASA and these are called the European Civil Aviation Conference (ECAC) countries. The ECAC was established by ICAO, and all 44 countries are member states of EASA.

Interestingly each member state of the EU remained a contracting state of the Chicago Convention, while the EU did not exist in itself. EU membership of ICAO was recommended by the Commission in 2002, but Article 92 of the Chicago Convention only permits adherence to the Chicago Convention and ICAO for individual States rather than regional organisations such as the EU. None the less the EU, EASA, do sit on some committees and does contribute to ICAO from time to time.

US Federal Aviation Regulations, EASA Regulations and the UAE Civil Aviation Regulations

It is essential that an Account Manager should have knowledge of the important, relevant regulations in the particular civil aviation organisation that they are accountable for, as the NAA will expect this and will expect to see evidence of this at the initial interview. Some NAAs insist the Accountable Manager and all the Post Holders attend a course on their responsibilities prior to appointment. This is an understandable requirement, especially for those who find themselves as Accountable Managers in civil aviation companies when aviation was not their previous industry of employment.

It should be remembered that the ICAO is not a regulator, a court or a sheriff and cannot write law or enforce the law on a member state. Each contracting member state must develop its own national laws and regulations and appoint its own sheriffs to be able to enforce the standards and practices desirable for civil aviation. Article 12 of the Chicago Convention is clear that every contracting state shall develop a code of regulations for civil aviation in their state. Article 37 is very clear that the regulations developed by each contracting state shall have the highest degree of uniformity. This has led to each contracting state developing the ratified law first and then the civil aviation regulations to be followed by all civil aviation companies in each contracting state. The advanced civil aviation countries with extensive civil aviation activities needed greater and wider-reaching laws than those with a less advanced civil aviation industry.

Today the main civil aviation regulations that regulate most of the civil aviation activity are:

- The USA the Federal Aviation Administration (FAA).
  - Ratified and legalised by the Federal Aviation Act.
  - Was a founding contracting member state to the Chicago Convention in 1944.

- Established the FAA in 1958 succeeding the Civil Aeronautics Administration.
- Develops, administers, enforces and oversees the Federal Aviation Regulations (FARs) in accordance with the Annexes and SARPs of the Chicago Convention.
• European Union, European Aviation Safety Agency (EASA).
  - Ratified and legalised by EU Regulations 1592/2002.
  - Did not become a member of the ICAO but did ratify the Chicago Convention in 2002.
  - Established EASA in 2002 then developed the EU Regulations on civil aviation in accordance with the Annexes and SARP's of the Chicago Convention.

Both the FAA, and FARs, and the EASA, and EU Regulations, have become the most significant national aviation authorities and civil aviation regulations used in the world today.

Boeing, Airbus, Rolls Royce, General Electrics, Prat and Whitney, Bell, Leonardo, Gulfstream, Dassault Falcon, Cessna, Piper, as well as hundreds of operators and maintenance and repair organisations are regulated and certified and audited by the FAA and EASA. There are also many companies in other contracting states such as Bombardier in Canada, Embraer in Brazil, Sukhoi in Russia, as well as all the international operators and airlines and maintenance and repair organisations.

The United Arab Emirates Regulations (UAE GCAA, 2021) are as follow:

• The United Arab Emirates, General Civil Aviation Authority (GCAA).
  - Ratified and legalised by the Civil Aviation Law.
  - Became a member of ICAO and signatory state of the Chicago Convention 1972.
  - Established the GCAA in 1996 then developed the Civil Aviation Regulations in accordance with the Annexes and SARPs of the Chicago Convention.

The UAE GCAA drafted and implemented the Civil Aviation Regulations (CARs) in order to meet its contracted commitment to the Chicago Convention, Arts 12 and 37. The CARs are constructed in a way that follows the Annexes and SARPs; their structure is similar to the structure of EASA's predecessor, the Joint Aviation Authorities, JAA, and the Joint Aviation Requirements, JARs, but do differ from time to time.

As indicated above, there are two major methods of thought and approach to the interpretation of the Annexes and SARPs in today's modern national aviation authorities civil aviation regulations—the FAA FAR approach and the EASA EU regulations approach. While both approaches are compliant with the Annexes and SARPs as Art 12 requires, the devil is in the detail of how they are structured and drafted. Many non-EU countries have adopted the

EASA EU Regulations or the JAA JAR formats as their template for their civil aviation regulations, for example Turkey, Ukraine and Serbia. The UAE GCAA has adopted an EASA and JAA style approach, not identical but similar as have many of the other modernised NAAs of the world. Some NAAs have adopted an FAA approach to their civil aviation regulations and structure, such as Canada's TC and Saudi Arabia's GACA. All are contracting member states, so their regulations should comply with Arts 12 and 37 of the Chicago Convention on International Civil Aviation, but remember, as said, the devil is in the detail, and the Annexes and SARPs are not heavily detailed documents but guidance documents with significant concepts and standards that need further developing and detailed drafting to become civil aviation regulations that can be implemented into the real civil aviation industry (Figure 1.2).

The structure of the FAA Federal Aviation Regulations

In the USA, Title 14 of the Code of Federal Regulations (14 CFR) is the Federal Aviation Regulations. These, in aviation circles, are referred to as the FARs, but "FARs" in the USA are also another set of regulations, the Federal Acquisition Regulations, which have nothing to do with aviation, and might cause confusion. The civil aviation regulations can be called the FARs or 14

Figure 1.2 A cascading structure of the Chicago Convention Annexes to NAA civil aviation regulations.

CFR, but usually, within the aviation industry, we call them FARs, so in this book we shall refer to them as such.

The FARs are separated into Volumes, Chapters, and Parts. In most aviation circles, the parts are referred to as referencing FARs (Table 1.1).

The important FAR Parts of particular interest and that are relevant and frequently used in the civil aviation industry are:

Airworthiness of aircraft: Chicago Convention Annex 8

Part 25 and Part 21: These regulations originate from Annex 8 of the Chicago Convention, Airworthiness. These regulations are important for *initial airworthiness* and design criteria of a fixed-wing civil airliner to obtain certification and a Type Certificate (TC) and a Supplemental Certificate (STC) and for *continuing airworthiness* to ensure continuing compliance with the original TC and airworthiness standard.

Each individual aircraft can only be released from the manufacturer for civil, commercial air operations in the USA once it satisfies Part 25 and obtains a TC from the FAA. Very often today, and in the past, not only will the NAA of the manufacturer's country issue the TC, but so will many other NAAs, particularly those who expect the aircraft to operate in their state and on their national register (Table 1.2).

Table 1.1 Important and relevant FAA FAR Parts

Part	Description
Part 21	Certification Procedures for Products and Parts
Part 23	Airworthiness Standards: Normal, Utility, Acrobatic and Commuter Airplanes
Part 25	Airworthiness Standards: Transport Category Airplanes
Part 27	Airworthiness Standards: Normal Category Rotorcraft
Part 29	Airworthiness Standards: Transport Category Rotorcraft
Part 33	Airworthiness Standards: Aircraft Engines
Part 39	Airworthiness Directives
Part 43	Maintenance, Preventative Maintenance, Repair and Alterations.
Part 61	Certification: Pilots, Flight Instructors, and Ground Instructors
Part 65	Certification: Airmen Other Than Flight Crewmembers
Part 91	General Operating and Flight Rules
Part 117	Flight and Duty Limitations and Rest Requirements: Flight crew Members
Part 119	Certification: Air Carriers and Commercial Operators
Part 121	Operating Requirements: Domestic, Flag, and Supplemental Operations
Part 125	Certification and Operations: Airplanes Having a Seating Capacity of 20 or More Passengers or a Payload Capacity of 6,000 Pounds or More
Part 135	Operating Requirements: Commuter and On-Demand Operations and Rules Governing Persons on Board Such Aircraft
Part 141	Flight Schools
Part 145	Repair Stations
Part 147	Aviation Maintenance Technicians Schools

Table 1.2 Examples of aircraft types that hold an FAA Type Certificate

Manufacturer	Aircraft Type	Aircraft Series or Variant
Boeing	B737	Classic 100/200/300/400/500 NG 600/700/800/900 Max 8/9
Boeing	B777	200/300
Airbus	A320	A318/A319/A320/A321-100, -200
Bombardier	Dash 8	100/200/300/400

Operations of aircraft: Annex 6

Part 91, 119, 121, 125 and 135: These regulations originate from Annex 6 of the Chicago Convention, Operations of Aircraft. These regulations are important for private operations, airline operations and charter operations. FAR 119 gives the details of the Certification of Air Carriers and Commercial Operators and defines different regulations depending upon the type of operations and the size of aircraft. These operations should be certified under Part 119; the FAA issues two types of air operators certificates: an Air Operating Certificate, (AOC) or an Air Carriers Certificate (ACC). Commercial operations is also referred to as "common carriage", and this means flying for payment or reward.

- **FAR 121** is for air carrier international operations, major airlines.
- **FAR 125** for non-commercial private operations of large aircraft of 20 seats or more or with a payload capacity of 6,000lbs or more; large private jets.
- **FAR 135** for on-demand charter operations (domestic or international) or limited scheduled airlines (domestic); for hire private jets; or commuter interstate airlines.

Part 91: This is not subject to Part 119 as it does not require Certification for Air Operations such as an ACC or an AOC. Part 91 is the general flying rules and private non-commercial aircraft with less than 20 seats, or under 6,000lbs. These aircraft should comply with FAR Part 91 to be allowed to operate on the US FAA register.

FAR 119: This gives all the regulatory requirements to obtain an ACC or AOC, including the regulatory requirements for the management personnel. This will be explored further in the book as it defines the regulated leadership required by the regulations, a very important and interesting subject with different approaches, depending upon the contracting states.

Part 145: Repair stations, or a Certified Repair Station (CRS) is one that meets the requirements of FAR 145. In industry terms, it may also be referred

18 *Introduction to aviation regulations and law*

to as a Maintenance, Repair and Overhaul Facility (MRO). In Europe, it is also referred to as an AMO, Approved Maintenance Organization, also certified to EU Regulation Part 145, but that will be described in the next section of the book. Under FAR Part 145, a CRS can conduct maintenance activities that it is certified for and that are detailed in that repair station's certificates rating, classification and operations specification (ops spec). FAR Part 43 and FAR Part 145 go hand in hand.

The structure of EU Civil Aviation Regulations (EU EASA, 2021)

All states of the European Union are legally bound to comply with the most current EU regulation on civil aviation, which is EU Basic Regulation 2018/1139. The original EU Basic Regulation on Civil Aviation was 1592/2002, created and ratified as the first EU civil aviation Basic Regulation in 2002 when the European Aviation Safety Agency, EASA, was created as a follow on from the Joint Aviation Authority, JAA, and each EU member states own NAA. Just as USA Federal Codes are sequentially numbered, so are EU laws and regulations. This is why the number does not mean much out of its sequence. The EU Basic Regulations are issued in the individual language of each of the 28 states. We shall refer to them from now on in this book as EU Regs, and when referring to them, we will be referring to the English language version.

The EU Regs have referring to it the Implementing Rules (IRs). The IRs are binding in their entirety and give details of the EU Regs and how they must be complied with. Also, the EASA issues Acceptable Means of Compliance (AMC) and Certifications Specifications (CS)—two documents that are non-binding—and, finally, it also issues guidance material (GM) that is again non-binding but explanatory on how to achieve the intent of the EU Regs, IRs, AMCs and CSs.

The EU Regs has 11 IRs. These IRs are broken down into Annexes that are further broken down into Parts, similar to the FARs.

For civil aviation companies such as airlines or aircraft maintenance and repair organisations, there are five very important IRs that we shall review in more detail, addressing the IR Parts and their IR CSs (Figure 1.3).

Some important and relevant EASA Parts and CSs are (Table 1.3):

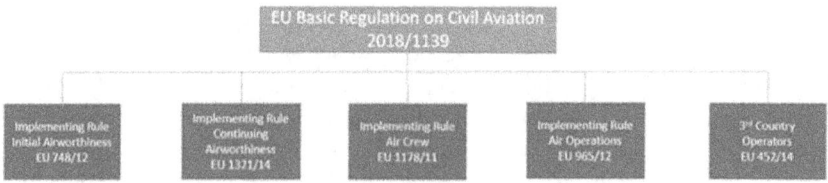

Figure 1.3 The EASA basic regulation structure.

Table 1.3 Important and relevant EASA Parts and CSs

Part 21	IR EU 748/12	Initial Airworthiness
CS 25	IR EU 748/12	Certification of Large Aeroplanes
CS 29	IR EU 748/12	Certification for Large Rotorcraft
Part M	IR EU 1321/14	Continuing Airworthiness
Part CAMO	IR EU 1321/14	Continuing Airworthiness Management Organizations
Part 145	IR EU 1321/14	Approved Maintenance Organizations
Part 147	IR EU 1321/14	Maintenance Training Schools
Part 66	IR EU 1321/14	Maintenance Staff Licensing
Part FCL	IR EU 1178/11	Flight Crew Licensing
Part ORA	IR EU 1178/11	Organization Requirements for Aircrew including Air Training Organizations ATO
Part ORO	IR EU 965/12	Organizational Requirements for an Air Operator
Part CAT	IR EU 965/12	Commercial Air Transport Operations
Part TRO	IR EU 452/14	Third Country Operators

The structure of UAE Civil Aviation Regulations

With the United Arab Emirates becoming a contracted state of the Chicago Convention in 1972, the same year it became a country, they were bound by Arts 12 and 37 to form a NAA and to implement the Annexes and SARPs of the Chicago Convention. The civil aviation law was implemented in 1991, and the General Civil Aviation Authority (GCAA) law was implemented in 1996 when the GCAA was formed. The GCAA then implemented the Civil Aviation Regulations (CARs) to comply with the Annexes and SARPs of the ICAO. The UAE GCAA has been a member of the ICAO Council for five years now. The Council is the governing body of ICAO.

In a very short period, the GCAA has not only adopted the Annexes and SARPs into the civil aviation regulations of the country, but it has also established a very well-managed, regulated and healthy civil aviation industry in its territory. It is truly a success story with regards to a young country signing the Chicago Convention and efficiently and effectively supporting civil aviation.

While the USA's FAA is an example of a founding member of ICAO, developing a well-established civil aviation regulation in the FARs and supporting a very successful civil aviation industry in its territory, the EASA of the EU is a very good example of cooperation of many ICAO members to harmonise civil aviation regulations throughout multiple contracted state territories, an example of Art 37. The UAE is an example of a young country efficiently and effectively developing and implementing civil aviation regulations, starting from nothing, progressing to a sophisticated and logical set of CARs.

In February 2006, a Memorandum of Understanding between the GCAA and EASA was signed to ensure continuing cooperation in rulemaking to enhance the regulations in the EU and in the UAE for civil aviation safety and airworthiness. This spirit of collaboration between the UAE GCAA and the

EU EASA has continued since then with regular working-together initiatives and regulatory harmonisation, just as Art 37 and the complete concept of the Chicago Convention encourage.

The CARs satisfies the UAE's commitment to Art 12 and 37 of the Chicago Convention as they are the regulations that must be followed and complied with by all civil aviation companies based or operating in the territory of the UAE. The CARs are supplemented by Civil Aviation Advisory Publications (CAAPs) that give guidance and advisory details to meet the intent of the CARs, similar to the FAR ACs and the EASA GM. With the CARs there is guidance material (GM), acceptable means of compliance (AMC) and interpretative and explanatory material for some of the regulations.

The CARs are separated into 11 Parts, Part I to Part XI, using Roman Numerals. The Parts address each specialist civil aviation activity. For example, CAR V, Airworthiness Regulations, Part CAR-145, Approved Maintenance Organizations (Figure 1.4 and Table 1.4).

Note the similarity in the numbering of Parts, at first appearing to harmonise with FARs and the EU Regs, 145 for maintenance, 21 for airworthiness certification and design, then we see further harmonised numbering between the CARs and EU Regs predecessor JARs CAR-OPS 1 for Aircraft Operations—Aeroplanes and CAR-OPS 3 Aircraft Operations—Rotary and CAR-M Continuing Airworthiness. It is similar even with sub Parts such as CAR-M, Sub Part-G CAMO, as well as many others. The similarity and harmonisation between the EU Regs and CARs goes beyond the numbering and notation to the details of the regulations and rules. The GCAA CARs were initially harmonised with the EU JAA JARs, but now the GCAA CARs can be said to be as much as 80 percent harmonised with the EU Regs and its Parts. Remember, the Chicago Convention encouraged harmonisation of the civil aviation regulations between contracting states in Art 37, and in that spirit, the EASA and the GCAA have a cooperation Memorandum of Understanding signed in 2006. It should be noted that the GCAA CARs are currently undergoing a harmonisation revision with the EASA regulations as per the GCAA Notice of Proposed Amendment 2020-12, (UAE GCAA, 2020). This book considers the CARs as they are in effect at the time of publishing.

Safety management and the civil aviation regulations

Safety management has been an essential and important part of civil aviation since the very start of the Chicago Convention in 1945. Article 3 and Art 44 of the Convention embed safety in the objectives of the ICAO and the Convention. The concept of a safer international civil aviation operation is detailed throughout the Articles and Annexes of the Convention, and the obligation of ensuring safety is placed on every contracting state. In 2010 the ICAO decided to consolidate all the safety considerations from six of the Annexes, i.e. Annex 1, 6, 8, 11, 13, and 14, into a single consolidated new Annex. In February 2013, Annex 19, Safety management (International Civil Aviation Organisation,

Introduction to aviation regulations and law 21

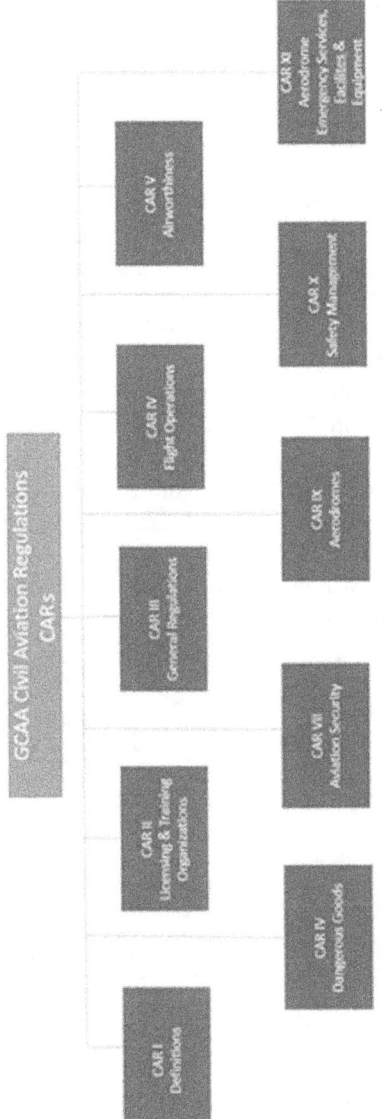

Figure 1.4 The structure of GCAA CARs.

22 Introduction to aviation regulations and law

Table 1.4 Important and relevant GCAA CAR Parts

Part FCL	CAR II	Flight Crew Licensing
Part 147	CAR II	Approved Maintenance Training Organisations.
Part 66	CAR II	Aircraft Maintenance Engineer Licensing
Part OPS 1	CAR IV	Air Operators Certificate for Fixed Wing.
Part OPS 3	CAR IV	Air Operators Certificate for Rotary Wing.
Part 21	CAR V	Certification of Aircraft
Part 145	CAR V	Approved Maintenance Organizations
Part M	CAR V	Continuing Airworthiness

2021) was issued, the first new Annex to be added to the Chicago Convention since Annex 18, Dangerous goods, was introduced in 1983. The FAA, EASA, and the GCAA, as well as every other contracting state of the Chicago Convention, then had to implement the new Annex into their regulations. In the UAE, CAAP 50 was issued in January 2015, which resulted in CAR X being issued in June 2016 (UAE GCAA, 2021).

In the US, the FAA issued FAR Part 5 (US FAA, 2021) in January 2015, along with AC 120-92 (US FAA, 2015), while in the EU, the EASA decided to follow the previous ICAO concept of keeping the Annex 19 safety elements in each particular regulations as the ICAO did previously. So safety management is dealt with in each specific EU Civil Aviation Basic Regulation (EU EASA, 2021), including Part FCL, Part 21, Part ORO, Part M, Part 145, etc. Later in this book, we shall review in detail how safety management is a very important part of the Accountable Manager's accountability and daily duty.

References

EU EASA, 2021. *Regulation 2018/1139 Basic Regulation on Civil Aviation* [online]. Available at: https://www.easa.europa.eu/regulations#regulations-basic-regulation.

EU Government, 2002. *EU 1592/2002, Establishment of the European Aviation Safety Agency*. Cologne: European Aviation Safety Agency.

French Government, 2021. *French Code des transports*. Paris: The French Government.

International Civil Aviation Organisation, 2021. *ICAO Annexes & SARP's*. Montreal: ICAO.

Russian Government, 2019. *Air Code of the Russian Federation*. Moscow: The Russian Federation Government.

The Chicago Conference, 1944. *The Chicago Conference of Civil Aviation Minutes & Articles*. Chicago, PICAO.

UAE GCAA, 2020. *NPA 2020-12 Civil Aviation Regulation Air Operations (CAR-AIR OPS)*, Abu Dhabi: General Civil Aviation Authority.

UAE GCAA, 2021. *GCAA Civil Aviation Regulations* [online]. Available at: https://www.gcaa.gov.ae/en/ePublication/Pages/CARs.aspx?CertID=CARs.

UAE Government, 1991. *UAE Civil Aviation Law Federal Act No 20 Establishment of Civil Aviation Regulations*. Abu Dhabi: UAE Department of Transport.

UAE Government, 1996. *The Establishment of the General Civil Aviation Authority & Civil Aviation Regulations*. Abu Dhabi: UAE Department of Transport.

UK Government, 2021. *UK Civil Aviation Act*. London: UK Government.
US FAA, 2015. *Advisory Circular 120-92B, Safety Management Systems*. Washington DC: Federal Aviation Administration.
US FAA, 2021. *14 CFR Federal Aviation Regulations* [online]. Available at: https://www.faa.gov/regulations_policies/faa_regulations/.
US FAA, 2021. *Federal Aviation Regulation Part 5, Safety Management Systems*. Washington DC.: Federal Aviation Administration.
US Government, 2021. *14 CFR Aeronautics & Space Federal Aviation Act*. Washington DC: US Government Department of Transport.

2 An introduction to the Accountable Manager

Now we have the knowledge and an understanding of the civil aviation authorities and their role and the civil aviation regulations and their legal requirements. We have also seen that the contracting state must set up a regulator that implements and oversees the regulations in accordance with the Annexes and SARPs of the Chicago Convention (ICAO, 2021 a–c). This regulator is referred to in the Convention as the National Aviation Authority (NAA) or, at times, the competent authority. This chapter will now examine the civil aviation companies that exist in a contracting state's territory. These civil aviation companies have been issued NAA approvals or NAA certifications, such as a Part 121 Air Carrier (US FAA, 2021 a–d) or OPS 1 Air Operator (UAE GCAA, 2021 a–c) to operate aircraft; a Part 145 Aircraft Maintenance Organisation (EU EASA, 2021 a–d) (UAE GCAA, 2021 a–c) to maintain aircraft; CS/Part 25 (EU EASA, 2020 a–c) or Part 29 (EU EASA, 2020 a–c) or Part 21 DOA or POA (EU EASA, 2021 a–d) (UAE GCAA, 2015) to manufacture aircraft or parts, design aircraft or parts or equipment; Part ORA ATOs (EU EASA, 2021 a–d) to train pilots, dispatchers; or Part 147 (EU EASA, 2020 a–c) (UAE GCAA, 2013) to train technicians and engineers in accordance with the NAA's civil aviation regulations. We will now review and examine how that certified or approved company satisfies and complies with the requirements of the civil aviation regulations through the leadership responsibilities of the executive manager of the approved organisations.

Often in a commercial organisational structure, the leading executive is referred to as the chief executive officer (CEO), the chief operating officer (COO), the managing director (MD) or the general manager (GM). In the regulatory organisational structure, the executive manager is referred to as the Accountable Manager (AM) or the Accountable Executive (AE). These titles, AM or AE, appear in the EASA Regulations, the FAA FARs and the GCAA CARs, as well as in many other civil aviation regulation of ICAO member states such as the Canadian TC, the Australian CASA, and many more.

In fact, almost all of the NAAs have adopted either title and term to identify the single person with the ultimate executive responsibility for ensuring the leadership for complete compliance with the civil aviation regulations. Interestingly,

DOI: 10.4324/9781003094685-3

the ICAO has only fleetingly referred to the Accountable Executive in Annexes 6 and 19, but not in Annex 8. This is interesting as the ICAO stays largely silent on executive leadership and accountability of that leadership. At the same time, the NAA regulators have identified that leadership and, more so, accountable leadership is a core tenant to a compliant operation, whether that is an air operator, aircraft maintenance organisation, a flying school or an airport in itself. Effective leadership and clear leadership accountability is an integral part of a safe and compliant civil aviation company.

As far as the NAAs are concerned, the two main aspects of regulatory executive leadership accountability and responsibility in a civil aviation company are:

- Ensuring the *adequate financial funding* is available to support a regulatory compliant company operation; and
- Ensuring an actual safe, secure, and *regulatory compliant* company operation.

In a careful review of these two aspects, we can see the executive AM is accountable. The definition of accountable is:

Oxford Dictionary:
Accountable: Responsible for your decisions or actions and expected to explain them when you are asked.

(Oxford Learners Dictionary, 2021)

Webster's Dictionary:
Accountable or Accountability: the quality or state of being accountable especially: an obligation or willingness to accept responsibility or to account for one's actions.

(Websters Dictionary, 2021)

Collin's Dictionary:
Accountable or Accountability: If you are accountable to someone for something that you do, you are responsible for it and must be prepared to justify your actions to that person.

(Collins Dictionary, 2021)

Wikipedia:
Accountable or Accountability: In ethics and governance, accountability is answerability, blameworthiness, liability, and the expectation of account-giving.

(Wikipedia, 2021)

We can see definite language emphasising that the person accountable has a substantial undertaking of legal responsibility, an obligation to accept responsibility and must be prepared to justify their actions, with answerability, blameworthiness and liability.

This means the Air Operating Certificate AM is accountable and responsible legally for the funding and for ensuring a compliant flight and continuing airworthy operation. The Approved Maintenance Organisation AM is also accountable and responsible legally for the funding and for ensuring a compliant maintenance operation of every aircraft maintained and released by their MRO. The same applies to each AM and AE in all approved and certified civil aviation organisations and companies.

Civil aviation regulatory responsibilities

The Accountable Manager and their regulatory responsibilities

The definition of the Accountable Manager in civil aviation is:

> The term "Accountable Manager" may be used to describe the single individual who is designated as the person responsible to a Regulatory Authority in respect of the functions which are subject to regulation, and carried out by an aircraft operator, an air navigation service provider, an aircraft maintenance and repair organization or an airport operator. That person is normally expected to be the person who has corporate authority for ensuring that all operations activities can be financed and carried out to the standard required by the Regulator.
>
> (Skybary, 2021)

The Accountable Manager is a very important part of the EASA Basic Regulations (EU Regs) and Implementing Rules and all its Parts. Many Chicago Convention contracting states adopt this very same approach where a single most senior executive is appointed by the organisation (owner, president, chairman or someone with full authority and power of attorney to act on behalf of the holding company) as the Accountable Manager to the civil aviation authorities. Note that the AM is appointed and not nominated, a difference we will look at later, but none-the-less needs to be accepted by the regulating NAA.

In the EU Regs 965/2012 (EU EASA, 2021 a–d), Part ORO AOC, the Accountable Manager is mentioned:

> Personnel requirements (a) The operator shall appoint an accountable manager, who has the authority for ensuring that all activities can be financed and carried out in accordance with the applicable requirements. The accountable manager shall be responsible for establishing and maintaining an effective management system.
>
> (EU EASA, 2021 a–d)

Again in the EU Regs 1321/2014 (EU EASA, 2021 a–d), Part 145 AMO, the Accountable Manager is mentioned:

The organization shall appoint an accountable manager, who has corporate authority for ensuring that all maintenance required by the customer can be financed and carried out to the standard required by this Part.

(EU EASA, 2021 a–d)

This term, Accountable Manager, is constantly used in EU Implementing Rules: IR, EU 965/2012 Operations 46 times, in IR EU 748/2012 Initial Airworthiness 41 times and in IR EU 1321/2014 Continuing Airworthiness 107 times.

One of the serious responsibilities of the AM is mentioned in the EU Regulations, where a declaration or a statement is required by the AM. EU IR 965/2012 or EU IR 1321/2014 and others require the AM to sign a declaration or statement that the company he or she leads is compliant with the regulations and shall always remain so. The AM signs many declarations and makes many commitments in accordance with the regulations. In law, a *declaration* is an authoritative establishment of fact. To make a false legal declaration is a criminal offence.

The guidance material of the EU regulations states each time that the intent of a declaration is to: (a) have the operator or organisation acknowledge its responsibilities under the applicable safety regulations and that it holds all necessary approvals; (b) inform the competent authority of the existence of an operator or organisation; and (c) enable the competent authority to fulfil its oversight responsibilities in accordance with the regulations on the operator or organisation.

Similarly, in the GCAA CARs the Accountable Manager concept is followed. The GCAA considered the AM role very important and wanted to ensure this was emphasised.

It was very clear what was expected by the appointment of the Accountable Manager by the Board, Chairman or owners, as well as very clear to the appointed Accountable Manager what was expected of them, that they issued a document called a Safety Alert No. 2018-07 (UAE GCAA, 2018) to clarify and extract from the regulations the accountability and responsibility of the AM. This safety alert, in one document, captures the regulatory responsibility of the AM in the UAE GCAA CARs but is very similar to accountabilities and responsibilities of the EU EASA and the other ICAO contracting states. The important points from the alert are as follows:

The intention of the Safety Alert 2018-7 is to:

a) Inform regulated organisations about the process and procedure for acceptance of a person appointed as Accountable Manager;
b) Inform regulated organisations about the non-liability of the GCAA with regards to acceptance of the AM and the appointed PHs;
c) Explain what the GCAA expects from the AM following his acceptance by the GCAA. …
   • An organisation holding an approval from the GCAA is responsible for appointing the Accountable Manager with the overall

- responsibility for the organisation to remain in compliance with regulation;
- The Accountable Manager is responsible for nominating Post Holders to deliver specific functions in relation to the management system of the organisation;
- The Accountable Manager is responsible for ensuring that there are initial assessments and periodic review of PHs' competence with suitable action taken when safety performance is compromised, which could include the provision of training, coaching environment whether their performance may be monitored or dismissed. ...
- Experience has shown that the Accountable Manager has a significant effect on safety and compliance issues:
- Organizations need to understand their (legal) responsibility in appointing Accountable Manager by establishing effective selection criteria;
- An approach towards performance-based regulation and risk-based oversight means that the GCAA will have a higher expectation on industry performance – directly linked to AM's competencies;
- SMS's effectiveness can only be as good as the leadership and participants.

In smaller organisations the Accountable Manager may also be a nominated Post Holder.

Seniority

One would expect that the Accountable Manager would be at a level in the organisation no lower than one that accepts direct reports from the nominated Post Holders required by the applicable standards. Though the appointee will often be the chief executive officer (CEO), president, managing director, general manager or similar title, it is not necessary for him/her to be the "controlling mind" of the organisation. It is perfectly possible for an Accountable Manager to be answerable to and directed by another person or persons, and still retain the appropriate level of authority to ensure that activities are financed adequately and carried out to an acceptable standard. The appointee need not be the person who sets overall company policy or objectives. The proposed organisation chart, terms of reference and letter of appointment (if applicable) can be used to demonstrate seniority. Evidence of directorship would also be helpful if held.

Budget

The appointee should be able to satisfy the GCAA that he/she has an operating budget or financial control limit, and that he/she had a meaningful input into determining the size of the budget. The exact financial details need not be disclosed, but the GCAA will need to be satisfied that governance exists, and is demonstrably appropriate to the scope of the operation. The appointee should be able to explain to the GCAA why he/she believes that the budget is adequate for the circumstances, and show evidence that he/she has the funds at their disposal without reference to a higher authority. If necessary, a written statement to that effect from such higher authority may suffice.

Standards

The appointee will be requested to show he/she has a basic understanding of the standards applicable to his/her organisation. For example, when it comes to an AOC holder, the following are the applicable standards:
The UAE Civil Aviation Authority:

- CAR-OPS 1 or/and 3 (as applicable);
- CAR-M;
- CAR-X; and
- CAR-145 (if applicable).

This understanding is essentially high level, with particular reference to the appointee's own role in ensuring that standards are maintained. The sections of the UAE civil aviation law that relate to AOCs should be understood, and the appointee should have a sound knowledge of the requirements of CAR-OPS that relate to the Accountable Manager and his/her function.

The appointee should also be able to demonstrate knowledge of the requirements related to the appointment of the persons within the organisation with designated responsibilities required under the relevant regulatory material.

For an AOC holder, such persons are:

1. The person responsible for flight operations;
2. The person responsible for crew training;
3. The person responsible for ground operations;
4. The person responsible for the compliance manager/quality manager;
5. The person responsible for accident prevention and flight safety programme/SMS;
6. Those persons required by CAR-M.706(c) and (d); and
7. In addition, those persons required by CAR-145.30 (b) and (c) may apply.

The GCAA will need to be satisfied that the appointee understands what the regulations require him/her to be responsible for, and can explain how the Post Holders have been selected and how their continuing competence will be monitored. The appointee should be prepared to explain the proposed policies on initial assessment, periodic review of managerial competence and provision of training where a need is identified. Significant changes in the operating environment or operational scope should be considered as possible review triggers. The GCAA also needs to be satisfied that he/she fully understands the significance of interrelated regulations such as CAR-X, CAR-M and CAR-145, and the reason and legal responsibility for signing the related exposition or operations manual commitment of the organisation to comply with the procedure specified therein.

The GCAA may require the appointee to attend an acceptable course designed for Accountable Managers (UAE GCAA, 2018).

Safety Alert 2018-7 (UAE GCAA, 2018) captures all aspects of the AM's accountable responsibilities and the exact expectations of the regulator. The regulator wishes to avoid the placement or appointment of an Accountable Manager that is unable to understand or enforce what they are accountable for. This has been the case in the past when Boards appoint an AM that is not sufficiently knowledgeable, has the wrong attitude or is just unaware of his or her accountable responsibilities. It must be understood that the Accountable Manager sets the culture of safety and compliance in the organisation—if he or she is not an evangelist of aviation safety and regulatory compliance, the organisation shall struggle with safety and compliance from its core.

Another contracting state, the Canadian Civil Aviation Authority, Transport Canada (TC), other than clearly detailing the Accountable Executive role in the civil aviation regulations, felt so strongly about the role that they also issued a specific document on the role, similar to that of the GCAA. This document is called "Selection of your Accountable Executive" (Transport Canada, 2021). Note that the Canadians do not call the position the Accountable Manager but the Accountable Executive (AE). This is a similar title used as the US FAA, which we shall review later in this charter. This TC document assists in addressing the AE accountable responsibilities at the selection stage of the position, giving guidance to a Board or organisation on who would be a suitable person for the role. This process of selecting the AM/AE will be reviewed further later in the book.

So, we have seen the UAE GCAA approach and the Canadian TC approach: both are contracting states to the Chicago Convention and both have the intention to ensure that the AM/AE understand their regulatory responsibility. Still, there is a slight difference in both approaches. The GCAA clarifies that the AM does not need to be the top executive "controlling mind" (UAE GCAA, 2018) of the organisation but can be reporting to another person, while the TC is not entirely clear on this point. The EASA currently does not offer an AMC or GM as the GCAA or TC do, but instead embed the AM responsibilities in the regulations, defining their function multiple times. In addition to ensuring that the AM understands their accountability, it is also essential for the Chairman of the Board, or whoever appoints the AM, to understand that they are required to empower the AM to be financially able to lead the organisation with regards to safety and compliance with the regulations. It is interesting that the TC, in particular, focuses on the document "Selection of your Accountable Executive, Appendix A & Appendix B" (Transport Canada, 2021), where the

An introduction to the Accountable Manager 31

nominee is assessed by the Board or Chairman for actual independence of leadership and ability to finance safety operations and compliance with the regulations. It is essential that the Board and Chairman understand this as important, and the AM understands his or her accountabilities.

Earlier, we looked at the AM signing declarations and statements. Upon the appointment of the AM, the Canadian TC will insist the owner or chairman of the board of the organisation signs a compliance statement appointing the AM (Figure 2.1), and the AM also signs the same statement accepting the appointment. This ensures both the appointee and the selected person understand the seriousness of the position and the accountability and responsibility that the position needs. This is also the first time the owner or chairman is involved with ensuring that they understand the appointment of the AM must come with the full delegation and full authority to fund and finance and make decisions without interference or restriction to ensure compliance with the civil aviation regulations. If at any time the AM feels he/she does not have the full authority and is being undermined or overruled or prevented from funding, the AM has a moral and legal obligation, as he/she is accountable, to make this

COMPLIANCE STATEMENT

I, _____, Certificate Holder for

_____, hereby appoint

_____ as Accountable Executive

I, _____ (name)

_____ (position title)

_____ (signature)

accept the responsibilities of this position for

_____ (name on certificate)

for the following certificates:

☐ Flight Training Unit   ☐ Manufacturer
☐ Approved Maintenance Organization   ☐ Air Operator

Figure 2.1 Canadian TC Accountable Executive compliance statement (Transport Canada, 2021).

known to the NAA. This is one of the challenging relationship issues between the AM and his employer that we shall examine in more detail later.

Interestingly the US FAA FARs take a different approach. No single responsible person is identified in the FARs for a civil aviation operation in Part 91 (US FAA, 2021 a–d), 121 (US FAA, 2021) or 135 (US FAA, 2020). In Part 145 (US FAA, 2021 a–d), we can see the first time the term Accountable Manager is used—in AC 145-9A the Accountable Manager is identified as:

> **Accountable Manager.** The person designated by the certificated repair station (CRS) who is responsible for and has the authority over all repair station operations that are conducted under part 145, including ensuring that repair station personnel follow the regulations and serving as the primary contact with the Federal Aviation Administration (FAA).
>
> **Note:** The FAA's definition of an Accountable Manager may differ from the European Aviation Safety Agency's (EASA) definition of an Accountable Manager; however, one person may serve both positions.
>
> (US FAA, 2017)

Interestingly, the FAA changed the title to AM for Part 145 Repair Stations, but FAR Part 5.25 for Safety Management (US FAA, 2021 a–d) details the title of the Accountable Executive and develops this in AC 120-92 (US FAA, 2015).

So note in the US, the term Accountable Manager is used in the maintenance regulations FAR Part 145, but Accountable Executive is used in the Safety regulations FAR Part 5, while in Canada, the TC uses the term Accountable Executive in the operations regulations CAR 106. In the EU and the UAE, the EASA and GCAA use the term Accountable Manager consistently in all regulations, as do many contracting states of the world that are harmonised with the EASA regulations.

So the FAA approach is to introduce the concept of a single senior Accountable Executive at the safety regulation level, rather than at the operational regulation level. It is applicable only for certain types of operations, such as FAR 121 Air Carrier, and not in FAR 135 as FAR 5 Safety Management is only mandated for FAR 121 operations and was mandated in January 2015. This is a different and interesting approach as it suggests that, previous to FAR 5 Safety Management, the FAA FARs did not have the concept of a single leading executive. FAR Part 5 uses the word "accountable" and insists and regulates that this person has the financial and human resource control qualities and leadership of ensuring compliance with the certification of the operator, which means in accordance with the regulations. It is also interesting that the FAA FAR Part 5 requirements for an AE are not required for other types of operations other than Part 121, such as FAR 135 AOC or FAR 125. This can be considered confusing: why is leadership (and safety management systems) important in one area of an aviation operation but not in another? Though the requirement for an AE is found in FAR Part 5 Safety Management regulations, it does mention clearly that the AE is accountable for operations in accordance with the certificate they hold, as well as for safety management and performance. This is clear in the following three sentences below describing the AE's accountabilities:

(1) Is the final authority over operations authorized to be conducted under the certificate holder's certificate(s).
(2) Controls the financial resources required for the operations to be conducted under the certificate holder's certificate(s).
(3) Controls the human resources required for the operations authorized to be conducted under the certificate holder's certificate(s).

(US FAA, 2021 a–d)

AC 120-92 further develops the identification of the AE in the same way as the Canadian TC did in their Accountable Executive document. The difference is the TC CARs insert the requirements for the AE in the operational regulation, and not only in the Safety Regulations. In fact, the FAA AC 120-92 uses almost the exact same flow chart as the TC to identify the Accountable Executive.

It can be noticed that the FAA approach to compliance with the ICAO Annexes and SARPs is slightly different than that of the EASA and, in fact, the rest of the world. This has shown that there are two main philosophies influencing the world of civil aviation regulatory: compliance and harmonisation with the Annexes and SARPs. While harmonisation does appear between many contracting states, it appears mainly with the EASA philosophy, which can arguably be said to be less similar to ICAO than the FAA, but none the less appears to be the favoured compliance style. Interestingly, the FAA approach to the Accountable Manager is slightly different from EASA and the rest of the world, where there are times that an air operation does not need an AM or Executive Leader to lead compliances and safety management. When they are mandated, the responsible accountabilities of the AM differ very slightly in the FAA and EASA regulations, but the concepts remain the same, as do the core responsibilities and core leadership requirements. This can be seen more clearly when we look at the mandated regulatory, organisational structure of a certified civil aviation operation in each contracting state, such as an EASA organisational structure for an air operator, EU Basic Regulations, IR Air Operations (Figure 2.2).

The AM is clearly responsible for leadership, financing and resourcing of the operation and training, and airworthiness of the organisation. In the EASA, the Safety Manager and the Compliance/Quality Manager are not Nominated Persons, but is a named person. The regulations are clear that the AM is the responsible person for both safety and compliance. (This shall be further examined later in the book.) The AM nominates the management team to the authority, NAA. The NAA then accepts or rejects the AM's nomination based on their appropriateness and qualifications for the position.

Below is an FAA organisational structure for an air carrier FAR Part 121 (Figure 2.3).

34 *An introduction to the Accountable Manager*

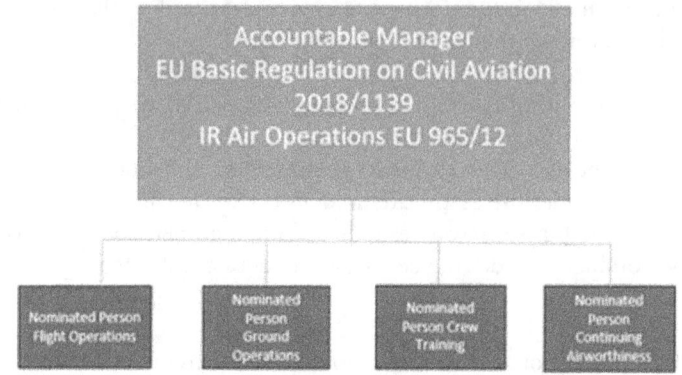

Figure 2.2 EASA AM and NP organisational structure (EU EASA, 2021 a–d).

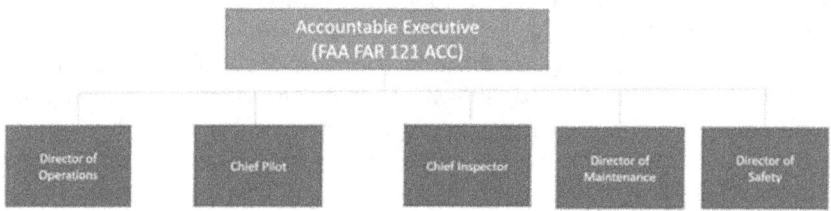

Figure 2.3 FAA AE and Management Personnel organisational structure (US FAA, 2021 a–d).

Here the Accountable Executive is clearly responsible for the leadership, financing and resourcing of the operation, and training, maintenance and safety of the organisation. In the FAA the Director of Safety (DOS) has a function called Internal Evaluation Programme (IEP) that is very similar to the EASA or GCAA Compliance/Quality Assurance function of managing the Q/CMS. The DOS IEP function is not a regulated or mandated function in the FAA regulated environment, but a voluntary function supported not by an FAR but by an Advisory Circular, AC 120-59B (US FAA, 2018). Similar to the EASA, the Accountable Executive is the ultimate responsible person for safety and for the IEP. The owner or president nominates the management team to the authority, who then accepts or rejects the nomination.

In the GCAA, an organisational structure for an air operator CAR Part Ops 1 or 3 (Figure 2.4) is as follows.

The Accountable Manager is clearly responsible for the leadership, financing and resourcing of the operation, and training, safety, compliance and airworthiness of the organisation. In the GCAA, all positions are nominated Post Holders including the quality, safety and security positions. The Accountable Manager nominates the management team to the authority, who then accept or reject the nomination.

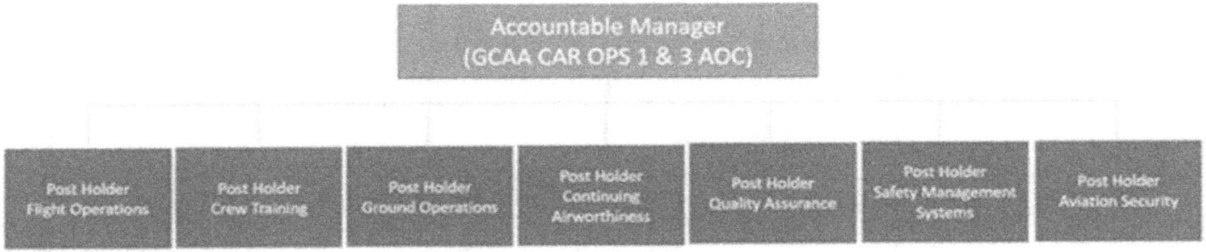

Figure 2.4 GCAA AM and NPH organisational structure (UAE GCAA, 2021 a–c).

Though the organisational structures look different, they are, upon closer examination, quite similar. The GCAA has mandated all the management positions as nominated Post Holders, but do allow duplication of positions in certain circumstances. This assists in keeping the operation lean at start-up, but all nominated Post Holders must pass the acceptance interview and be qualified as required by the GCAA CAR. The EASA does not make the compliance/quality management position a nominated position. They are, in fact, an appointment that the authority must accept.

With regards to accountable and regulatory leadership, the FAA approach is to separate the types of operations, Parts 121, 135, 125 and 91. At the same time, the GCAA does not do so; all are treated the same. The EASA has recently adjusted the regulations to include non-commercial complex operations (NCC), such as large private jet operations, but even then have a definite need for the Accountable Manager. The FAA goes on to make the Accountable Executive's appointment dependent on the type of operation mandated for: only FAR Part 121 air carriers, but not for Parts 135, 125 or 91, and makes the AM appointment mandatory for Part 145 repair stations. It is clear in the EASA and GCAA regulations that the AM is the accountable leader for a safe and compliant operation. It is a little harder in the FAA regulations to identify who is the ultimate accountable leader in Part 135 or 125 operation as the application for a Part 135 operation lists three management personnel, i.e. the director of operations, the chief pilot, and the director of maintenance with no need for a leading Accountable Executive. FAR 125, Part 91 is not a certified operation, so it is even harder to identify who the leader is, and who is responsible in these cases.

It is clear in EASA, the GCAA regulations and the FAA FAR 121 regulation, as it is with many other NAAs, that the AM plays the leadership role that is accountably responsible for compliance with the regulations for flight and ground operations, airworthiness, maintenance, safety, training and aviation security. He or she is legally liable and, by signing statements, indicate they understand this and accept this position of responsibility and accountability. They also state that they have the independent authority to act and supply funds and hire qualified personnel to ensure a safe and compliant operation. We shall now look closer at the two roles of quality/compliance management and safety management, areas that the AM is definitely responsible for, but has an appointed person to assist them with this accountability.

The quality management system

The Quality Management System, or more correctly the Quality Monitoring System (QMS), exists clearly in the EASA and GCAA regulations, and is also referred to at times as the Compliance Monitoring System (CMS), depending upon whether the regulatory environment is operations, airworthiness or maintenance, as it swaps between them. The ICAO Airworthiness Doc 9760 (ICAO, 2020) and in Annex 8 (ICAO, 2021 a–c), as well as in the EASA regulation Part

M or 145, all refer to ensuring that regulatory and procedural audit is maintained as part of a QMS that is overseen and managed by a quality manager who is appointed and answers to the AM. In contrast, in EASA EU Reg 965/2012, it is referred to as a Compliance Management System and overseen and managed by a compliance manager. In practice, QMS and CMS are the same, and provided the manager is qualified, they can be appointed as both the quality manager for airworthiness and maintenance and the compliance manager for operations and is frequently referred to in EASA regulations as the management system. The AM is clearly responsible and accountable for the Management System and in fact leads the administration of the management system.

QMS and CMS have their origins in the ISO 9001 quality management systems (ISO, 2015), "Plan, Do, Check, Act". Leadership is a very important aspect of the QMS, and the culture of quality and compliance comes from the top leader, the Accountable Manager. A failure of the AM to create a culture of compliance, quality and continuous improvement shall cascade down to directors, managers and staff, resulting in the failure of the company to regard compliance and quality as a very important part of the corporate operation.

It is clear in the EASA and GCAA civil aviation regulations that the Accountable Manager, remains responsible and accountable for the continuous monitoring of compliance of the organisation with the regulations, even though they nominate (or name) a quality/compliance manager. This can be seen easily as the Accountable Managers are the signatories of the quality manual that includes the quality policy statement, a commitment to quality and compliance standards. At no time should the Accountable Manager mistakenly assume that the quality/compliance manager is ultimately responsible for compliance in the company (Figure 2.5).

In EASA, the AM-appointed manager for QMS/CMS is not a Nominated Person, but a named person in the ops spec and OMA, acceptable to the regulator. At the same time, in the UAE GCAA CARs, they are a nominated Post Holder, but in all the AM retains the responsibility and accountability for quality, compliance monitoring and actual compliance with the civil aviation regulations. It is required by the civil aviation regulations that the AM is aware of the non-conformities with the regulations or with company procedures, as well as any corrective action to be taken on any finding of non-conformity. The regulations require the quality or compliance manager to have access to the AM in order to report back, giving continuous feedback of audits and compliance issues. A formal quality/compliance meeting should take place and should be minuted at least twice a year.

So it is clear that the AM is responsible and accountable for compliance with the regulations and the company procedures. This includes the establishment of an effectively resourced and funded quality/compliance monitoring system and management system. The AM is also to appoint a quality/compliance manager. This exists in most NAA CARs and that person is either nominated or proposed by the AM, but is approved or accepted by the NAA. That manager assists in the implementation and administration of the QMS/

Sample Quality Policy Statement

Europa Aviation Limited, EAL, aims to be a trusted partner to its clients by providing consistent, reliable and high quality services.

We are committed to providing our staff with the resources and opportunities to develop their initiatives, talents and creativity to maximize their contribution to the success of our Company and the continued satisfaction of our clients.

Quality performance is one of the cornerstones of our culture and is considered a personal responsibility of all employees. To maintain quality performance of all business units at the highest level, the following aims are pursued:

- Complying with statutory obligations, standards, specifications and codes of practice relevant to quality management;

- To cultivate and maintain the commitment to continual improvement and communicate our goals and objectives to every one of our employees;

- The provision of all necessary resources and support to ensure the effective operation of the Company's Quality Management System (QMS);

- The involvement of all staff in the continuous improvement of the Company's processes and procedures; and

- Regular monitoring and review of all company systems and processes through an audit programme to ensure ongoing compliance and continual improvement.

We are committed to achieving these objectives by incorporating a QMS that is integrated into every part of our operation. This QMS is based on the International Standard ISO 9001:2015 and all relevant EASA regulatory requirements relating to the EAL AOC, CAMO and AMO.

Our Quality Management System is approved by my self being the CEO and must be adhered to by all employees both management and staff, involved in the delivery of services to clients, ensuring safe and compliant flying operations, aircraft maintenance and other support activities.

Mr. Hans Smitt

CEO & Accountable Manager

Europa Aviation Limited

Figure 2.5 An EASA or GCAA company quality policy statement signed by the Accountable Manager.

CMS and perhaps also in authoring the quality/compliance manual. It is, however, the AM who remains accountable and responsible for signing the quality/compliance statement—a significant commitment and undertaking in itself. It is essential that the AM and QM/CM have a very close working relationship and the QM/CM has access to the AM to give correct feedback and updates on compliance issues. The required minimum twice annually meetings are questionable if that frequency is really adequate for the AM to be fully aware and be knowledgeable of their accountability for compliance. In practice, an AM who takes quality and compliance seriously conducts monthly briefs from the QM, reviewing findings from audits, especially reoccurring findings and level 1 or 2 findings. The AM would be briefed by the QM on the root causes of significant findings and how the company is addressing those root causes. If the root cause is not identified and corrected, it is highly likely that the non-conformity shall re appear at a later stage. It is highly recommended that an AM undergoes basic QMS training to understand the concepts and theories behind QMS, auditing and non-conformity management, and continuous improvement. QMS or ISO 9001 training is enlightening and does change the outlook of a leader regarding the attention to detail, compliance management and the value of audit. There is a wide variety of software available to assist the quality/compliance manager in managing the audit cycle and non-conformity/finding management.

Similarly, the NAA will conduct audits on the operator. It is expected that the AM is present to meet with the NAA and attend the AOC or AMO audits. The frequency of audits reflects the NAA's compliance opinion of the AOC or AMO. The more frequent the audits, the more concerned the NAA is of the compliance of the AOC or AMO. A normal audit cycle would be one NAA audit every 12 months. Anything more would suggest the AOC or AMO is being monitored by the NAA or the NAA have concerns on compliance or other important issues. This should be used as an important guide for the AM on the opinion of the NAA on the management system that the AM is accountable for.

So, to summarise, it is clear that the QMS/CMS is the ultimate responsibility of the Accountable Manager. They are the custodians and champions, ensuring the corporate culture is one of quality and compliance from the very top of the board room to the flight deck and to the hanger floor. Understanding the pillars of QMS and supporting the quality/compliance manager in addressing audit findings is essential, as is the installation of a continuous improvement culture where procedures and processes are constantly audited and, where needed, improved. It is also very important to understand that the QMS process is predominantly focused on regulatory compliance, and is effective on other non-regulatory procedures such as service and customer satisfaction. While perhaps the QMS/CMS manager will be very busy on regulatory audits, addressing findings and with regulatory compliance issues, the system is very effective on non-regulatory oversight and audits, such as customer service or other service-related processes. This is taking an ISO 9001 approach that has its origins in customer satisfaction.

A final interesting question to be considered is who audits the quality system? The answer is the regulating NAA. The NAA expects the AM to publish an audit programme for the year that the QM, along with his qualified auditors, shall implement. The AM is accountable for the QMS, which includes the definition and implementation of the audit programme and the coordination with the NAA, who shall conduct their audits on the civil aviation company, the AOC, AMO, DOA, CAMO or otherwise. It is recommended that the AM has good knowledge of the QMS, perhaps attending not only an aviation QMS course but an ISO 9001 course also. The concept of QMS, compliance management and continuous improvement is an excellent one that can be applied to all aspects of business, not only the civil aviation regulatory aspects.

In the FAA operations regulations, FAR 121 and 135, there is a different approach and requirement for the quality/compliance monitoring. There are, in fact, no regulations mandating the QMS function. The FAA instead makes the system of compliance audit voluntary and refers to in an Advisory Circular 120-59B (US FAA, 2018) calling it the internal evaluation program (IEP). The IEP has all the traits of a QMS as well as a safety management system and is regarded as a function under the director of safety (DOS), who should have a manager of the internal evaluation progamme (MIEP) with the qualifications and capability of internal auditing, tasked with administering and running the IEP (QMS) function including all audits and finding management. The AC also goes on to recommend that the IEP does not stop at regulatory and safety evaluation, but also customer service evaluation, perhaps more close to ISO 9001 than the EASA or GCAA QMS regulations, as customer service and continuous improvement are the core concepts of ISO 9001. If an air carrier is seeking to obtain IOSA approval they must have a QMS or IEP programme in place.

The safety management system

In this section of the book, we shall review two important safety management systems that should exist by law in a civil aviation company. Only one of them is mandated by civil aviation regulations, the aviation safety management system (SMS), as in Annex 19 of the Chicago Convention and ICAO. The other system has legal accountabilities but the requirements are not in the civil aviation regulations, rather in the occupational health and safety regulations for any type of operating civil aviation company or otherwise. To start with, we shall review the civil aviation SMS requirement and the responsibilities and accountabilities for the Accountable Manager to be aware of.

We have seen that the AM is the custodian and responsible person accountable to the civil aviation regulator, the NAA, for the quality and compliance management of the civil aviation organisation he or she manages. We saw that continuous improvement is desirable as a management concept. The exact same exists for the safety management system, where the AM is also not only the custodian but also the legally responsible and accountable person for the safe and compliant operation of the company. It should also be understood that the QMS system ensures continuing compliance is established, and also it does this with the SMS system—the QMS audits the SMS to ensure continued compliance with the NAA safety regulation that are required as a result of the latest ICAO Annex.

ICAO Annex 19, the most recent Annex, introduced the concept of safety management in aviation, making it a SARP. The NAAs took this new Annex and developed civil aviation regulations. It is the responsibility of the NAA to ensure that a state safety programme (SSP) is established, and this requires each operator or maintainer in civil aviation to develop their own SMS in accordance with the SARP and Annex. We saw earlier that an SMS is embedded into every operational and airworthy regulation in EASA, while in the GCAA CARs it has a stand-alone regulation in CAR X (UAE GCAA, 2020). Just as the Am signs the quality policy statement committing to its effective implementation in the organisation, they also sign the safety policy statement with the exact same intention to ensure implementation of the safety culture and all its procedures and processes. Just as the AM can assign a quality/compliance manager to administer the process of the QMS, so can they appoint a safety manager. Interestingly the FAA FAR 121 is the only operational regulation that calls for the AE to be responsible for the SMS and to accept accountability for the safe operation of the air operator under FAR 121. As with the EASA equivalent, the FAA AC 120-92 (US FAA, 2015) calls for the AE to ensure a safety culture exists, with the four components of the SMS programme:

1 Safety policy documented, endorsed and practised by the Accountable Executive.
2 Safety risk management, where risk and hazards are identified and mitigated.
3 Safety assurance, similar to QMS, where audits are conducted to identify non-compliances.
4 Safety promotion through AE evangelising and training.

Embedded into the four components of the SMS is the concept of open reporting, a just culture and risk management, where hazard identification exists as a common practice. Also where the management of change (MoC) is a controlled process that is frequently practised for identifying risks for each change the company goes through. Another core activity of the SMS is the emergency response plan (ERP): the SMS requires that an effective ERP is identified within the company and organisation.

The AC 120-92 goes on to further say that, "The Accountable Executive has the ultimate responsibility for safety management within the organization". The specific duties of the AE are looked at in more detail in the discussion of Sec 5.25 below.

Section 5.25: Designation and responsibilities of required safety management personnel

a) Designation of the accountable executive

The certificate holder must identify an accountable executive who, irrespective of other functions, satisfies the following:

(1) Is the final authority over operations authorized to be conducted under the certificate holder's certificate(s).
(2) Controls the financial resources required for the operations to be conducted under the certificate holder's certificate(s).
(3) Controls the human resources required for the operations authorized to be conducted under the certificate holder's certificate(s).

(4) Retains ultimate responsibility for the safety performance of the operations conducted under the certificate holder's certificate.

(b) Responsibilities of the accountable executive

"The accountable executive must accomplish the following:

(1) Ensure that the SMS is properly implemented and performing in all areas of the certificate holder's organization.
(2) Develop and sign the safety policy of the certificate holder.
(3) Communicate the safety policy throughout the certificate holder's organization.
(4) Regularly review the certificate holder's safety policy to ensure it remains relevant and appropriate to the certificate holder.
(5) Regularly review the safety performance of the certificate holder's organization and direct actions necessary to address substandard safety performance in accordance with Sec. 5.75.

(US FAA, 2015)

Just as the AM/AE is required to draft and sign the quality policy statement, they must do the same with the safety policy statement. More than a commitment, this is, in fact, an undertaking where the AM/AE accepts their accountability to the regulator and regulation for compliance and safety (Figure 2.6).

The same definition and signing of the safety policy statement is required by EASA regulations and the GCAA CARs, using the term Accountable Manager, while in the FAA, the term used is the Accountable Executive (Figure 2.7).

As we now understand the AM's responsibilities with SMS, we can start to see a similarity to the QMS and CMS. The AM accepts responsibility and accountability for the SMS, enabling and championing a culture of safety and compliance, supporting the audits and finding management, supporting education and training, and supporting the appointed safety manager in accomplishing the SMS tasks. All of these responsibilities are very similar to the QMS/CMS; the one significant difference is the use of hazard and risk identification methods. The SMS studies a project or task prior to its accomplishment and identifies the risk and hazards in doing that task, followed by inserting risk mitigation actions to reduce the hazards effects or likelihood before the task is accomplished. This means the SMS is *proactive*, while an audit of QMS is a *reactive* strategy, identifying shortfalls retrospectively by conducting audits and correcting non-compliances. While both systems have many similarities, this is the main difference between a corrective reactive QMS and mitigating proactive SMS. If both QMS and SMS are applied effectively in a civil aviation company, you have created a system where the AM has clear visibility and knowledge of how the company is performing with regards to compliance with the regulatory accountability and responsibility. This protects the organisations' licenses and, therefore, their ability to operate and participate in the business, with the correct processes of management of change and risk/hazard identification, with

SAMPLE SAFETY POLICY STATEMENT

The Executive Management of Aircraft Airlines Limited (AAL) recognizes that an effective Safety Management System (SMS) is vital to the success and longevity of the Company. Therefore the Executive Management is committed to implementing and maintaining a fully functional SMS and to the continuous improvement of the level of safety throughout AAL.

- Executive Management of AAL will establish specific safety-related objectives and will periodically publish and distribute to all employees those objectives and plans.

- These safety objectives will be monitored, measured, and tracked to ensure overall corporate safety objectives are met. All employees and individuals in the company have the responsibility to perform their duties and activities in the safest practical manner.

- AAL Executive Management is committed to providing the necessary financial, personnel, and other resources to establish and maintain a fully functional SMS.

- AAL Executive Management is dedicated to establishing a confidential employee reporting system to report all hazards, accidents, incidents, and safety issues without fear of reprisal.

- Activities involving intentional disregard for FAA regulations, company policies and procedures, illegal activities, and/or drugs or alcohol may be subject to disciplinary action.

- As a component of the SMS, AAL Executive Management is committed to establishing, maintaining, and periodically exercising an emergency response procedure and plan that provides for the safe transition from normal to emergency operations.

Executive Management will convey this expectation to all employees through postings, intranet site, company newsletter, and any other means to ensure all employees are aware of the company's SMS, their duties and responsibilities, and our safety policy.

This safety policy will be periodically reviewed by Executive Management to ensure it remains relevant and appropriate to the company.

Ms. Mary Smith

Chief Executive Officer and Accountable Executive

Aircraft Airlines Limited

Figure 2.6 An FAA company safety policy statement signed by the Accountable Executive.

mitigation actions or activities and tasks as a daily part of operating. Then the AM can be assured that the company is operating safely always, assessing and anticipating possible events in advance and in compliance with the regulations. It should be said and understood that ensuring the company is operating safely is the primary moral accountability of any Accountable Manager.

Two other very important aspects of SMS that have a significant effect on the company are detailed in ICAO Annex 19 (ICAO, 2021 a–c) (ICAO, 2021 a–c), regulated in EASA under Part ORO (EU EASA, 2021 a–d) and under GCAA CAR Part X (UAE GCAA, 2020) are also covered by FAR Part 5 (US FAA, 2021 a–d). These are the Management of Change (MoC) and the Emergency Response Planning (ERP). Both MoC and ERP are part of the SMS programme

Sample Safety Policy Statement

In Europa Aviation Limited, EAL, Safety is a core function and an integral part of the way we conduct our business. We are committed to developing, implementing, maintaining and continually improving our strategies and processes to ensure that the highest standards of Safety are achieved.

As the Accountable Manager of the Company having the ultimate responsibility for the conduct of the organization's affairs and the full authority for human and financial resources, I have established the following commitments as part of our efforts to demonstrate and implement a highly effective and efficient Safety Management System (SMS):

- No economic priority or commercial pressure shall overrule our efforts to achieve the safest operations;
- Highly competent staff and the required financial and technical resources will be allocated to implement, manage and carry out safety strategies and processes to support this Policy;
- In the delivery of our services, the Company shall meet and exceed whenever possible customer expectations;
- If a conflict arises between Safety, production and/or customer requirements, Safety shall prevail;
- The Company shall comply with all applicable legal requirements, standards and "best practices";
- Everyone has a role to play in communicating this Policy and safety principles at all levels, in fostering an organizational culture of safe practices and procedural compliance, in effectively reporting safety issues, and in initiating preventive/corrective actions in a just, consistent and transparent manner;
- Safety objectives and standards of Safety performance must be established, measured and regularly reviewed in our aim to continually improve the effectiveness of our SMS;
- Contractors shall comply with and adhere to this Policy, safety guidelines and operational procedures outlined in our documented manuals and management systems;
- The Company shall review the SMS periodically to ensure continual improvement, suitability, adequacy and effectiveness;
- The Company shall establish and implement hazard identification and risk management processes in order to eliminate or mitigate safety risks associated with our business activities to a point which is "as low as reasonably practicable";
- The Company shall clearly define employee accountabilities, responsibilities and acceptable behaviors for the delivery of safety;
- Safety communication schemes and training programs shall be implemented to ensure all employees diligently perform their safety obligations and to promote workforce awareness on safety hazards, risk mitigation and lessons learned from our safety investigative processes.

Every employee has an individual responsibility to strictly comply with this Policy and to implement the Safety Management System principles and guidelines within Company activities, procedures and/or programs. Heads of Departments shall also implement a "Safety Performance" based approach within their own sections. Ultimately, we all have a duty to act in accordance with our Safety regulations and legislation legislations, and to carry out our work in a manner that protects ourselves, our assets and all of our stakeholders.

Mr. Hans Smitt

CEO & Accountable Manager

Europa Aviation Limited

Figure 2.7 An EASA or GCAA company safety policy statement signed by the Accountable Manager.

An introduction to the Accountable Manager 45

with the intention of developing a management system that is prepared and organised, thus resulting in risk-mitigating. This concept of a well-managed and organised approach to projects or organisational changes results in a reduction in hazards and risk. This culture of MoC comes from the AM and cascades down to each employee. There is also a possibility that an AM will experience a significant adverse or unfavourable event, perhaps even an emergency. The concept of ERP prepares the organisation for executing the best possible managed approach and best possible outcome from an unfortunate event. ERP includes the rehearsal and drill of events such as fires, crashes, bomb threats and other possibilities. Again, the adoption of ERP in the organisation starts with the AM.

It can be seen that both MoC and ERP are very sensible approaches to change, projects and events. MoC can be used in routine situations, such as for the replacement of a senior employee or the introduction of a new aircraft type or a new capability within the company. MoC is the concept of clear and documented appropriate project management of new tasks, using project management technics such as leadership, terms of reference, planning, meetings, minutes and action items. But it also includes the risk and hazard identification report with resulting risk mitigation actions and tasks identified. This is an important part of SMS and is the responsibility of the AM, often delegated in task to the safety manager, but not delegated in accountability or responsibility. Similarly, the ERP is a systematic written plan that is rehearsed frequently within the company to ensure preparation for emergency scenarios from aircraft crashes to office building fires. Again, this is the responsibility and accountability of the AM but who often delegates in the task to the safety manager. Rehearsals or drills, or simulations of unfortunate or even catastrophic events, is a healthy way of ensuring the organisation is as ready as they can be to react in the best way to the time when such an event or incident should happen. The AM should ensure the organisation is ready and practised in managing unfortunate emergency events.

Occupational and environmental safety and health programme

Just as with the aviation SMS programme, the Occupation and environmental safety and health (OHS) programme must be the responsibility and accountability of the top management and is, by law, a mandatory requirement for operating companies, aviation or otherwise. When the SMS regulations came out as a result of Annex 19 from ICAO, then followed by the OSH (which is not an ICAO requirement but a local country law), there were attempts to merge them both into one document and one system, but the NAAs did not agree to this and insisted that the aviation SMS documents and programme were separate from the OSH and the EHS programmes. The NAA had nothing to do with OSH or EHS and the ICAO Annexes, and nothing to do with their regulation or their oversight. The OSH regulations in many territories originate from other regulators such as the Department of Transport and

Department of Labour, which have regulations for all industries, not just civil aviation regulations. The stance of the NAA is that they regulated in accordance with the ICAO SARPs and Annexes. The OSH does not have its origins in the SARPs or Annexes. So, while the Accountable Manager would perhaps prefer to merge both programmes for efficient use of resources, it has been rejected until now from most NAAs.

The main motivation for a country to mandate that organisations develop and implement an occupational health programme can be found in the World Health Organization (WHO), Art 2 of its Constitution. It includes promoting the improvement of working conditions and other aspects of environmental safety and hygiene. In this case, the WHO is like ICAO, while the regulator of OSH is the DoT in the UAE, like the NAA. Though we need to be clear that the OSH programme is not required or regulated by the NAA and the NAA prefers the programme is managed outside of the SMS programme. It often turns out that small to medium organisations give the OSH responsibility to the same manager as they give the SMS responsibility to, the safety Post Holder.

The OSH programme should address all determinants of workers' health, including risks for disease and injury in the occupational environment, social and individual factors, and access to health services. The accountable executive for this responsibility is more often than not the AM of the AOC or AMO, as he or she has the finances and resources at their disposal to ensure compliance—non-compliance can result in the loss of the commercial operating license (not AOC or AMO) and also significant fines.

The OSH programme and requirements are similar to the SMS where a senior executive, such as the CEO, COO or the AM/AE, is accountable and responsible for compliance with these regulations. The neglect of them or deviation from them resulting in an incident or accident is a criminal offence. It is a requirement to produce a policy statement, just like SMS, to develop an OSH culture through training and promotion. Where exactly OSH and SMS authority start and finish is sometimes a little grey, but it is said anything before the aircraft steps is OSH and anything after the aircraft first step is SMS.

Just as the SMS programme has a policy statement signed by the AM, so does the OSH programme (Figure 2.8).

Note that in the US the FAA and OSHA, Occupational Safety and Health Administration, have issued an MoU to work together to ensure the regulations overseen by both regulators do not conflict with each other. This has started in the cabin with flight attendants.

The Accountable Manager and their relationship with the NAA

We have seen that the chairman, or the board presents their candidate Accountable Manager to the NAA. The NAA expects the board to present a qualified candidate that has knowledge of civil aviation regulations and an exact understanding of the accountabilities that the position undertakes. The NAA

Occupational Safety and Health Policy

Europa Aviation Limited, EAL, believes that it is a fundamental moral and social duty to provide a safe and healthy working environment, and to foster an accident-free workplace while meeting all relevant occupational health and safety legislations. No economic priority or commercial pressure shall overrule health and safety at work.

In our aim to achieve a high level of OSH performance, our company has implemented an active aviation OHS Management System to provide a structured approach to the management of risks inherent to our activities. As an integral part of this system, our company is committed to:

- Complying with all applicable local and federal OSH laws and regulations, in particular, the countries Occupational Safety and Health Systems Framework (OSHAD SF) and the countries Department of Transport OSH requirements;
- Establishing and implementing risk management processes in order to eliminate or mitigate risks associated with our business activities;
- Defining employee accountabilities and responsibilities for the delivery of safety;
- Ensuring all employees are provided with adequate and appropriate safety information and training to ensure they are qualified and competent to perform their functions;
- Establishing and maintaining an effective Safety Reporting System for reporting information concerning OSH issues;
- Establishing and measuring safety performance against realistic objectives and targets;
- Ensuring that contractors and service providers adhere to our OSH Policy, guidelines and procedures;
- Implementing audit and assurance programs to monitor performance and compliance;
- Allocating the required human and financial resources to support this Policy and associated management programs;
- Enforcing OSH as one of the primary responsibilities of management and employees;
- Conducting annual management reviews to ensure continual improvement, suitability, adequacy and effectiveness of our OSH Management System.

It is the responsibility of Heads of Department to integrate this policy within Company activities, procedures and training programs. Through our proactive management of hazards and risks, it is essential that all Company employees strictly comply with this Policy and diligently implement the OSH Management System in their area of responsibility. All employees have a duty to act in accordance with our OSH regulations and legislations, and to carry out their work in a manner that protects themselves, other workers and the environment.

Mr. Hans Smitt

CEO & Accountable Manager

Europa Aviation Limited

Figure 2.8 A company safety and health policy statement signed by the CEO and Accountable Manager.

frequently rejects a candidate either based on their lack of civil aviation knowledge or based on their inadequate delegated financial and control authority. Remember, the AM must have the authority to finance the safe and compliant operation of the company as well as the full authority to hire and fire personnel required to ensure that compliant and safe operation. Also, they must have the authority to nominate to the NAA and directly manage each of the required Post Holders. While the chairman and the board can express opinions on required regulatory staff and required regulatory procedures, the AM must have the independent authority delegated to him or her to make Post Holder staff decisions, as well as the management of funds, and also the independent delegated authority to spend funds to support regulatory compliance. We shall review the Post Holders later in the book and their role in reporting to and supporting the AM in their effort to ensure a compliant and safe operation.

The first interaction between the NAA and the AM for a new company applying for an AOC or AMO or DOA or other civil aviation approval or certification, is in the pre-application phase, where the AM presents the NAA application form. If any of the Post Holders are recruited at this time, it is also expected that the AM presents his or her nominations while submitting the application. The NAA would expect the AM/AE, the first person recruited, to manage the establishment of the organisation, ensuring it is in accordance with the civil aviation regulations. Also, it is the AM/AE who signs the compliance undertaking, a part of the application form to the NAA, for any civil aviation company approval or license. This is in the case of a new company; in the case of an established company the AM should still be presented, and the declaration and undertakings are still to be signed and renewed with the name and signature of the newly appointed AM or AE. The NAA shall conduct an interview of the potential new AM and examine their knowledge of civil aviation regulations and their role, ensuring they understand the accountabilities and responsibilities that are given to them as per their position, should they be accepted. The NAA will spend time examining the delegated authority that is given to the applicant AM to ensure they do, in fact, have full signatory authority to finance a safe and compliant operation as well as the ability to hire and fire the required civil aviation personnel. It is not unusual for the NAA inspector at the interview to ask many times for proof of the delegated authority from the board. In fact, the FAA requires a letter of delegation from the chairman or the board to the named AM. They specifically say in that letter the exact authority and amount of finance that has been delegated to the applicant. It should detail the exact amount that they, as the AM/AE, have at their disposal to fund a safe and compliant operation. The FAA shall comment if they feel it is insufficient or otherwise. The UAE GCAA do something similar at the initial interview where they expect a letter from the owner of the company, clearly stating that they shall delegate and empower the named AM to run the company and have available funds for a safe and compliant operation. Without this letter, there is always doubt that the AM can, at their own discretion, fund airworthiness activities and aviation training and aviation safety management to ensure complete compliance with the civil aviation regulations as a priority above other company spending. This can be an area of conflict between the AM and the owner or chairman as it can also be between the AM and the NAA. It should be remembered by all AMs that they sign a declaration when assuming the position, that they have authority to and can fund a compliant operation. To fail in this or to falsely sign that declaration knowing that they do not have the finance or authority at their disposal, can be criminal under civil aviation law.

GCAA CAAP No 8 (UAE GCAA, 2017), now replaced by AMC 08 (UAE GCAA, 2021 a–c), explains the application process for a civil aviation company—in this case, an AOC—and explains the Accountable Manager must be accepted by the GCAA:

8.2.5 Management/Post Holders Qualification Resumes

8.2.5.1 General

The application for nominated personnel acceptance including Accountable Manager and Post Holders are via the E-services. The application form GTF-NPA-001 is to be completed and should include a brief resume containing information on the individual qualifications, certificates, ratings, and experience of personnel selected for at least the following, or equivalent, positions.

(a) Accountable Manager
(b) Post Holder Flight Operations
(c) Post Holder Continuing Airworthiness (if applicable)
(d) Post Holder Crew Training
(e) Post Holder Ground Operations
(f) Post Holder Aviation Security
(g) Post Holder Quality Assurance
(h) Post Holder Safety Management System (SMS)

Applicants must ensure that only qualified and trained personnel are appointed for the above appointments in addition to those in-charges of Flight Safety, Security and Cabin.

On case to case basis the GCAA may consider a person to hold more than 1 of the nominated posts.

Operators are advised that a lack of technical management appointments during the application process will delay the process. The GCAA will assess the applicant's qualifications and experience as well as their managerial ability. A knowledge test in the form of an interview or written test will be conducted before the nominated accountable manager and Post Holders are accepted.

An AM/PH is initially approved for 3 months and renewable by a maximum another 3 months. If the PH doesn't meet expectations during any of these 2 periods, he will be revoked. An AM/PH is required to attend a PH course during the 3 first months.

8.2.5.2 Expected Qualifications and Level of Experience

The qualifications and level of experience of Post Holders and key operational staff will vary according to the scope and size of the proposed operations. Post holders and key operational staff shall have an understanding with Human Factors and Human Performance limitation besides the following specific requirements.

8.2.5.2.1 Accountable Manager

To serve as an Accountable Manager, a person must have the qualifications, experience and authority as specified in CAR OPS 1 or 3.

(UAE GCAA, 2021 a–c)

Once accepted by the NAA, the AM then is accountable and responsible for compliance with the regulations and for the definition and implementation of the QMS and SMS. It is essential that the AM starts and continues with a relationship that is open and transparent with NAA. The NAA shall nominate a principal inspector for the company, and the AM, along with the quality Post Holder or Nominated Person, shall develop a relationship of mutual respect and communication should be cultivated. The inspector wants the company to be safe and compliant, and that is exactly what the AM is accountable for, so their relationship is built upon common objectives and should be the basis of an open and transparent relationship. Some Accountable Managers may prefer to leave the relationship building with the NAA to his quality Post Holder and other Post Holders, but as the AM is accountable to the NAA, they should build a good working relationship with the NAA and have regular contact, instilling a level of confidence that the AM is taking his task seriously and putting the compliance with the regulations as a priority. An AM that delegates most communication with the NAA to a subordinate to relieve himself of the burden could be seen as an AM that does not prioritise their civil aviation regulatory accountability and responsibility. Good judgment should be used by the AM when deciding when to visit, meet with or communicate the NAA and when to delegate this task to another person.

At times, in order to minimise the expense at starting up a new company, the AM could possibly also hold another position, perhaps a Post Holder position. This is permissible provided they are qualified to hold the positions, for example, the AM is also the Post Holder of flight operations or the Post Holder of safety.

It is recommended that, prior to NAA audits, the AM should be present at the launch meeting with the NAA inspectors. The task of coordinating with the NAA can then be delegated to a Post Holder, perhaps the quality Post

Holder or quality manager, who is delegated as the main point of contact for the NAA within the civil aviation organisation. In fact, the quality manager is often the preferred point of contact for the NAA as they are accessible, highly qualified in the regulations and workings of the NAA, and often the AM is very hard to get in contact with because of their busy schedule running the company. It should be noted in the FAA FARs, and in the EASA EU Civil Aviation Regulations, the quality manager or director is not in fact, a Post Holder or Nominated Person. In EASA they are an accepted person by the NAA but not nominated. At the same time, in the GCAA, the quality manager or quality director is a nominated Post Holder position, nominated by the AM to the NAA. In order to be accepted by the GCAA, he or she should qualify and pass the requirements. The relationship between the AM and the quality manager is very important as the AM is accountable and responsible for the QMS but relies on the quality manager to administer the day-to-day running of the QMS and compliance management and oversight system. It is often said that the quality manager keeps the AM legal, compliant and out of jail.

Below, we look the times the AM interacts with the NAA through forms and declarations. These are very serious interactions, and the AM should fully understand their implications:

- Undertaking to comply with the civil aviation relegations by signing the application for an approval or license for the company they represent.
- Undertaking that the company is compliant with the civil aviation regulations by signing the compliance statement for the company.
- Signing the quality and compliance policy statement, as this sets the compliance culture for the company.
- Signing the safety policy statement, as this sets the safety culture for the company.
- Signing the Aircraft Maintenance Programme, a critical technical document that details how the fleet is kept airworthy in accordance with the OEM and NAA's requirements.

These signatures are more than assurances to the NAA, but commitments and undertakings that carry liability. The AM has to be sure that the management system in place is sufficient, so when they sign these documents, they are, in fact, not only real and current but effective and applicable. The NAA expects the AM to understand each document and its relevance to the continuing compliance, safety and airworthiness of the company. Still, even before they sign these documents, the presented AM to the NAA must first be able to convince the NAA inspector that they are knowledgeable and qualified for the position. For some NAAs, this includes confirming that they have attended appropriate training or coaching, or presenting their CV as a qualified person having knowledge in civil aviation. The NAA shall conduct an interview of the presented candidate that can take anything from one hour to four hours where probing questions are asked, and their knowledge of the task at hand is reviewed. This sets the stage for the relationship between the AM and the NAA. Normally, the NAA inspector conducting the interview will be the principle inspector assigned to the company that the AM represents. Should the AM be presented by an existing approved company, the inspector will explore their knowledge of the existing company and the business it exists in, as well as the history of that company. This will be a chance for the NAA inspector to highlight any concerns the NAA has with the existing company in its compliance and address previous and historical findings, and an opportunity to inform the new possible AM of their opinion of the company. The NAA will expect the candidate to have a good knowledge of the current audits and findings, in particular the open findings. An indication of a company's compliance record with the NAA is the frequency of audits conducted by the NAA or if the company is, in fact, on a watch. These tell-tale signs will give the AM candidate a clue as to the status and reputation of the company that he or she is about to be in charge of and accountable for. Preparation by the AM candidate is required, as is the understanding that their acceptance into the position by the NAA is not a formality. The candidate should consider the consequences of being presented to the NAA and that this initial interview could result in them not being accepted by the NAA to take the position. Again, preparation, training and coaching are recommended. It is not unusual that the candidate is not accepted at this first presentation and further training is required, before re-presenting the candidate a second time once training has been conducted. As much as 18 months can pass before the NAA accepts the AM as now having adequate knowledge. Also, the AM could be rejected as not being appropriate for the position, but this is very rare. The board and chairman would need to appoint an interim solution to fill the AM position in the meantime.

The NAA inspector is an agent of the law and has the authority to exercise civil aviation law and take measures when the law is not followed or when a person or company is in contravention of the law. This means the inspector should be treated with respect, and it should always be understood this is a legal matter—compliance with the civil aviation regulations is the law.

If we review the times that the AM interacts with the NAA other than at the start of his or her appointment or when signing forms and declarations, it is normally at pre-audit meetings when the NAA come to the company to conduct an audit. The pre-audit meeting is when the NAA presents their plan to audit the company, perhaps the AOC or the AMO. At the meeting, the NAA principle inspector will present the NAA audit team and the audit schedule for the coming days. It is very important that the AM is present to show support and respect to the NAA and show they understand the importance of compliance and the audit as part of the QMS continuous improvement and compliance management system. To delegate sending another Post Holder to this meeting would not be recommended as it could appear that the AM is too occupied to be concerned with the NAA and compliance. The frequency of audit is a reflection by the NAA on the confidence of compliance that they have in the company. Anything less than 12 months would indicate that the

NAA has issues or concerns with the company's compliance. Anything more than 12 months suggests the NAA has confidence in the compliance of the company with the regulations. The AM should be aware of the NAA's confidence in the company and should be aware of the concerns the NAA has, if any, with the company. It is recommended the AM knows the last audit findings, how the company addressed them and whether they closed them or not. This will give the NAA confidence that the AM is involved with compliance management and aware of his accountabilities.

If the AM is new to aviation or has climbed the ladder through a non-technical or non-operational career path, it is highly recommended that the AM as a candidate, prior to taking up the role, undergoes civil aviation regulation training and reads this book. Some states shall mandate that all AM candidates attend a civil aviation regulations course that includes civil aviation QMS and SMS subjects and human factors in aviation. This will assist the newly appointed AM in understanding their accountabilities and will go a long way to appeasing the NAA, further assisting the AM in getting to a place where their appointment can be accepted. It is not recommended that an AM candidate meets the NAA for their interview unprepared and unknowledgeable of the regulations, safety and quality/compliance.

Fiduciary corporate responsibilities

A fiduciary is a person that holds a legal or ethical responsibility to act in the interest of a third party. The fiduciary responsibilities are usually to take care of finances, investments or assets in a responsible way that maintains the value of the assets or investments or a way that facilitates the appreciation of the value of the assets or investment. It is a legal responsibility or legal accountability for the fiduciary. This responsibility is contracted through a legal appointment such as a contract of services or an employment contract. An attorney-client relationship is a fiduciary responsibility where the attorney is the fiduciary to consider and act in a way that is in the best interest of the client at all times. A director of a company has a fiduciary responsibility to act and manage the company he or she is a director of, in a way that is in the best interests of the shareholders of the company. The CEO of an airline or any civil aviation company, whether they are a director of the board or not, can, in their employment contract, undertake a fiduciary responsibility to act at all times in the interest of the shareholders or owners of the airline. In many cases, we have seen the CEO of a civil aviation company can also be the AM presented to the NAA. This means the CEO has the fiduciary accountability to the shareholders by law to manage the company in a way that is in their interests, protecting their investment, as well as, regulatory accountability to the NAA to ensure the company operates in a manner that is compliant with the civil aviation regulations and in a safe and airworthy way. There is no doubt that an airline or civil aviation company does not exist to be a perfectly compliant operation that is unprofitable or unsustainable, but exists to be both a profitable and sustainable business that rewards investors and shareholders with dividends. Both these legal responsibilities and accountabilities can, at first glance, be seen to be in conflict with each other, but really protecting the civil aviation license or NAA approval is in the interest of the shareholders and owners. To lose the licence due to non-compliance or operating the company in a non-safe method would be to remove the company's ability to operate and generate revenue. So, putting compliance with the civil aviation regulations as a priority is, in fact, a satisfactory action to comply with the CEO's accountable responsibilities, but again it is not always seen that way when times are tough and spending is controlled due to difficult financial constraints. The challenge of the CEO is to manage a compliant operation while being a profitable business. The chief financial officer (CFO) then has a role to play, which the CEO must lead. The CFO, as a natural controller of spending, must realise that the CEO, if they are the AM, or whoever is the AM, has full authority to spend and hire and fire Post Holders to ensure compliance and a safe and airworthy operation. The relationship between the AM and the CFO is a very sensitive relationship, and if the CEO is the AM and the CFO reports to them, this eases the tension and possible areas of conflict. However, if the AM is not the CEO but a person of equal seniority to the CFO it can mean that the CFO might resist or object to spending and try to persuade the more senior CEO that the spending the AM wishes to make should not be approved. Then the AM is compromised in meeting his civil aviation regulatory accountability.

The relationships of the chairman, the CEO and the CFO are a challenge for the CEO to manage on a governance level. The relationship of the CEO, CFO and the AM, if the CEO is not the AM, shall be explored further later in the book. The triangle of regulatory and fiduciary accountable responsibility that occurs when the AM is not the CEO is one that is of great concern for the NAAs. It should be realised that a situation where the CEO is not the AM creates a sensitive and a complex challenge that we shall further examine.

Corporate leadership

A corporation is a legal entity that exists to represent its owners or shareholders in daily operations. It can trade, take loans, hire staff and enter into contracts, as well as many other business activities. A corporation can be for both profit or non-profit and has limited liability, which means the owners and shareholders can participate in the profits of the corporation by taking dividends, but they themselves have no personal liability for the debts. The owners and shareholders should appoint a board of directors (BoD) that runs the governance and fiduciary oversight of the corporation. The BoD should appoint a management board who have day-to-day responsibilities to run and operate the corporation and are responsible for executing the business plan strategy identified by the CEO, which is approved by the BoD. The BoD do not carry personal liability for the corporation's debts, but do have a duty of care to the corporation that can incur liabilities if it is shown there is neglect on their part. Both the owners and shareholders can have a claim on the BoD if they are seen to neglect their duties and responsibilities. Also, the staff and public can also have a claim on the BoD if negligence and wilful neglect or fault arising from a director's breach of their duties results in damage or loss.

In US corporations, the top director of the management board is delegated to the executive authority to run the corporation on a daily basis. This person is often called the Chief Executive Officer (CEO) and defines strategy and the strategic direction of the corporation or company, often in the form of a business plan. The CEO may or may not be invited to be a member of the board of directors, but is still delegated to act as the executive director. The delegation of authority should be from the board of directors in the form of a board resolution that clearly states the CEO's level of authority for decision making and for spending. The CEO understands the reason the corporation exists and its intentions and desired direction. Reporting to the CEO is the president, who works very closely with the CEO and is responsible for executing and implementing the strategy of the CEO. In smaller corporations, the CEO is also the president, called the CEO and president in one title. The CEO reports to the chairman of the board, who manages the board of directors. A balance of power often exists between the chairman of the board of directors and the CEO. The CEO defines strategy and the business plan that the chairman and the board of directors approve. Then the CEO executes the business plan. The chairman and the BoD's position is one of governance while the CEO position is a managerial position. Careful thought should be taken prior to inviting the CEO to the board—to make the CEO both governance and management can, at times, create conflict and even overload the CEO.

Vice presidents (VPs) report to the president. VPs are subject matter experts in their areas of responsibility.

In the UK, the CEO is often called the managing director (MD) and the directors report to them. Directors are specialists in their area, managing the day-to-day operations of their speciality, much like VPs. In the UAE, often the term general manager (GM) is used to describe the CEO or MD. It is important to understand that directors of the board are different from directors who report to the CEO or managing director. Directors of the board sit on the board deliberating on governance issues and strategy, while the day-to-day functional directors manage their speciality operations, implementing the approved defined strategy.

If we recall the regulatory requirement of the AM, the CEO or MD, if adequately empowered with delegated authority, fits the bill of a cooperation leader and of a regulatory compliance leader where both positions carry legal accountabilities. The corporation accountabilities are explained and detailed in the corporation and company law of the country, while civil aviation regulatory accountabilities are explained in civil aviation regulations and the aviation law of the country. If the CEO or MD is also a board member, he or she will be very busy as there are governance responsibilities as a board member, day-to-day management responsibilities as a CEO or MD, and civil aviation responsibilities as the AM. It is normally the case that the CEO of the company is also the AM presented to the NAA for acceptance, but it can be found sometimes that the AM position can be a person in the company other than the CEO that also reports to the CEO, such as the COO. This person shall only assume the AM position if successfully presented to and accepted by the NAA, after sitting an AM interview and satisfying the required financial and company management authority. It has been seen before in large corporations, such as flag carrier airlines, that a chief operating officer (COO) is presented as the AM to allow the CEO to focus on business and strategy, especially if the CEO is also a member of the board of directors. This leaves the daily operations management including regulatory compliance and safety oversight to the COO. Also, the CEO may not be an aviation person and is not comfortable in taking on the AM role. Since aviation qualifications are not a mandatory requirement of the NAA for a presented AM, knowledge and understanding of the civil aviation regulations, aviation safety and aviation compliance are. This is where a COO, who is an aviation professional, can take on the role and accountabilities confidently, allowing the CEO to focus on their board and fiduciary responsibilities. It should be noted that in the cases of the CEO not being presented to the NAA as the AM but another person is, the NAA shall investigate carefully for evidence that whoever is presented, such as a COO, has the required delegated financial budget, financial authority and management authority to satisfy the needs of the AM role. It is a sensitive decision for the CEO not to be the AM and should be made only after careful deliberation and understanding of its implications.

Financial leadership

The top executive responsible for managing the finances of a corporation is the chief financial officer (CFO). As the top finance executive, one of their priority aspects is enabling a culture and environment of financial responsibility within the corporation. This does have key challenges, including communication of policies and procedures across the corporation, developing and monitoring internal controls, as well as developing and maintaining effective financial reporting and cash finance management processes. The CFO reports to the CEO, and this relationship is perhaps the single most important relationship in the corporation outside of the civil aviation regulatory environment. The CFO supports the CEO in defining the vision and strategy by ensuring the financial implications are identified and are understood. The CFO also supports the CEO in executing the vision and strategy by ensuring the finances are available and that all financial issues are managed efficiently and in a timely manner. The CFO is more than a financial controller or a treasurer; he or she is a financial strategist managing the funds of the company, including the spending and, very importantly, the cash flow. The CFO ensures the company is solvent and able to trade and operate using its funds to support the business plan and strategy and, when new funds are needed, manages the banks and loans. Though the CFO is not fiduciary accountable, he or she has legal procedures to follow and adhere to. Failure to do so can lead to legal action. Though they are not the CEO, the CFO contributes heavily in getting the corporation to a decision on whether to take a strategic direction or investment. The CFO will assess the financial feasibility of such strategies, and then ensure the funds are available for the venture. The CFO also has no civil aviation regulatory responsibility or accountability at all, unless they are also the AM, accepted by the NAA. It is not impossible for the CFO to be the regulatory AM, but it would be highly irregular, and the NAA might ask the question, if is the CFO is proposed as the AM, what role does the CEO play? While CFOs have gone on many times to become CEOs of aviation companies, it would be very irregular for a practising CFO to hold the AM position at the same time.

The US executive search company Russel Reynolds, in 2016, surveyed more than 100 CFOs at leading US companies. The survey found there were strategic benefits to a strong CFO–CEO relationship:

- 82% of CFOs surveyed gave their CEO high marks for overall effectiveness.
- A majority of CFOs said they trusted their CEOs.
- Less than half of the respondents gave CEOs a high score when it came to their ability to coach and develop the CFO.
- 49% of CFOs surveyed said they had a "very strong" relationship with their CEOs.
- The survey found that structural factors have surprisingly little impact on the relationship.
- 70% of CFOs rating their CEO relationship as very strong say they provide their boards with exposure and access to their direct reports.
- For CFOs with weaker CEO relationships, only 40% say they do the same.
- 98% of CFOs with "very strong" CEO relationships say they are comfortable bringing difficult issues to their chiefs.
- 29% of CFOs who reported weak relationships with their CEOs said they are comfortable tackling tough topics with their bosses.

(Russel Reynolds, 2016)

Another US executive search company based in Washington, CFO Selection Ltd, published on their website tips for making the relationship between these top executives work or to explore how a broken one can be mended (CFO Selections, 2017). These tips are also very relevant to the position of the aviation AM and their CFO:

1 Both must be open with each other, have mutual trust and respect and a shared vision.
2 The skills and personality of the CEO and CFO need to complement each other.

3   The CFO should maintain a self-awareness and realise how they are perceived.
4   The CEO gets to deliver the good news, and the CFO is charged with delivering bad news.
5   Healthy tension at times can be productive—accept that rifts are going to happen.
6   Always present a united front.
7   The CFO is a strategic partner and advisor, not a bean counter.
8   A CFO is not expected to be the CEO's "best" friend.
9   The CFO needs to have very high integrity, independence and courage.
10 A good CFO should easily offset his or her cost through value creation, direct cost savings and risk mitigation.
11 The CFO must have a mindset to deliver business results, as opposed to primarily managing the financial organisation and reporting the results.
12 Cultivate the relationship from day one. The CFO reports to the CEO except in extraordinary cases—it's the single most important relationship CFOs must get right from the outset.

When it works well, the collaboration between a CEO and CFO creates a value greater than the sum of its parts, giving the company the power to leap past the competition. If the relationship goes bad, it can tear an organisation apart (CFO Selections, 2017).

So it can be seen that the CEO must nurture and use the relationship with the CFO to assist in defining, documenting, presenting to the board and justifying and implementing strategic decisions. An aviation example would be the decision on which aircraft to buy for the fleet renewal plan. A full financial review is required, as is funding options or a decision on what new route to open up next when a full financial study and feasibility must be done, perhaps led by the CFO. Any reply to tenders must be with the CFO's involvement as they will know the cost implication of executing the tender should the corporation win the project. So while the CFO is not the CEO, they are very involved in many of the activities the CEO conducts. In a listed company, the CFO and the CEO need to be separate people, but in a private company, it is possible that the CFO and the CEO are filled by the same person who may also even be the AM (Table 2.1).

In an aviation context, the CEO runs the corporation and the operation, makes aircraft decisions, training decisions, marketing decisions, fleet decisions and personnel decisions—all supported by good financial sense analysed by the CFO. The CFO is not the decision-maker but an advisor of decisions from a financial point of view. If the CFO, or any other position than the CEO, becomes the decision-maker and the ultimate approver of all decisions, this would be in contradiction to the regulatory accountability of the CEO if he or she is the AM and also the delegated fiduciary authority of the CEO unless the corporate fiduciary is, in fact, the CFO. But it is very unlikely that the regulatory AM is the CFO. A situation may occur where the CFO becomes so

Table 2.1 Objectives of the CEO vs the CFO

CEO vs CFO	
CEO	CFO
Leads the organisation and oversees all departments.	Leads and oversees the finance department.
Is responsible for the strategy of the organisation and sees the big picture.	Responsible for supporting the organisation's strategy with financial resources and creates company-wide budgets.
Has broad scope of duties including managing operations and public relations, making business decisions and leading change.	Has a narrower scope of duties than the CEO, focusing only on activities relevant to the finance department including hiring, training, operations and communications.
Evaluates business risks and gains.	Evaluates financial risks and gains.
Liaises with all stakeholders.	Liaises with stakeholders when it comes to finances (e.g. bankers, investors).
Finds ways to ensure profitability and corporate success.	Monitors profitability and enables corporate success.
Is ultimately accountable for overall organisational performance.	Is ultimately accountable for financial planning and reporting.
May come from any background (including, sales, operations, etc.).	Usually comes from a finance/accounting background.

significant in a corporation and becomes the de facto CEO where the actual named CEO is comfortable for many reasons to take a back seat. This is dysfunctional and if the CEO is the AM, it could violate civil aviation regulations in practice, although maybe not on paper. It is better, if the board has lost faith in the CEO and would prefer the CFO to take the reins, that it is done properly through promoting the CFO to the CEO's position and replacing the CFO, or giving them both positions. This might not pass compliance checks or internal audits as the CEO and CFO positions should be separate for compliance issues for a publicly traded company, but still might be acceptable in a privately owned company.

Reporting to the board

As we mentioned earlier, the CEO reports to the board that is led by the chairman, and perhaps the CEO and/or the CFO are also a board members. Later in the book, we will review organisational structures and the challenges with each possible reporting structure. For now, let's consider and review how the reporting to the board is managed (Figure 2.9).

Note the VPO in this case is same as director of operations—both are different names for the Nominated Person for flight operations. Generally, the NAA do not mind if you used vice president of director titles as long as you are consistent (Figure 2.10).

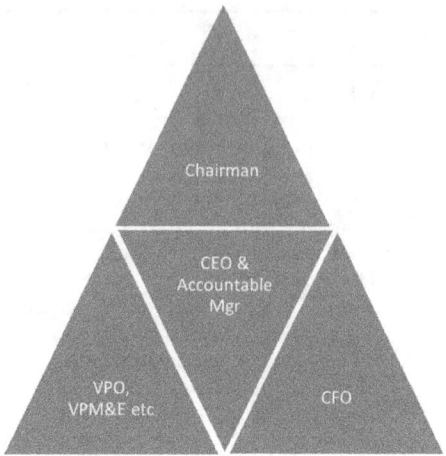

Figure 2.9 The triangle of authority when the CEO is the Accountable Manager.

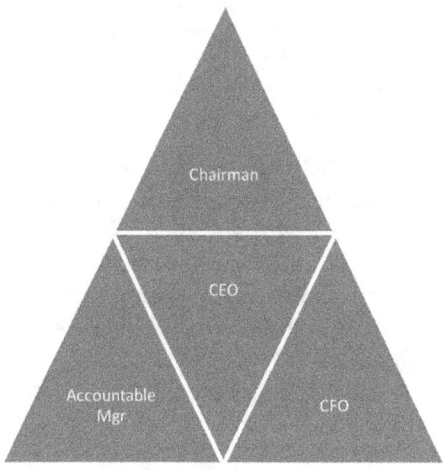

Figure 2.10 The triangle of authority when the CEO is not the Accountable Manager.

The CEO is recruited by and reports to the chairman and board. The CEO's continuing employment depends on the continuing support of the chairman and the board. In this scenario, the CEO presents the business plan, the annual budget, the corporate strategy and the financial reports for board approval and board direction. The reporting is supported by the CFO with financial data, such as profit and loss and cash flow analysis and the financial status of the company to date and compared to the year's board approved budget. Though the CEO takes the lead, the CFO is an integral part of reporting to the board and, in fact, in many ways, is the chief architect of all financial reports and financial data that goes to the board. In order to fulfil their responsibilities, board members must be able to rely on financial information that is:

- **Accurate**: Information must be reliable and accurate. Resolve any question about the quality of record-keeping or accounting first.
- **Timely**: Information should be available to the board within two or three months at the latest.
- **In context**: Information should be presented in relationship to the history, goals and programs of the organisation.
- **Appropriate**: No one-size-fits-all financial report exists. Reports must be designed to communicate information specific to the organisation's current circumstances in a format that matches the knowledge level and role of board members.

(Propel, 2021)

Financial reports should be on the agenda at every board meeting. The CEO should regularly present to the board the organisation's details, like:

- **Income statement** detailing income and expenses for the period versus those in the approved budget year to date, YTD;
- **Balance sheet** showing the corporations assets and liabilities; and
- **Budget**, which should be based on strategic realistic plans and should be approved each year by the board prior to the start of the fiscal year.

In addition to these, once a year, the board should review:

- The annual financial reports and an audit report; and
- The compulsory tax return information.

As well as corporate and financial information, the board should receive a report from the CEO and AM on the regulatory compliance and safety management of the corporation. This is where the AM comes into play. The board must take an interest in the safety and compliance record of the corporation. They must keep an eye on the state of the relationship between the corporation and the NAA. It should be aware of the last NAA audit findings and the open non-compliances, with a description from the AM on why they remain open and the action plan to close and address each item. While these items are perhaps not the reason an owner or shareholder has invested in an aviation corporation, these are very important items that enable the corporation to maintain its safety and compliance standards and hence its licences and approvals. If the CEO is not the AM, it would be of concern that the Board isn't getting a real picture of the state of the corporation with regards to regulatory issues including safety and compliance. Perhaps the company is making great profits, utilising staff and assets to the maximum, at the cost of neglect in compliance, maintenance, training, oversight and safety operations. This might not be a priority for a CEO who is not the AM—their eye is on return on investment for their owners and shareholders as that is what keeps them in the job, and the chairman rates their performance annually on the return, not necessarily compliance and safety.

In the scenario that the CEO is the AM, he or she shall have full authority to make funding decisions and strategic decisions that fully consider regulatory compliance and safety. Remember, violations of the regulations are a criminal act carrying personal liability. Also, in this scenario, the CEO has access to the chairman and the board, and can report on the compliance and safety status of the corporation, thus bringing a compliance and safety reporting culture to the very top management ranks. Their mindset will constantly be on making a sustainable profit in the frame of the regulations and safety, and their decision-making in taking the company forward will always be with judgment in the context of the regulations and safety.

The board represents the owners and shareholders of the corporation. It is in their interest to ensure the company performs financially well, generating revenue, but more so profit. Generating revenue means new business, new lines of income, maximising the use of resources, while generating profit can also mean cost-cutting, lean management, getting your expenses as low as possible, so that as much as possible of your revenue is profit. The CEO has to manage this expectation while at the same time, if they are the AM, manage the safe and compliant operations as well as spending on training, maintenance, qualified staff, new systems and new procedures. These activities at a first glance may appear not to contribute to profit but are instead expenses that take away revenue from being profit. The CEO AM has to be knowledgeable and skilled to convince the board, who have the right to continue or terminate their employment, that spending on compliance and safety issues are in the interest of the owners and shareholders because "Safety = $"—accidents and incidents are extremely costly and can ruin a civil aviation company.

A safe and compliant corporation equals a healthy, successful, profitable and sustainable corporation. If the CEO is not the AM, their business and strategy focus might be different than if they were also the AM. If the CFO accompanies the CEO to board meetings, and the CEO is not the AM, how they brief the board might be quite different than if the CEO was also the AM. The NAA will be very interested in the scenario where the CEO is not the AM, and the AM is a staff member reporting to them, such as a COO. The NAA will want to see the COO's delegated authority to spend and control compliance and safety. The NAA will be very interested if the AM does not have access to owners and shareholders directly or through the board. It is preferred by the NAAs that the top executive has regular access to the owners and shareholders directly or through the board to be able to clearly express the status of their main regulatory duty and accountability. One accident or incident would cost the corporation millions in both reputation and finances. An AM who is also the CEO then has full responsibility and accountability so is in control and has full ability to report to the board on regulatory, compliance and safety issues.

The AM must remember they have the accountable responsibility, and they must set an example of compliance and regulatory respect. The top executive sets the culture of the company, the AM as the top executive such as the CEO has then the ability to establish a culture of safety and compliance. If is the AM is not the top executive, the question must be asked: can they set that corporate culture that aids in safety and airworthiness and shows respect and compliance for the regulations while not being the top executive of the company?

So we can see the senior executive, the CEO, along with the CFO, have many fiduciary responsibilities to the board to ensure they are running a sustainable and profitable business, taking care of the owners and shareholders investments while adhering to the tax laws and financial laws of the country the corporation exists in. These are additional fiduciary responsibilities to those in the interests of the owners and shareholders. In addition, if the CEO is the also AM, they must report to the board on the state of the safety culture and regulatory compliance issues the corporation faces, to ensure that the board understands the industry they are in, the sensitive nature and peculiarities of the civil aviation industry and where the danger and the hazards exist. The AM must bring the board the safety reports and audit reports highlighting the issues that exist and recommending the measures to take. If the AM is not the CEO, then the CEO must give the AM access to the board to ensure the board understands the AM's challenges and responsibilities.

References

CFO Selections. (2017). *Understanding the Relationship between the CEO—CFO—The Ultimate Partnership*. Retrieved from https://www.cfoselections.com/perspective/understanding-the-relationship-between-a-ceo-and-cfo-the-ultimate-partnership.

Collins Dictionary. (2021). *Accountable*. Retrieved from Collin's Dictionary: https://www.collinsdictionary.com/dictionary/english/accountable#:~:text=If%20you%20are%20accountable%20to,your%20actions%20to%20that%20person.

EU EASA. (2020a). Regulation 1321/2014, Part 147 Approved Maintenance Training Organisations. Cologne: European Aviation Safety Agency.

EU EASA. (2020b). Regulation Certification Specification 25 for Large Aeroplanes. Colonge: European Aviation Safety Agency.

EU EASA. (2020c). Regulation Certification Specification 29 Large Rotorcraft. Colonge: European Aviation Safety Agency.

EU EASA. (2021a). Regulation 1178/2011, Part ORA ATO Air Training Organisations. Colonge: European Aviation Safety Agency.

EU EASA. (2021b). Regulation 1321/2014, Part 145 Aircraft Maintenance Organisations. Colonge: European Aviation Safety Agency.

EU EASA. (2021c). Regulation 748/2012, Part 21 Airworthiness & Environmental Certification. Colonge: European Aviation Safety Agency.

EU EASA. (2021d). Regulation 965/2012 Air Operations. Cologne: European Aviation Safety Agency.

ICAO. (2020). *Document 9760, Airworthiness*. Montreal: International Civil Aviation Organisation.

ICAO. (2021a). Annex 19, Safety Management. Montreal: International Civil Aviation Organisation.

ICAO. (2021b). *Document 9859, Safety Management Manual*. Montreal: International Civil Aviation Organisation.

ICAO. (2021c). ICAO Annexes & SARP`s. Montreal: International Civil Aviation Organisation.

ISO. (2015). ISO 9001 Quality Management Systems. Geneva: International Organisation for Standradisation.

Oxford Learners Dictionary. (2021). *Accountable*. Retrieved from Oxfords Learner Dictionary: https://www.oxfordlearnersdictionaries.com/definition/english/accountable?q=accountable.

Propel. (2021). *Board Communication: Reporting Financial Information*. Retrieved from https://www.propelnonprofits.org/resources/reporting-financial-information-board/#.

Russel Reynolds. (2016). *The Power of Industry-Leading CFO-CEO Relationships*. Retrieved from https://www.russellreynolds.com/insights/thought-leadership/leadership-squared-the-power-of-industry-leading-cfo-ceo-relationships.

Skybary. (2021). *Accountable Manager*. Retrieved from Skybary Aviation Library: https://www.skybrary.aero/index.php/Accountable_Manager#:~:text=The%20term%20'Accountable%20Manager'%20may,an%20aircraft%20maintenance%20and%20repair.

Transport Canada. (2021). Canadian Aviation Regulation 106.1 & 106.2 Selection of the Accountable Executive. Montreal: Transport Canada.

UAE GCAA. (2013). Civil Aviation Regulation 147, Approved Maintenance Training Organisations. Abu Dhabi: General Civil Aviation Authority.

UAE GCAA. (2015). Civil Aviation Regulation Part 21, Certification of Aircraft & Related Products. Abu Dhabi: General Civil Aviation Authority.

UAE GCAA. (2017). *Civil Aviation Advisory Publication 8*. Abu Dhabi: General Civil Aviation Authority.

UAE GCAA. (2018). Safety Alert 2018-7, Accountable Manager Acceptance Process. Abu Dhabi: General Civil Aviation Authority.

UAE GCAA. (2020). Civil Aviation Regulation Part X, Safety Management Systems. Abu Dhabi: General Civil Aviation Authority.

UAE GCAA. (2021a). *Acceptable Means of Compliance 08, Issuance or Renewal of an AOC or POC*. Abu Dhabi: General Civil Aviation Authority.

UAE GCAA. (2021b). Civil Aviation Regulation Part 145, Aircraft Maintenance Organisations. Abu Dhabi: General Civil Aviation Authority.

UAE GCAA. (2021c). Civil Aviation Regulation Part OPS 1 & 3, Operations Regulations. Abu Dhabi: General Civil Aviation Authority.

US FAA. (2015). Advisory Circular 120-92B, Safety Management Systems. Washington DC: Federal Aviation Administration.

US FAA. (2017). Advisory Circular 145-9A, Guide for Developing & Evaluating Repair Stations & Quality Control Manuals. Washington DC: US Federal Aviation Administration. Retrieved from FAA AC: https://www.faa.gov/documentLibrary/media/Advisory_Circular/AC_145-9A.pdf.

US FAA. (2018). Advisory Circular 120-59B, Internal Evaluation Programs. Washington DC: Federal Aviation Administration.

US FAA. (2020). Federal Aviation Regulations Part 135, Air Carrier & Operator Certification. Washington DC: Federal Aviation Administration.

US FAA. (2021a). *Federal Aviation Regulation Part 121, Air Carrier Certification.* Washington DC: Federal Aviation Administration.
US FAA. (2021b). *Federal Aviation Regulation Part 145, Aircraft Repair Stations.* Washington DC.: Federal Aviation Administration.
US FAA. (2021c). *Federal Aviation Regulation Part 5, Safety Management Systems.* Washington DC.: Federal Aviation Administration.
US FAA. (2021d). *Federal Aviation Regulation Part 91, General Operating & Flight Rules.* Washington DC: Federal Aviation Administration.
Websters Dictionary. (2021). *Accountable.* Retrieved from Merriam-Webster Dictionary: https://www.merriam-webster.com/dictionary/accountability
Wikipedia. (2021). *Accountable.* Retrieved from Wikipedia: https://en.wikipedia.org/wiki/Accountability

3 Leadership of the Post Holders

An introduction to the Nominated Persons, Nominated Post Holders and Management Personnel

The management team that the Accountable Manager leads is made up of highly qualified and experienced aviation experts in their particular disciplines. These professional positions are referred to as Nominated Post Holders or Nominated Persons in the civil aviation regulations. The leadership skill of the Accountable Manager is how to ensure these professionals are supported financially in their regulatory obligations while ensuring a sustainable commercial company prevails. The relationship of the Accountable Manager with each one of these expert specialists is an essential aspect of successful leadership in any civil aviation company. This is one of the many challenges of the Accountable Manager, spreading the budget to each one of the specialist disciplines who are constantly advising the Accountable Manager on matters of safety and compliance with the civil aviation regulations, as well as the very best practices to employ that give the company a competitive edge as well as compliant operation. This chapter will explore in detail these essential relationships and explain the sensitivities of each.

We will first examine the regulations on the required Post Holder positions that are to be nominated by the Accountable Manager. These slightly differ depending upon the territory the company operates in and is approved by.

EASA 965/2012 ORO.GEN.210 Personnel requirements

(a) The operator shall appoint an **accountable manager**, who has the authority for ensuring that all activities can be financed and carried out in accordance with the applicable requirements. The accountable manager shall be responsible for establishing and maintaining an effective management system.

(b) A person or group of **persons shall be nominated** by the operator, with the responsibility of ensuring that the operator remains in compliance with the applicable requirements. Such person(s) shall be ultimately responsible to the accountable manager.

(EU EASA, 2021 a–c)

EASA 965/2012, as well as the GCAA CAR OPS (UAE GCAA, 2021 a–c) and the FAA FAR 121 (US FAA, 2021 a–c), not only require an Accountable Manager to be appointed and presented to them, they also need the AM to nominate the management personnel to run the civil aviation company. If we remember earlier many times in the book, we referred to the management team specialists in each civil aviation discipline, depending upon the type of company such as an AOC, an AMO, an ATO or a CAMO or a DOA, different Nominated Persons (NPs), or Nominated Post Holders (NPHs), that are required to be in place for a compliant operation. In most NAA jurisdictions, such as EASA or GCAA, the management personnel are referred to as Nominated Persons or Nominated Post Holders. In the FAA jurisdiction they are referred to as Management Personnel. A NP is a regulatory required position that holds responsibility for a particular set of regulations and responsibilities. They are selected and nominated to the NAA by the Accountable Manager. They then undergo an interview and test by the NAA to see if they are qualified and acceptable to the NAA to hold the position they are nominated or named for. The regulations detail the minimum required qualifications for each regulatory position. While the AM remains accountable to the NAA as the person to be held responsible for a compliant and safe operation, the NPs, in each of their specialisation are essential to assisting the AM in meeting his accountabilities. While they are not accountable like the AM, as Post Holders, they do have regulatory responsibilities to meet, and failure to meet those responsibilities can result in losing their nomination by the AM or losing their acceptance as a NP by the NAA and even legal criminal action.

We will now look closer at the required management team for an EASA and GCAA Air Operator's Certificate. The management personnel required by the regulations are nominated by the Accountable Manager to the EASA regulator in an application called Form 4.

Accountable Manager: He/she is the ultimate executive that is accountable for all compliant and safe operations of the company. He or she must have access to funding safe and compliant operations. He or she is not only accountable for complete compliance, but is also the signatories to the safety and quality programmes. They must prove to have uninterrupted direct access to the funds, direct access to the board and chairman, and empowered to make the important decisions themselves. They should have knowledge of the civil aviation regulations, the safety management system, the compliance/quality management systems, and what it means to be an accountable manager. The Nominated Persons or Post Holders must have a direct reporting line to the Accountable Manager.

Nominated Person/Nominated Post Holder Flight Operations: The most senior member of the flight operations department responsible for managing all the crew and for setting all the flight operations standards and ensuring the flight operations safety standards are established and adhered to. Normally he/she is a qualified professional pilot with or having held at one time an airline transport pilots licence or a commercial pilots license as applicable and having being qualified on similar types of aircraft to those operated in the AOC. If he or she is not a professionally qualified pilot, he or she must have a deputy that is a qualified professional pilot. The NP or NPH Flight Operations must report directly to the AM with no in-between line manager. This person is nominated to the NAA as the Post Holder or Nominated Person and will have to pass an interview and a test set by the NAA, for their nomination to be accepted.

Nominated Person/Nominated Post Holder Continuing Airworthiness: The most senior member of the continuing airworthiness department responsible for managing all the airworthiness staff and for ensuring all maintenance management systems are in place and compliance with all continuing airworthiness requirements for the fleet of aircraft and components in accordance with Part M (EU EASA, 2021 a–c) (UAE GCAA, 2021 a–c). Also ensures the airworthiness safety standards are established and adhered to. Normally he/she is a qualified aircraft engineer or technician with an engineering or technical degree or a maintenance technician/engineer's license. If the person is not a professionally qualified aircraft maintenance engineer, he or she can substitute with years of experience and airworthiness courses. The NP or NPH Airworthiness must report directly to the Accountable Manager with no in-between line manager. This person is nominated to the NAA as the Post Holder or Nominated Person and will have to pass an interview and a test set by the NAA for their nomination to be accepted.

Nominated Person/Nominated Post Holder—Crew Training: This is the most senior member of the training department, responsible for managing:

- all the training crew such as pilots and flight attendants;
- safety and emergency procedural trainers;
- for ensuring all training standards are in place for the fleet of aircraft for ensuring all training standards that are in place are applicable and effective and being applied and followed by all pilots and crew.

Normally he/she is a qualified pilot with a training background such as a TRE or TRI with knowledge of the types of aircraft the company operates. The NP Training must report directly to the Accountable Manager with no in-between line manager. This person is nominated to the NAA as the Post Holder or Nominated Person and will have to pass an interview and a test set by the NAA for their nomination to be accepted.

Nominated Person/Nominated Post Holder—Ground Operations: This is the most senior member of the ground operations department, responsible for managing all of the ground operations staff and all of the ground operations procedures. He/she also ensures the ground operations safety standards are established and adhered to. Normally he/she is a career ground operations person with knowledge of aviation safety. The NP Ground Ops must report directly to the Accountable Manager with no in-between line manager. This person is nominated to the NAA as the Post Holder or Nominated Person and will have to pass an interview and a test set by the NAA for their nomination to be accepted. It should be noted that the majority of accidents and incidents happen on the ground; this position should be aware of methods and procedures to maximise the avoidance of ground accidents to aircraft and personnel.

Nominated Person/Nominated Post Holder—maintenance (if Part 145 AMO) (EU EASA, 2021 a–c) (UAE GCAA, 2021 a–c): This is the most senior member of the aircraft maintenance department, responsible for managing all the maintenance staff and for ensuring all maintenance tasks are carried out by the correctly qualified aircraft maintenance technicians or engineers for the fleet of aircraft and components in accordance with Part 145. Also, he/she ensures the maintenance safety standards are established and adhered to. Normally he/she is a qualified licensed aircraft engineer with a maintenance licence and experience on the types of aircraft in the fleet of the company. The NP Maintenance must report directly to the Accountable Manager (AMO) with no in-between line manager. This person is nominated to the NAA as the Post Holder and will have to pass an interview and a test set by the NAA to accept their nomination.

In the FAA FAR Part 145 Aircraft Repair Station (US FAA, 2021 a–c), the relevant management personnel is referred to as the Director of Maintenance.

Three very important other regulatory required positions that are not EASA Nominated Persons but are GCAA Nominated Post Holders (UAE GCAA, 2021 a–c), are the following:

1. **Manager/Nominated Post Holder Quality and Compliance**: The most senior member of the Quality / Compliance department, responsible for managing all the Quality and Compliance Management and Audit staff and ensuring all required regulatory audits are carried out correctly in accordance with the published and NAA accepted audit plan. Normally he/she is a qualified aviation quality professional and qualified aviation auditor coming from either maintenance or engineering background or from an operations background with quality and audit qualifications and experience. He or she should be highly knowledgeable on the civil aviation regulations and the main focal point for the company with the NAA. In a large complex operation, the NAA might ask for the airworthiness and operations function of quality/compliance management to be split between two specialist managers. This position must be extremely close to the Accountable Manager as this person administers and oversees the quality management system and compliance management system of the company on behalf of the AM, who is the signatory of the Quality Statement. In some jurisdictions, such as the UAE GCAA, this position is held in such high regard and is also a Nominated Post Holder position, while in other jurisdictions such as EASA, it is not a Nominated Person position but a named position in the ops spec and OMA. In the FAA regulations, such a position does not exist as a mandated position but is encouraged and, when it does exist, is referred to as the Internal Evaluation

Programme Manager (IEPM) (US FAA, 2021) (US FAA, 2018). The manager of the QMS must report directly to the Accountable Manager with no in-between line manager. This person is perhaps the most important link between any civil aviation company and the NAA. The manager of the QMS manages all communications and coordination between both the company and the NAA and the non-compliance and finding rectification management within the company, as well as the most important regulatory advisor to the AM, keeping him honest and out of a non-compliant situation or position with his accountabilities. One interesting question is, while the Quality/Compliance Manager is responsible for the audit of the company, who is responsible for the audit of the Quality Manager and the Quality department? The answer is the NAA. The NP/Quality Manager must be named to the NAA and even if not a NP such as in EASA, must undergo an NAA interview for acceptance in the position. An important note is in an EASA Part 145 (UAE GCAA, 2021 a–c): the Quality Manager is a Nominated Person, but in an EASA AOC a named person.

2. **Manager/Nominated Post Holder Safety Management Systems**: The most senior member of the Safety department, responsible for managing all the Safety Management and Safety Audit staff and ensuring all required regulatory safety oversight and audits are carried out correctly in accordance with the safety regulations. Normally he/she is a qualified aviation safety professional coming from an operations background with safety and audit qualifications and experience. He or she is highly knowledgeable on the civil aviation safety regulations and the main coordinator with each Post Holder to ensure they are implementing the correct procedures and process for safety management in their discipline. This position must be extremely close to the Accountable Manager as this person administers and oversees the safety management system of the company on behalf of the AM who, is the signatory and Champion of the Safety Statement and corporate safety culture. In some jurisdictions, such as the UAE GCAA, this position is held in such high regard it is also a Nominated Post Holder position, while in other jurisdictions, such as EASA, it is not a Nominated Person position but is a named position in the ops spec and OMA. In the FAA regulations, this position is mandated only for in Part 121 (US FAA, 2021 a–c) air carrier operations under FAR Part 5 (US FAA, 2021 a–c) (US FAA, 2015). The manager of the SMS must report directly to the Accountable Manager with no in-between line manager. This person is perhaps the most important person in supporting the AM in setting the very best safety culture in the company as possible. It is important to realise that the manager of the SMS is not responsible for conducting the SMS activities in each specialised department, but responsible for setting the procedures and processes for each Post Holder to follow, and ensure the SMS regulations are met and complied with. For example, establishing management of change procedures for the Post Holder Flight Operations to follow, or establishing hazard identification procedures and processes for the Post Holder Maintenance to follow and comply within their department. At times mistakenly, Post Holders

think it is the responsibility of the manager of the SMS to undertake the task responsibility, but it is actually the responsibility of the relevant Post Holder. Often Flight Data Monitoring (FDM) falls in the responsibility of the SMS department. In some small organisations, the NAA might permit the doubling up of responsibilities between the manager of the QMS and SMS, but the person should be qualified. In earlier years of SMS, a system called FOQA (Flight Operations Quality Assurance) existed, SMS now encapsulates FOQA. The NP/Safety Manager must be named to the NAA and even if not an NP such as in EASA, shall undergo an NAA interview for acceptance in the position.

3. **Manager/Nominated Post Holder Security**: The most senior member of the Aviation Security department responsible for managing all the Security Management and ensuring all required regulatory security oversight is carried out correctly in accordance with the security regulations. Normally he/she is a qualified aviation security (AvSEC) professional, coming from an operations back ground with security qualifications and experience. He or she should be highly knowledgeable on the civil aviation security regulations. Again, in some jurisdictions, such as the UAE GCAA, this position is held in such high regard it is also a Nominated Post Holder position, while in other jurisdictions such as EASA, it is not a nominated person position. The Manager of the AvSec must in some jurisdictions report directly to the Accountable Manager with no in-between line manager, but in others not. Often in smaller organisations, the Post Holder Ground Operations or the Safety Manager takes on this responsibility of the security manager. It should be noted that due to the sensitivity of the position, some jurisdictions insist on a certain nationality to hold the position. In the GCAA jurisdiction the NPH Security manager must be nominated to the NAA and shall undergo an NAA interview for acceptance in the position.

Different NAAs take a different approach to the Post Holders or Nominated Persons or Management Personnel. For example, lt us compare EASA, GCAA and the FAA for their requirements of Nominated Persons or Nominated Post Holders or management personnel for an air operator.

Note that an EASA Quality Manager for an AMO or CAMO can also be the Compliance Manager in an EASA AOC, if the person is qualified and acceptable to the NAA (Table 3.1).

Furthermore, as we seen earlier, it is interesting to note that in the EU the EASA regulator does not require the compliance, safety or security managers or directors in an AOC to be Nominated Persons (EU EASA, 2021 a–c), but EASA does require in a Part 145 AMO (EU EASA, 2021 a–c) that the Quality Manager is a Nominated Person, while in the UAE the GCAA call them Nominated Post Holders in both AOCs and AMOs (UAE GCAA, 2021 a–c) (UAE GCAA, 2021 a–c). Also, in EASA the AOC Compliance Manager and Safety Manager are referred to as a Named Person in the ops spec and OMA and should be presented to the regulator but not nominated. Furthermore,

Table 3.1 EASA, GCAA, FAA Nominated Persons, Post Holders and management positions (EU EASA, 2021 a–c) (UAE GCAA, 2021 a–c) (US FAA, 2021 a–c)

Position	EASA EU 965/2012 Nominated Persons	GCAA CAR OPS Nominated Post Holders	FAA FAR 121 Management Personnel
Top Accountable Person	Accountable Manager	Accountable Manager	Accountable Executive
Flight Operations	Nominated Person Flight Operations	Nominated Post Holder Flight Operations	1. Director of Operations 2. Chief Pilot
Ground Operations	Nominated Person Ground Operations	Nominated Post Holder Ground Operations	Director of Operations
Continuing Airworthiness	Nominated Person Continuing Airworthiness	Nominated Post Holder Continuing Airworthiness	Director of Maintenance
Maintenance	Nominated Person (AMO) Maintenance	Nominated Post Holder (AMO) Maintenance	Director of Maintenance
Crew Training	Nominated Person Crew Training	Nominated Post Holder Crew Training	Chief Pilot
Quality	Nominated Person (AMO) Quality	Nominated Post Holder Quality	Director of Safety / Manager of Internal Evaluation Program
Compliance	Manager (AOC) Compliance	Nominated Post Holder Quality	Director of Safety / Manager of Internal Evaluation Program
Safety	Manager Safety	Nominated Post Holder Safety	Director of Safety
Security	Manager Security	Nominated Post Holder Security	Director of Operations

in the US FAA regulated territories, the director of safety is required to be nominated only for an Air Carriers Certificate Part 121 (ACC) (US FAA, 2021 a–c). It should be noted that currently in EASA and GCAA regulations there is no need for a Safety Management System for Part M (UAE GCAA, 2021 a–c) or Part 145 (UAE GCAA, 2021 a–c), but this is changing.

It should be noted that the FAA does not mandate or regulate the Quality/Compliance Management System but recommend it in an Advisory Circular AC 120-59B (US FAA, 2018), and call the process of compliance management the internal evaluation program (IEP). We have reviewed this earlier in the Accountable Manager's responsibilities and QMS. The IEP responsibility falls under the control of the Director of Safety or manager of the IEP (US FAA, 2021 a–c) (US FAA, 2018).

In a small operation, the NAA might allow the doubling up of Post Holder positions for a single person to take. This is subject to the person being qualified and accepted by the NAA for both positions. For example:

- The Post Holder Flight Operations and Post Holder Ground Operations
- The Post Holder Quality and Post Holder Safety
- The Post Holder Continuing Airworthiness and Post Holder Maintenance

This is normally allowed by the NAA for a small operator of up to 21 employees or a start-up company wanting to keep a lean, cost-effective management team for the start-up period.

The relationship between the Accountable Manager and the Post Holders

The Accountable Manager is the person who nominates the Nominated Persons (EASA), Nominated Post Holders (GCAA) or the management personnel (FAA) to the NAA for review and acceptance for the positions. They must also report directly to the Accountable Manager. The AM must pay attention to each NP and not only ensure they are qualified and trained correctly for the position he/she nominates them for, as well as ensuring they have adequate funds for financing operations in accordance with the regulations. The AM must also spend time working with and supporting the NP's ensuring regulatory compliance with each area of civil aviation operations of the company, reviewing the findings and non-compliances. While the AM is accountable by law for a safe and compliant operation, the NP shares responsibility for their area of specialisation. Should the NP fail to meet the standards expected to be compliant within the company, and it is identified in an internal audit conducted by the quality or compliance department or external audit by the NAA, a non-compliance finding shall be raised against the department meaning the NP. The level of severity of the non-compliance shall be noted against the finding; for example, a Level 1 finding is to be corrected immediately before the next flight, a Level 2 finding is to be corrected no longer than three months to be exactly defined by the auditor, or a Level 3 finding which is categorised as an observation only, with no time frame for correction. The AM must be aware of and regularly review the non-compliances and findings with the Quality/Compliance Manager and also with the NP that owns the finding and discuss the rectification action to address and close the non-conformity. The AM must support the NP in closing the findings and getting to the root cause of why the finding occurred, and addressing the root cause to ensure it does not reoccur again. Recurrent findings or findings not being addressed in time can be a reflection of the inability or lack of competence of the NP holding the non-conformity, or a lack of interest of the AM. In the case of a non-capable NP, it is essential that the AM address the capability issue by training the NP through management support or some other action, perhaps even dismissal and replacement of the NP.

We have now identified the three most important relationships for the Accountable Manager to manage.

1. Firstly, between the Accountable Manager and the chairman and board, his employer. Where the Accountable Manager must report to the chairman and board on the state of the company, he or she is responsible for and report on their fiduciary responsibilities of profit and loss.
2. Secondly, the relationship between the Accountable Manager and the regulator, the NAA. This is an essentially important relationship where the Accountable Manager must show complete understanding and attention to regulatory compliance with the civil aviation regulations to maintain the licenses and approvals granted to the company by the NAA to operate as a civil aviation company.
3. Thirdly, the very important relationship is between the Accountable Manager with the nominated and named persons: where each nominated person reports directly to the Accountable Manager, where the Accountable Manager must lead, coach, and support the NP in meeting both his accountabilities and, in turn, the NP's responsibilities in accordance with the civil aviation regulations.

This balancing of accountabilities and responsibilities is the challenge of the Accountable Manager, needing a skilled executive capability that understands corporate fiduciary management, civil aviation regulatory compliance, and professional aviation leadership. Reliance on the Nominated Person team is essential, where the AM always understands that the Quality/Compliance Management System (QMS) and the Safety Management System (SMS) is his or her responsibility. The Quality Manager and Safety Manager are essential in supporting the AM in meeting his or her accountabilities. These two relationships are very important, as are all NP relationships, but these two relationships and these two functions are indicators of the regulatory and safety health of the company. For example, when many audit findings are unaddressed, or many hazard identifications are not mitigated satisfactorily, or an increase in ASR's and FDM exceedances, or an increased rate of NAA audits on the company reflecting a loss of faith in the compliance and safety culture. The compliance and the safety culture comes from the top executives and percolates down to every person in the company. A non-attentive or delinquent AM will set a similar corporate culture, which will inevitably result in a delinquent compliance and safety culture throughout the company. The biggest challenge is at times of a difficult economy where the attention of the CEO/AM is predominantly on the fiduciary and financial state of the company. After all, having a wonderfully compliant and safe operation that does not make a profit is not sustainable and is a delinquency of the fiduciary responsibility of the CE/AM. Similarly, to neglect compliance or safety and allow the regulatory authorities to stop or put a limitation on the operation, it will also mean a non-sustainable operation even if it is profitable. So attention to both sides of the responsibilities is essential, and this is why sometimes a large civil aviation company might allocate the AM duties to someone other than the CEO, but, as stated earlier, this must pass a careful examination from the NAA to ensure that person who holds the AM role has the correct delegated power of authority and the correct finances to run and fund a regulatory compliant civil aviation company. It appears it is preferred by the NAA that the top executive is also the Accountable Manager on most occasions, for good reasons.

Now we shall review each Nominated or Named Person in the EASA or Post Holder in the GCAA regulated environment and review the support that they need from the Accountable Manager to ensure the accountability responsibilities are met by the AM as well as the regulatory responsibilities of the NP/PH.

The Nominated Person Flight Operations: The Accountable Manager must first nominate a correctly qualified and capable person. If accepted by the NAA, the AM must ensure funds are available to recruit the correct amount of flight and cabin crew in respect of the flight duty periods and flight time limitations. Also, the AM must ensure the funds are available to correctly operate the aircraft in accordance with the correct standard operational procedures. All of these standards are stated in the civil aviation regulations. Very often, the relationship between the AM and NP FOps is a close relationship, as efficient and effective flight and cabin crew and aircraft management are essential to the success of the operation, while ineffective management can result in non-compliance with the regulations as well as an extra expense or lost opportunities. It is very desirable to have a well-run flight operations department that can contribute extensively to minimising operational costs, efficiently and effectively utilising the crew and the aircraft.

The Nominated Person Crew Training: The Accountable Manager must firstly nominate a correctly qualified and capable person. Then, if accepted by the NAA, the AM must ensure the funds are available to set the standards of flying training, to ensure they are carried out efficiently and to ensure they are effective and if not revised. The crew training NP is essential to setting the standards in training that affect the standards of operations. It is the AM's responsibility to ensure the funds for the correct training and operational standards are available. This is a very important relationship as simulator training is very expensive and has to be scheduled months in advance. The AM must support the NP crew training to ensure the companies training standards support compliance and safe operations. It is very desirable to have an efficiently and effectively trained operating crew as that has a significant effect on reducing operational costs.

The Nominated Person Ground Operations: The Accountable Manager must firstly nominate a correctly qualified and capable person. Then, if accepted by the NAA, the AM must ensure the funds are available to set the standards of ground operations, to ensure they are carried out well, and to ensure they are effective and if not revised. The ground operations NP is essential to setting the standards of the ground operation. It is the AM's responsibility to ensure the funds for the correct ground operational standards are available. This is very important as the majority of accidents and incidents with aircraft happen on the ground and result in very expensive damaging events. The AM must support the NP ground operations to ensure the company's training standards support compliance and safe operations. Well trained efficient ground crew have a significant effect on reducing operational costs from turnaround times to minimising ground incidents and delays.

The Nominated Person Continuing Airworthiness: The Accountable Manager must firstly nominate a correctly qualified and capable person. Then, if accepted by the NAA, the AM must ensure that funds are available to manage and support the maintenance of the aircraft. Even more so than crew training, maintenance is the most expensive part of operating aircraft after the actual aircraft purchase. Careful management of compliance and effective maintenance supported with qualified engineers, compliant parts and tools, and taking aircraft off operations for scheduled maintenance is an essentially important task. It is the AM's responsibility to ensure the funds are available for supporting the continuing airworthiness and maintenance of the aircraft and all its components. The selection of maintenance facilities and the coordination of planning maintenance visits is a very important management task. While the aircraft is not operational, it is not making revenue, which can put the company's fiduciary financial targets in a sensitive state. A well-run continuing airworthiness department can have a large effect on maintenance cost reduction. It is desirable to have an efficient and convenient fleet maintenance plan accepted by the whole company.

The Quality/Compliance Manager: The AM must firstly nominate a correctly qualified and capable person. Interestingly this is not a nominated person position in an EASA AOC (though it is in an EASA AMO) but is a nominated post holder in the GCAA. In EASA, it is described as an accepted named person or position required for the management system. The named person is for the NAA to decide on. The AM must ensure the funds are available to conduct the QMS and the correct amount of internal and external audits required to ensure confidence in compliance. It is also essential that the AM supports the correction of non-compliances and findings, with a continuous improvement philosophy being part of the corporate culture. While the AM is the signatory of the Quality Statement, it is the Quality Manager that is the administrator and facilitator of the QMS. It is the Quality Manager that keeps the AM in compliance with their quality/compliance monitoring accountabilities. The relationship between the Quality Manager and the AM is perhaps, along with the Safety Manager, the most important relationship for the AM with any of his reporting staff. The Quality Manager has their finger on the pulse of the operation and is in frequent communication with the NAA. It is he or she that really knows the status of compliance and the status of the NAA's opinion of the company. The Quality Manager is a very important guide and advisor to the Accountable Manager, and close regular compliance review meetings must take place, where the Quality Manager advises and reports to the AM the results of audits, the management of closing findings, the status of compliance within the company in every department. The relationship of the Quality/Compliance Manager and the other post holders is also very important. The AM must support a harmonious relationship where the quality/compliance manager's role is seen not as a policeman but as a service provider that helps all to continually improve. A further point to be considered is, while the AM encourages a culture of complete compliance, they should listen to the Quality/Compliance Manager on the occasion that a regulation can be met with through an alternative means of compliance (AMOC), supported by an acceptable equivalent safety case study, to be presented to the CAA for acceptance and approval, and signed by the AM.

The Safety Manager: The AM must firstly nominate a correctly qualified and capable person. Again, this is not a Nominated Person position in an EASA AOC but is a Nominated Post Holder in the GCAA. In EASA, it is described as an accepted named person or position required for the management system. The named person is for the NAA to approve. In the FAA regulatory environment, it is also a nominated director part of the required management personnel for air carriers. The AM must ensure the funds are available to support the SMS. The SMS is required to ensure safety confidence in every department process. It starts with the procedures, like hazard identification, the management of change to flight data monitoring, emergency response planning and others, with a safety philosophy being an integral part of the corporate culture. While the AM is the signatory of the safety statement, it is the Safety Manager that is the administrator and facilitator of the Safety Management System. It is the Safety Manager that keeps the AM in compliance with his or her safety regulatory accountabilities and had a very significant influence on the company being a safely operating company. The relationship between the Safety Manager and the AM is perhaps, along with the compliance manager, the most important relationship for the AM with any of his reporting staff. The Safety Manager has his or her finger on the pulse of the operation and is in frequent communication with the NAA. It is the safety manager that really knows the status of safety within the company. He or she is a very important guide and advisor to the AM, and close regular safety review meetings must take place, where the safety manager advises and reports to the AM the results of safety findings, management of change, safety audits, the status of safety management within the company in every department. All of this reflects the safety health of the company.

We can see that the AM relies heavily on the productivity of the Nominated Persons/Post Holders and the better the relationship between them the better the company can run. The AM management styles may differ where some may practice a hands on approach with each PH or some may have a more hands off approach, but it should be realised that while the Post Holders/Nominated Persons have regulatory responsibility, it is the AM that has the regulatory accountability. This presents the challenge of what is the degree of involvement and the level of "hands on approach" that the AM must establish to ensure they are involved and aware of the company being safe, secure, airworthy and compliant.

References

EU EASA, 2021a. *Regulation 1321/2014 Part 145, Aircraft Maintenance Organisations.* Cologne: European Aviation Safety Agency.

EU EASA, 2021b. *Regulation 1321/2014, Part M, Continuing Airworthiness.* Cologne: European Aviation Safety Agency.

EU EASA, 2021c. *Regulation 965/2012 ORO.GEN.210, Personnel requirements.* Cologne: European Aviation Safety Agency.

UAE GCAA, 2021a. *Civil Aviation Regulation Part 145, Aircraft Maintenance Organisations.* Abu Dhabi: General Civil Aviation Authority.

UAE GCAA, 2021b. *Civil Aviation Regulation Part M, Continuing Airworthiness.* Abu Dhabi: General Civil Aviation Authority.

UAE GCAA, 2021c. *Civil Aviation Regulation Part OPS 1 & 3, Operations Regulations.* Abu Dhabi: General Civil Aviation Authority.

US FAA, 2015. *Advisory Circular 120-92B, Safety Management Systems.* Washington DC: Federal Aviation Administration.

US FAA, 2018. *Advisory Circular 120-59B, Internal Evaluation Programs.* Washington DC: Federal Aviation Administration.

US FAA, 2021a. *Federal Aviation Regulation Part 121, Air Carrier Certification.* Washington DC: Federal Aviation Administration.

US FAA, 2021b. *Federal Aviation Regulation Part 145, Aircraft Repair Stations.* Washington DC.: Federal Aviation Administration.

US FAA, 2021c. *Federal Aviation Regulation Part 5, Safety Management Systems.* Washington DC: Federal Aviation Administration.

4 Organisational structures in a civil aviation company

The organisational structure of a civil aviation company is very important. The reporting lines need to conform to the civil aviation regulations, where the regulator requires that the Accountable Manager must be the direct reporting manager for each of the Nominated Persons / Post Holders. The regulator also requires that the Accountable Manager is the top executive or is at least in a very senior position, with direct access to the chairman and the board. This chapter will review how an organisational structure can be designed so that the regulators will accept it, and will also look at organisational structures that have been rejected as not compliant or acceptable to the regulator. The chapter will then go on to look at the job description of an Accountable Manager and what is important with regards to the duties the AM is responsible for in that job description.

A correct organisational structure and why

In the first organisational structure (Figure 4.1), the AM is also the chief executive officer (CEO) and reports directly to the chairman of the board. This means he or she is in control of all funds and can support financially and with authority a regulatory compliant operation in accordance with the regulations. The CEO has direct fiduciary responsibility, is responsible to the Chairman and the Board for running an appropriately governed corporation, and is accountable to the NAA for running a compliant civil aviation operation. There is no doubt who is in charge and who is making the funding decisions. Reporting to the CEO/AM are all the regulatory required position holders: the chief financial officer (CFO), chief commercial officer (CCO), chief information officer (CIO) and the chief people officer (CPO). The CEO/AM has to balance decision-making and strategy between the sometimes not completely compatible objectives of seeking safety and regulatory compliance, and that of managing a sustainable and economical business. The CEO/AM, as the company's top executive and leader, controls the finances and the hiring and firing, and sets the corporate culture.

In the second organisational structure (Figure 4.2), the regulatory required positions and functions are separated from the corporate fiduciary positions

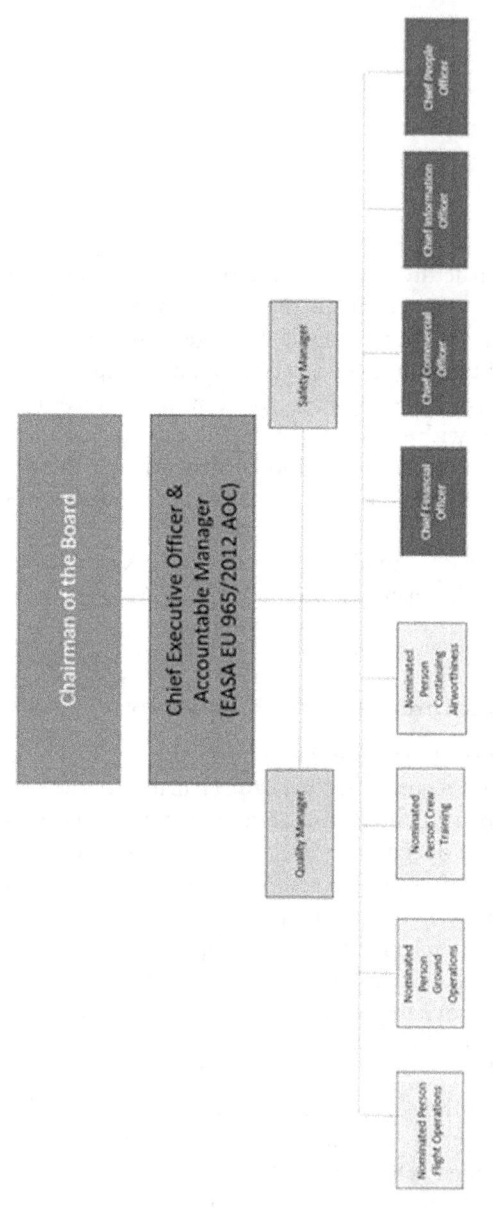

Figure 4.1 Organisation structure 1 for an EASA EU 965/2012 AOC (EU EASA, 2021).

Organisational structures in a CAC 81

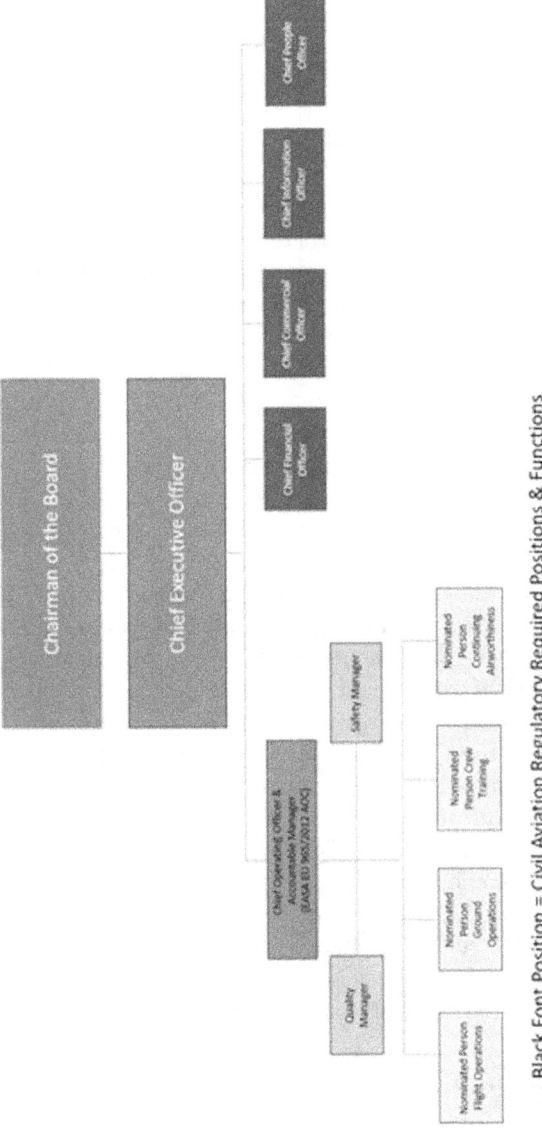

Figure 4.2 Organisation structure 2 for an EASA EU 965/2012 AOC.

and functions. The CEO remains the top executive and leader but is not the accountable manager presented to the NAA and therefore does not have any accountability to the NAA for compliance with the civil aviation regulations. A position has been created, called the chief operating officer (COO) that is presented as the AM to the NAA with the full accountability for a regulatory compliant operation. Note also that the CEO reports to the chairman, but the COO/AM does not. The CEO controls the finances and has the hire and fire capability, but the COO/AM does not. The fiduciary positions and functions report not to the COO/AM but to the CEO. This structure is permitted only if the COO has a financial capability and budget in his control to fully fund a compliant operation, and only if the COO/AM has full authority to hire and fire the nominated persons that do report directly to him or her. The NAA will have to be satisfied that, in such a structure, a COO/AM who does not control the CFO or the CPO does, in fact, have (a) full financial control to fund a compliant operation and to hire and fire nominated persons and (b) the influence to establish a safety and compliance culture within the company. Finally, the COO/AM must have access to the Board to report on safety and compliance issues and the state of the AOC. The NAAs will only allow this organisational structure if these requirements are satisfied, and it can be shown to them that the AM has funding sources available as well as hire and fire authority for the regulatory positions and functions. This structure can be advantageous for a large operation, as it frees the CEO to focus on corporate strategy and fiduciary responsibilities, relieving the AM of fiduciary responsibilities. It should be realised though the Fig 4.2 structure is acceptable, it would be of detailed interest to the NAA, and full investigation and full disclosure must be presented to the NAA to accept the presented COO as the AM. It must be made very clear that the COO is the AM and can meet the demands of the AM, as having the authority to fund and support a compliant civil aviation company, meaning he or she, and not the CEO, can approve the release of funds for operations, maintenance, training and to hire and fire the nominated persons. The COO, in this case, is the safety and compliance policy signatory and champion, but not being the top executive means it might be challenging for the COO to be able to set the corporate culture of safety and compliance. The CEO being the top executive in the company may be more of a visible and influencing leader in the organisation. For such a structure to work, the CEO and COO must have a close professional relationship, and the NAA needs to be convinced that the COO/AM's delegated authority is adequate.

A wrong organisational structure and why

In this structure (Figure 4.3), the CEO is also the AM, but the nominated persons do not report to him or her but to the COO. This structure is not acceptable to the NAA as they require the nominated persons to report directly to the AM and not through anyone else. The COO position in this structure is not in a regulatory position and is not recognised by the NAA. If the COO were

Organisational structures in a CAC 83

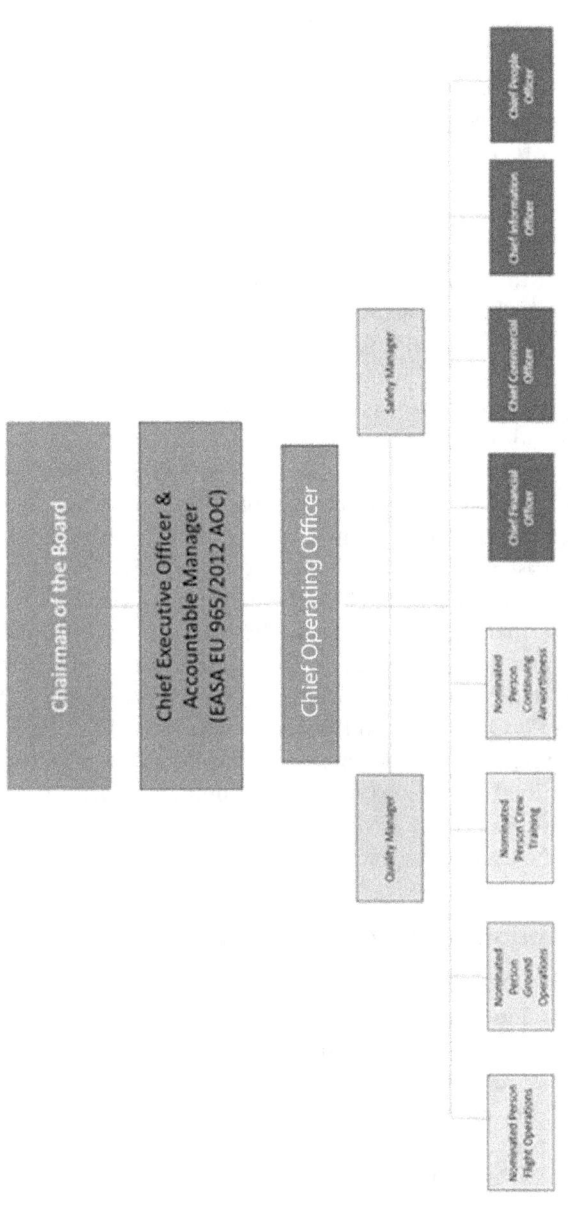

Figure 4.3 Organisation structure 3: A wrong structure for an EASA EU 965/2012 AOC (EU EASA, 2021).

also the AM with full financial and management authority to fund and run a compliant civil aviation operation, it could be acceptable with some assurances to the NAA of his or her authority and access to the board.

In this structure (Figure 4.4) a position called deputy AM has been created to relieve the CEO from the daily AM duties. This position of deputy AM does not exist in the civil aviation regulations, so it is of no concern to the NAA at all; in fact, it is a violation of the civil aviation regulations, in that the nominated persons must report directly to the AM. While it is understandable that a very busy CEO wishes to have assistance and relief from routine daily regulatory issues, the creation of such a position is irrelevant to the NAA and cannot be in any way a delegation of the CEO's duties as the AM. While a CEO can delegate tasks and projects; but he or she cannot delegate accountability or responsibility in terms of the civil aviation regulations and to the NAA. So, while a deputy CEO is a possibility to assist the CEO in the latter's daily tasks it is of no interest to the NAA and should not affect in any way the relationships of the post holders and the AM. The position should not appear on the organisational chart as anything but an assistant to the CEO and AM rather than a deputy in between the AM and the PHs.

It should be noted that there are times that the AM is not available or contactable and cannot carry out his accountable duties, such as the time they are sick or on leave. Most regulations have a rule that when the AM or any nominated person is away from base on leave or sickness or duty travel, they must nominate and inform the NAA of the person who stands in for them for the period of time they are away from the base. In the case of the AM, it is a nominated person or post holder that stands in. In the case of a NP or PH, it is another NP or their trained and qualified deputy, if acceptable to the NAA. In the case of the CEO, who is also the AM, it would not be accepted that the CFO takes on the position, unless he is qualified and acceptable; it would normally be the NP flight operations or NP continuing airworthiness. In a small company, it is possible for the AM to stand in for the NPs, provided this is acceptable to the NAA, and they are qualified.

The job description of the Accountable Manager

A job description (JD) is a company document that in detail defines the job requirements, job duties, job accountabilities, job responsibilities, and skills required to perform a specific position. A more detailed JD can be developed with key performance indicators (KPIs) that can be used as a performance management tool. Let us review from all we know so far, what would the JD of the CEO/AM for an EASA air operator, AOC, and maintenance company (AMO) look like. We are going to use a simple template that many companies use today. In this instance, we are considering the essential qualifications to be those of leadership and competent management. Aviation expertise and experience are an added value at recruitment but if absent at the beginning they must be very quickly learned (Table 4.1).

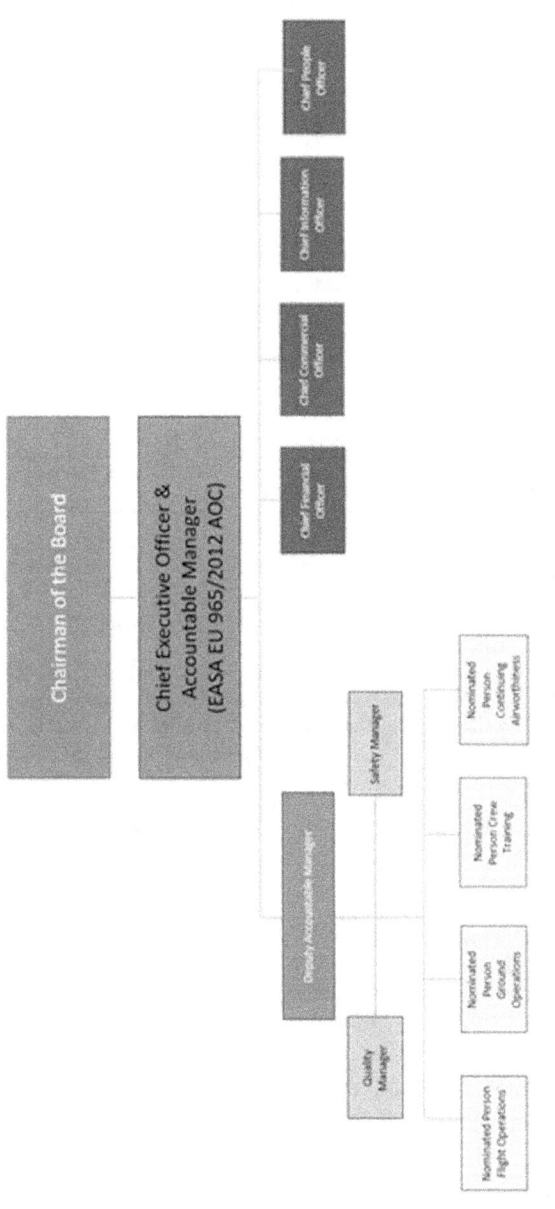

Figure 4.4 Organisation structure 4: A wrong structure for an EASA EU 965/ 2012 AOC (EU EASA, 2021).

Table 4.1 A job description for the Accountable Manager

1. Job Details

Job title:	Chief executive officer and Accountable Manager (CEO & AM)	**Reports to:**	The chairman of the board
Division:	Aviation	**Department:**	CEO

2. Job purpose

The CEO and AM has two main functions. The first function is a regulatory function. The AM is responsible to the civil aviation authorities to ensure continued compliance with the civil aviation regulations and to ensure the maintenance of the AOC and the AMO approval. The second function is a fiduciary function, to lead in an efficient and effective way the commercial and technical operation of the fleet, all assets and also all personnel required to compete profitably in the aviation industry.

3. Organisational structure

Please refer to the attached organisational structure

4. Main responsibilities/duties

Regulatory:
- Is initially qualified for the AM position and continues to be accepted by the NAA as the AM.
- Maintains an excellent corporate relationship with the NAA, promoting all regulatory values in the company.
- Ensures the company remains in complete compliance with the CARs to ensure continuation & validation of the company's AOC and AMO at all times.
- Ensures the QM system is intact, meets the CAR requirements and is applied within the company at all times; & that the company promotes a continuous improvement ethic and culture.
- Ensures that the SMS is intact, meets the CAR requirements & is applied within the company at all times & that the company promotes a safety ethic and culture.
- Ensures the compliance management system is intact, meets the CAR requirements and is applied within the company at all times; & that the company promotes a regulatory compliant ethic and culture.
- Nominates and maintains qualified nominated persons to hold the positions required by the CARs.
- Manages the nominated persons on a daily basis, ensuring the company's quality, safety & compliance culture is effectively cascaded to them.

Others:
- To lead the commercial and financial management of the company to ensure a well-run, profitable and sustainable company competing in the aviation business, maximising shareholder value at all times.
- Ensure the very best use of the company's assets, including its fleet, in an efficient and effective way, minimising downtime and non-utilisation to enable the company to best compete effectively and efficiently in the aviation business.
- To ensure the very best use of the company's people, in an efficient and effective way.
- To maximise training and development to ensure the knowledge and skill set of the people is at a level that enables the company to compete effectively and efficiently in the aviation business.

Table 4.1 Cont.

- To ensure that every item of expenditure is justified, and approved and contributes to the efficient and effective running of the company to best compete in the aviation industry.
- To report to the board with financial and commercial reports as required by the board.
- To ensure the development & management of an annual budget that is presented and approved by the board.
- To ensure minimum deviation from the approved budget, obtaining the correct authorisations for variances if they occur.
- To ensure that the corporate public image of the company is one of a great company at all times.
- To ensure that the company operates within the laws of the land and the regulations of the financial institutions at all times.

5. Qualifications/requirements

Education
Essential:
- Bachelor degree in business, management or finance

Desirable:
- Bachelor Degree in Aviation Business or Aviation Management;
- Aviation qualification such as aircraft maintenance license, pilot licence, dispatcher licence, etc; or
- Master degree in business administration.

Experience & Knowledge:
Essential:
- Experience and knowledge acceptable to the civil aviation to qualify as an AM;
- Experience in reporting to a board of directors and shareholders;
- A detailed understanding of the civil aviation regulations, aviation SMS/QMS and the obligations of an AM.
- Strong people leadership skills.
- Minimum of ten years' experience in a senior executive such as CEO/COO/MD/VP, etc.
- Experience in commercial operations on an international scale with knowledge and acute awareness of international business dealings.
- Strong finance and budgeting experience or background.
- Detailed experience in leading a profitable company in a highly complex regulated industry.
- Experience in negotiating multi-million dollar, multi-year contracts.
- Competence in contract review and preparation.

Desirable:
- Ten years in commercial aviation.
- Having held a post holder position or a senior position in an aviation company.
- Competence in setting a competitive price structure for aviation services.
- Knowledge of company capabilities.
- Knowledge of international aviation market pricing.
- Knowledge of competitor pricing structure as well as their strengths and weaknesses.
- Knowledge of upcoming trends in the market.
- Knowledge of contracts and business law.

(*continued*)

Table 4.1 Cont.

Skills:

Essential:
- Strong personality.
- Excellent written and spoken English.
- Presentable.
- Charismatic and empathetic with strong leadership abilities.

- Proven ability to listen, advice and counsel at all levels.
- Ability to get the best out of people.

Desirable:
- Multi lingual

6. Competencies

Competency	Level < dependent on the job>
Negotiation skills	Proficiency Level 3
Customer focus	Proficiency Level 3
Change leadership	Proficiency Level 3
Attention to detail	Proficiency Level 3
Planning and organising	Proficiency Level 3
Decision making	Proficiency Level 3
Coaching	Proficiency Level 3
Communication	Proficiency Level 3
Result focused	Proficiency Level 3
Performance management	Proficiency Level 3
Integrity	Proficiency Level 3

It is one opinion that aviation experience and qualifications is not a prerequisite to take on the CEO and AM position. This opinion also says that this is a complex business leadership role with a focus on fiduciary responsibility, ensuring that the company can operate with the lowest cost base while at the same time generating the largest revenues, thereby making the largest profits. It is suggested that the knowledge required of the AM can be learned on the job utilising the relevant expert post holders for the detailed aviation expertise required.

If we look at past CEOs of airlines, many in fact were not aviators or with aviation experience. On many occasions these CEOs were from other industries, and we can see that they had significant success in their role. It would be interesting to know how on these occasions the CEO gained the necessary level of understanding of civil aviation and the regulations, of safety management systems and quality management systems to pass the NAA accountable manager interview. It has been a frequent complaint of the NAAs that the proposed AM was not prepared adequately for the NAA interview with the required level of knowledge, resulting in an awkward rejection of them holding the position.

One very successful CEO took over the top executive leadership role at one of Europe's largest airlines, although coming from a very different industry.

This person held the CEO position for seven years and the AM position for five years. This leadership resulted in an excellent fiduciary leadership tenure and an equally successful regulatory compliance tenure, so this proves it is very much possible.

Reference

EU EASA. (2021). Regulation 965/2012 Air Operations. Cologne: European Aviation Safety Agency.

5 Ethical leadership and the Accountable Manager

We have identified two kinds of accountable responsibilities as an AM: regulatory accountability and fiduciary accountability. In reality, there is also a third responsibility. Not only as CEOs/AMs, are we accountable by law to the regulations and by fiduciary responsibility to the shareholders, but we also have a moral and ethical duty to manage and lead in a way that respects human life and the environment. It can be said our ethical and moral accountabilities can be described in three aspects.

The passengers

Whether it is aircraft design, aircraft production, engine manufacturing, avionic part manufacturing, pilot training, or airline operations, commercial aviation is all about creating a sustainable industry where we can transport passengers around the world. We have an ethical duty to every one of those passengers who flies on the aircraft or passes through the airports that we have been involved in creating, establishing or managing, to ensure that passengers are transported safely and securely and to protect their lives as best we can. This means:

- not cutting corners in safety;
- not using regulatory loopholes to exploit a situation in our favour;
- not finding methods of reducing the cost that means reducing quality in the level of safety or of service; and
- not overlooking designs or procedures that could be better.

Protecting the lives of those who travel with us or using our products and services is an important aspect of ethical leadership that AMs/CEOs should remind themselves of regularly. Making a profit at any cost is not ethical and should not be a priority of the leadership, while ethical and moral leadership should be.

The employees

The AM has a legal duty to manage employees within the labour law, and an ethical duty to every employee who works under him or her, thereby enabling employees to work in a safe and secure work environment where they can express themselves and develop their capabilities. This means:

- fair recruitment systems that give equal opportunities to all groups of people, not favouring one particular group;
- fair remuneration to staff carrying equal responsibilities;
- fair development and training of staff ensuring they are equipped sufficiently in order to correctly do their jobs.

There is also a social, societal responsibility where taking school leavers and placing them on an apprenticeship programme and taking graduates and placing them on internships is to be encouraged. Treating the staff respectfully as a priority is an important aspect of ethical leadership as this then, in turn, ensures that the staff treats the customers with equal or more respect. Treating the employee as a "king" as much as the customer very often results in high customer satisfaction, since the employees understand the importance of respect and feel worthy in their job, resulting in them treating the customer with greater worth. Many leaders, in their focus to meet their accountable manager responsibilities and their fiduciary responsibilities, perhaps overlook their less obvious ethical responsibilities. Later in this chapter, we shall talk further about the ethical behaviour of leadership and how it cascades throughout the company.

The environment

Finally, the AM has an ethical and moral duty to minimise the impact our operation, service, or product has on the environment, trying our best to reduce the impact on the environment as much as possible. When buying aircraft, we should consider their environmental impact. We should put pressure on the manufacturers to develop and produce more environmentally friendly aircraft and systems. The products we use in our services should be used with consideration for their impact on the environment. When maintaining the aircraft or production of aviation products such as aircraft, engines, parts and equipment, the methods we use should be with consideration for careful disposal of waste and recycling wherever possible. Aviation is one of the most challenging industries to be ethically and environmentally cautious. Environmental impact is definitely a challenge, from the noise pollution of the aircraft near local towns, to air pollution from gas emissions coming out of the engines, to the land pollution needed to build the airports and factories we need to operate out of. The AM can influence the decision on buying aircraft and aviation products. preferring environmentally friendly aircraft and products. Many Accountable Managers today are part of lobbying groups, asking the big manufacturers (Boeing, Airbus, etc.) to produce less environmentally damaging products and aircraft.

The AM/CEO's challenge is to be

- as professional as possible in how the company flies, maintains its aircraft, operates and serves;
- as professional as possible in being regulatory compliant;
- as lean and profitable as possible; and
- as responsible as possible in our fiduciary duties.

It is possible to neglect to give enough importance to the environment, the passengers, and the employees. Aviation leadership today involves balancing the regulatory, fiduciary, and ethical aspects of running the company. The culture of the company comes from the top and cascades down through the directors and managers. If ethical leadership is part of the culture, if priority is given to the passenger's welfare, the employee's welfare, and the environmental welfare, then the culture will reflect this all through the company. It can be said if we prioritise ethical leadership, regulatory compliance and safe operations, then, in an ideal world, profitability will naturally follow, as ethical leadership means responsible professional leadership that has only a positive effect on a commercial company.

Just as the company's safety culture comes from the leadership and cascades down to the top management and to the staff, so does the ethical culture. A toxic leadership will poison the managers, which creates a toxic work environment. Disrespect shown by the leaderships will result in disrespect shown by the employees to both their co-workers and the customers. Any leaders, in aviation or otherwise, should be aware that they set the corporate culture tone. They should be aware of the dark traits that have been detected as a personality trait of many existing or aspiring CEOs and leaders. The "dark personality traits" (Paulhus & Williams, 2002) or "wicked behaviours" are very often seen in CEOs. These are traits of narcissistic behaviour, Machiavellianism, and psychopathic behaviour. All three seem to be frequent personality traits of ambitious and determined leaders. If these traits are not recognised and kept in check, a very toxic culture can permeate from the top executive leadership to the managers and then to the lower staff members. Ethical leadership will prevent "wicked behaviours" from winning or taking a grip. Some methods to help prevent the dark traits from appearing could include:

- A confidante that has permission to mention or advise the CEO on delicate issues that have ethical aspects to them;
- A corporate code of conduct that defines how we treat each other while at work and is referred to frequently as a process to help us re-gauge our behaviour.

It has been documented that the practice of corporate bullying, where the leaders

- often criticise directors in public;
- encourage aggressive competition between directors; or
- support lounge-style meetings where personalities are discussed openly

are all unethical forms of behaviour not to be encouraged. High functioning successful leaders do very often focus so much on the success target that the ethical journey is forgotten, and casualties are left behind by their desire to succeed. Ethical leadership is less common than you would hope. Humble and credible CEOs who are ready to openly discuss their strengths and weaknesses with their team, or are ready to seek feedback without retaliation, are not frequently found in the C Suit team (senior executive positions, such as the CEO, COO and CFO). A machismo environment where co-workers openly have extreme views, and practice disrespect is frequently seen. These are not traits that good leaders should exercise or encourage. Very often, overconfident leadership with high self-importance is a dark trait found in many leaders today. It would be recommended that to prevent an unethical culture from getting a hold on your corporate culture, a CEO should be very careful to avoid the toxicity of displaying the "dark traits", frequently gauging and reviewing their behaviour and leadership style and apologising for times they don't get it exactly right.

An airline that accelerates its growth very fast, with a leadership that is very result-focused, can create a culture of aggressive behaviour within the staff: for example, frequent use of bad language, with managers expected to work very long working hours, coupled with an attitude of performance achievement at any cost can create a very toxic work environment and a very damaging corporate culture. This can result from ethical leadership being low on the priorities of the CEO, and while it is separate from the AM's accountable responsibilities, such a culture is surely not conducive to a culture of compliance and safety, and perhaps will take the company down the dark road that can only result in an unfortunate ending.

Being an ethical leader is about values

There is a difference between being a boss and being a leader. A boss orders, while a leader guides. A boss manages while a leader inspires. A boss directs while a leader coaches. A leader is concerned about how he or she makes their employees feel and how he or she sees his or her relationship with the employees. A good leader feels responsible for inspiring, guiding, coaching, and nurturing the employees to help them improve and develop. An ethical leader leads by example.

According to Kiely Kuligowaski of *Business News* (Kuligowaski, 2020), an ethical leader will be concerned with moral and virtuous behaviour. Such a leader will practice seven values in his or her daily leadership journey:

1. Have a clear understanding of and defining his or her values.
2. Hire people with similar values.

3   Promote open uncriticised communication.
4   Beware of self-opinion bias.
5   Lead by example.
6   Identify his or her role models.
7   Show that he or she cares for himself or herself, so that he or she is able to care for others.

In aviation, being an ethical leader involves more than simply saying you wish to create a culture of respect, compliance, and safety. The AM creates a safety and compliance statement to develop a safety and compliance culture, and should similarly develop and draft an ethics statement, a code of ethical conduct not only while conducting business but always while at work.

- **Actions matter more than words.** Ethical leaders do not make false promises. If they make a promise, they do whatever they need to in order to keep it. Always act in an unselfish and kindly way to every one of your staff. As a golden rule, never treat the janitor any differently from how you treat the CFO. As much as possible, lead by example and "walk the talk".
- **Provide appropriate training and coaching.** Ethical behaviour should always be emphasised through training and coaching opportunities. Schedule sessions that drive home how treating others in an ethical way promotes a positive workplace. Create ethical coaches within the company.
- **Practice good communication.** Remain transparent in all business dealings. Never lie or mislead others for the benefit of the business or yourself. Keep employees and associates in the loop about all dealings. For example, if your company must downsize, let staff know far in advance.

Empathy in leadership is important

The ability to understand and listen to people you lead and to share their feelings is a very powerful method of forming a relationship with people you lead. As the AM you are leading some very qualified people that themselves have some very serious responsibilities. For example, the director/Post Holder of Flight Operations will perhaps have the largest team under his or her leadership, from aircraft captains to flight attendants and dispatchers—people responsible for the front line service and the on time delivery of the service, people who can make a massive difference in the company's success. It is very important that the AM recognises the contribution of such a person and tries to understand the operational challenges they face on a daily basis. The AM must spend time with each director and PH/NP and give them time, support them and listen to them and remember they are in it with you, with the same objectives and targets. If the company`s strategy is defined and correctly cascaded to the directors and managers, then they shall share the AM's KPIs. Respectful, empathetic leadership will result in a better outcome than a hard line "do your job" attitude.

One of the responsibilities of leadership is defining a long-term strategic vision for the organisation and establishing some short-term goals for the employees to attain in order to transform the strategy into reality. This is where the definition of the strategy and communication of that strategy through cascading of the strategic targets is important.

However, what separates mediocre leaders from those who excel at leading others is how the great leaders understand that their focus should not be simply directed to whether goals are achieved or not. Rather, their focus is also on fulfilling the collective purpose of creating something meaningful, in a civil aviation company that should be a safe, compliant and sustainable company.

Being a leader is a pleasure and a privilege. Those that we lead deserve respect and gratitude. This should be reflected in your daily behaviour and dealing with staff and in fact all others suppliers and customers. This is the start of ethical leadership.

References

Kuligowaski, K. (2020). *How to Be an Ethical Leader: 7 Tips for Success*. Retrieved from https://www.businessnewsdaily.com/5537-how-to-be-ethical-leader.html#:~:text=Remember%20actions%20matter%20more%20than,how%20you%20treat%20the%20CFO.

Paulhus, D., and Williams, K. (2002). The Dark Triad of Personality: Narcissism, Machiavellianism, and Psychopathy. *Journal of research in personality*.

6 A tool kit and SOPs for the Accountable Manager

Now that we understand the important aspects of the AM's role, let us review and remind ourselves of the very important functions that the AM is accountable for, recapping on both the regulatory responsibility and accountability and the corporate fiduciary responsibility and accountability.

Civil aviation regulatory accountability

ICAO and the Chicago Convention: The AM should understand the origins, the evolution, and motives for the structure of civil aviation in today's world, the attempt of ICAO to standardise operations through the Annexes and the SARPs that drive common standards in civil aviation to promote harmony of operations, safety, and cooperation between contracting states.

Civil aviation regulations: The AM should understand the evolution of the state's civil aviation regulations from the Annexes and the SARPs.

The civil aviation regulator: The AM should understand that the AM is the primary responsible and accountable person in a civil aviation company who is held accountable and liable by the civil aviation regulator for a safe and compliant civil aviation operation. The AM should understand that he or she signs an undertaking that the company he or she leads will have the funds at his or her control and support from the Board for him or her to lead a compliant and safe operation.

Quality Management Systems: The AM is the primary person responsible for the QMS system and signs the company's compliance/quality statement to commit to a compliant and audited operation with the civil aviation regulations. The AM should encourage a culture of continuous improvement.

Safety Management Systems: The AM is the primary person responsible for the SMS system and signs the company's safety statement to commit to a safe operation with a safety culture throughout the company. The AM should take a detailed interest in the safety review board functions. The AM should encourage a culture of safety and risk mitigation though out all the functions of the company.

The appointment and leadership of nominated persons: The AM has the responsibility to ensure the appointment and the continued support and

DOI: 10.4324/9781003094685-7

leadership of the nominated persons required by the civil aviation regulations. When the NPs are found not to be competent in their field, the AM must take action.

Fiduciary accountability

Corporate leadership: The AM, if also the CEO, has the responsibility to report to the chairman and the board to ensure that the interest of the owners and shareholders are looked after with sensible business decisions and that the company is run in a responsible and legally compliant way.

Financial leadership: The AM, if also the CEO, along with the CFO, has the responsibility

- to ensure that the company finances and accounts are managed correctly and in accordance with commercial regulations;
- to ensure that all taxes are paid, and all financial commitments are met;
- to return to the owners, shareholders and investors a reasonable return on their investment, through sensible financial and cash flow management.

The Accountable Manager's tool kit

Today, aviation executives have available to them many methods and systems and software to help them manage their daily tasks and their accountabilities effectively. Even though the AM has a team of post holders and nominated persons who report to him or her, he or she must pay attention to his or her accountabilities, and know the status of these accountabilities, with a method of oversight and understanding. This is an important issue: the AM cannot delegate the accountabilities, so should have a good all-round up-to-date knowledge of the company's status.

To assist the AM to prioritise and organise their tasks while being knowledgeable of the important aspects of the company they are accountable for, we have developed a "tool kit" that consists of:

a   AM NAA "Interview preparation guide".
b   AM "Timetable" of oversight activities and meetings.
c   AM "Dashboard" of important information.

This tool kit is to assist the AM or accountable executive in preparing and also in meeting the complex demands of the position of CEO and AM.

A preparation guide for the NAA Accountable Manager interview

The AM ideally is the leading executive in the company, for example, the CEO or MD. The chairman and the board are responsible for selecting and managing the CEO. Once they have done so, they are responsible for presenting them to the NAA for acceptance. This is not for approval, as he or she is not a nominated person or nominated post holder but a person for the position of AM accepted by the NAA. Anyone accepting the position needs to remember the job description did say the individual must be acceptable to the NAA to hold the AM position. This requires knowledge and capability in the skills necessary for the role. The chairman has to realise that if he and the board select a person who has no aviation qualification or experience, it will require the investment of time and training for the selected person to be ready to present to the NAA. It is not advisable to present the candidate raw with no brief, no training and no preparation. The NAA will not be impressed or satisfied, which could damage the relationship the company has with the NAA. So it is recommended that if a qualified and capable person is selected for the position, they can prepare with a short course on being the AM and also prepare with a brief from the post holders for safety and compliance to get familiar with the SMS and statement, as well as the compliance management system and statement. If the person nominated as AM is a senior post holder from within the company, it should be relatively easy, as the NAA would have knowledge of the person. Similarly, if the person is from the industry but from another aviation company within the same country, the NAA should already know the person, again making the process easier. But if the person is not known to the NAA and, particularly, is not an aviator or a person from the aviation industry, preparation is required—lots of preparation.

Let's start with the NAA AM interview and how the proposed AM should prepare for and approach the interview.

We are aware that the AM is proposed for the position by the chairman, owners, or the board of the company to the NAA of the country. It is the responsibility of the NAA of the country, as a member state of the ICAO and a signatory of the Chicago Convention, to ensure that the civil aviation regulations of their state are implemented and overseen. This involves accepting and approving the management positions, ensuring the proposed or nominated managers are competent, qualified and capable for their role. The highest level of the manager is the AM. While the AM is an accepted position rather than an approved nomination, the application process is the same in what is traditionally in the EASA world called a Form 4.

The NAA is being asked to accept a presented AM who has full authority to:

- finance;
- manage the post holders; and
- manage the compliance with the civil aviation regulations.

So knowledge of the regulations is required, as is knowledge of the accountabilities of the AM. To assist the candidate presented to the NAA, we have developed a table of reference subjects to guide and assist in the candidate's preparation. The table assumes a candidate from outside the industry, but the same expectation from the NAA exist whether the nominee is from inside or outside the industry. It should be noted that all of these subjects are covered in previous chapters of this book. Reading and studying this book should adequately prepare the candidate for the interview.

For a non-aviation industry professional to take on the role may require 12 to 18 months of training and introduction. This might mean that a temporary stand-in is required. It is better this be volunteered by the chairman and company rather than be imposed by the NAA after a failed interview. Some of the most successful CEOs and AMs have come in from outside of the industry. They have undergone 12 to 18 months of intense training and coaching to become a very effective and capable AM. To go to the NAA interview without very careful and thorough preparation is strongly not advised. NAAs have complained regularly about ill-prepared candidates and the damage this does to the company and to the industry. The interview is not a formality; it is not a sure thing. The AM is the most senior leadership position in a civil aviation company as far as the regulator is concerned. The post requires a qualified and appropriately capable person ready to assume the accountabilities and responsibilities of the role (Table 6.1).

A timetable of meetings for the Accountable Manager

This timetable will assist the AM in confidently overseeing, gathering, and analysing information easily, ensuring

- awareness of his or her accountable responsibilities;
- using the information to make wise, informed strategic decisions; and
- confidently brief and report to the board.

We shall use the scenario of an EASA or GCAA AOC holder managing a fleet of internationally operating aircraft.

Regulatory accountabilities

By following the timetable (Table 6.2), the AM will have complete knowledge, visibility, and oversight of all their regulatory responsibilities. This six months cycle of reviews will enable the AM to be aware. It will also facilitate post holder leadership, by having the nominated AM meet with the post holders to build the relationship, and by supporting the post holders by giving them the time together with the AM to build an understanding of support and communication. These are two essential success factors for the AMs to be executing their accountable responsibilities. Many AMs are tempted not to stick to the schedule, and instead to delegate attendance at the meetings and ask the post holders to brief them on these accountable responsibilities. For the AM not to attend these meetings will mean that the AM will not have the required

Table 6.1 A preparation guide for the Accountable Manager NAA interview

Accountable Manager knowledge Subjects	Details and depth of knowledge
ICAO and the Civil Aviation Regulations	1. Have a broad knowledge of where the regulations originate from and how they are brought into effect in the country in which the AM is going to be working. 2. Have a broad knowledge of the structure of the civil aviation regulations in the territory. 3. Have a broad knowledge of the role of the CAA in the territory. 4. Have detailed knowledge of the approvals and licences the company holds and the applicable civil aviation regulations. 5. Have detailed knowledge of the licensed aviation professionals in the company and their qualifications. 6. Have a broad knowledge of the regulations requiring the PHs to be in place. 7. Have a detailed knowledge of each current PH, as their broad responsibilities. 8. Have detailed knowledge of where the regulations detail the AM's role and the AM's accountable responsibilities. The NAA is looking to determine if the candidate is knowledgeable of the origins and the structure of civil aviation regulations as well as the basics of aviation regulations. They will focus on the regulations applicable to the specific approvals the company currently has in place.
The Safety Management System (SMS)	1. Have detailed knowledge of what SMS is. 2. Have detailed knowledge of the company's SMS. 3. The applicant should have the safety statement to refer to. 4. Have a broad knowledge of the company's current safety challenges. 5. Have a broad knowledge of any recent safety audit findings and how they were addressed. 6. Have detailed knowledge and a copy with you of the company's last safety review board meeting report. It would be useful if the applicant has attended an aviation SMS course and participated in multiple coaching sessions with the Safety Manager.
The Quality/ Compliance Management System (Q/CMS)	1. Have detailed knowledge of what Q/CMS is. 2. Have detailed knowledge of the companies Q/CMS. 3. Have the Quality/Compliance Statement with you to refer to. 4. Have a broad knowledge of the company's current compliance challenges. 5. Have a broad knowledge of any recent compliance audit findings and how they were addressed. 6. Have detailed knowledge and a copy with you of the company's last Quality/Compliance review board meeting report. It would be useful if, in addition, the applicant has participated in multiple coaching sessions with the Quality/Compliance Manager.

Table 6.1 Cont.

Accountable Manager knowledge Subjects	Details and depth of knowledge
Management Responsibilities as the Accountable Manager	1. Be able to prove you have been presented by the chairman of the company as the AM to the NAA. 2. Be able to prove and describe how you have the delegated authority and the financial authority, and the budget to spend that is adequate to support the safety and compliance of the size of operation you are accountable for. 3. Be able to prove and describe how you have the delegated authority to hire, fire, and train the NPs and PHs, as well as all aviation professionals. 4. Present the declarations the AM has to sign and explain what each one means and how you are confident in signing these declarations. 5. Describe how the chairman and the board will support your requirements in running a safe and compliant operation. 6. The NAA officials are likely to ask you to prove you have delegated full authority with a budget at your fingertips to support safe and compliant operations. Be prepared for this being asked multiple times. The NAA wants to confirm you are as fully delegated to run the company as the regulations require. They are interested that you have a budget at your disposal and the complete ability to hire and fire. They want to be assured you have been given full authority from the chairman and that all PHs report to you.
Training and Development in Preparation for the position	1. Prove that you have been trained in aviation SMS. 2. Prove that you have been trained on the duties of the AM and civil aviation regulations. 3. Prove that you have been fully briefed on the company's past and current compliance and safety culture. 4. Prove that you have read the last audit and safety reports and that you have a detailed knowledge of any significant findings or incidents the company may have had. 5. Prove that you have industry-current knowledge of important regulatory, safety, technical or operational events. 6. Understand fully the fleet and the capability you are about to be accountable for. 7. Understand in detail the company's approval and licence list and what each one means. Have the capability list with you. The NAA wants to see that the seriousness of the position is understood and the correct training and preparation have been taken by the candidate. This is not just an added-on function of the CEO but a priority responsibility with real legal accountabilities, fully understood by the candidate. Again it would be useful to have attended an AM course and to have participated in multiple coaching sessions with the previous AM or a suitably qualified coach.

Table 6.2 A timetable of regulatory meetings for the Accountable Manager

Daily Task **Daily Morning Operations Meeting** 08:00 30mins to 1 hour Operational Fleet status review **Operations Control Centre, OCC.** • Accountable Manager • NP/PH Flight Ops **CHAIR** • NP/PH Ground Ops • NP/PH Continuing Airworthiness • Manager/PH Security	**Review Time Frame: Yesterday / Today / Tomorrow (YTT)** • Where is the fleet? • Did the fleet depart on time? • Did the fleet arrive on time? • What is the airworthiness status of the fleet? (ETOPs/MEL/Defects/ADs/AMP). • What is the security status of the stations and destinations? • Were there any events or incidents?
Weekly Task **Accountable Manager / Post Holder General Coordination Meeting altogether.** • Accountable Manager **CHAIR** • NP/PH Flight Ops • NP/PH Ground Ops • NP/PH Continuing Airworthiness • NP/PH Training • PH/Mgr Quality/ Compliance • PH/Safety Mgr • PH/Security Mgr	• Week past Significant Safety Items / MOCs / Hazards • Week ahead Audit Timetable Review Internal/ NAA • Remaining Open Audit Significant Item Findings (Level 1 and 2) • Week Past ASR/ROSI Significant Item Review • Remaining Open Significant Non-Conformity Findings • Week Past Significant Items / Incident / Events
Monthly Task **Accountable Manager / Post Holder General Support Meeting, One on One (with each individual PH/NP)**	• How are you in meeting the regulatory compliance and safety requirements in your department? • Do you have any issues to be brought to the AM's attention? • Do you have any significant open or recurring non-conformities/findings that should be discussed with the AM?
Monthly Task **Accountable Manager Compliance Review with PH/Quality Quality/ Compliance**	• Full brief on the regulatory compliance status of the company and a review of all audits and open non-conformity findings (NCRs). • Full brief of NAA relationship Items and NAA audit plan • Review of completed company audit plan internal and external: are they being accomplished on time?

Table 6.2 Cont.

Monthly Task **Accountable Manager Safety Review with PH/ Mgr Safety**	• Full brief on the SMS compliance status of the company and a review of all audits and open Non Conformity Findings, NCRs. • Full brief on ASRs / ROSIs /VORSIs / MOCs and Hazards identified and open. • Review of Flight Data Management issues and corrective action.
3 Monthly Task **Accountable Manager / Post Holder, Fleet Maintenance Planning Review.** • Accountable Manager • NP/PH Flight Ops • NP/PH Ground Ops • NP/PH Continuing Airworthiness **CHAIR** • NP/PH Training • PH/Mgr Quality/ Compliance • PH/Mgr Safety • PH/Mgr Security	• Short Term Fleet Maintenance Plan Review = next 3 months, when, what and where. • Medium Term Fleet Maintenance Plan Review = next 12 months • Long Term Fleet Maintenance Plan Review = next 60 months
3 Monthly Task **Accountable Manager / Post Holder, Fleet Reliability** • Accountable Manager • NP/PH Flight Ops • NP/PH Ground Ops • NP/PH Continuing Airworthiness **CHAIR** • NP/PH Training • PH/Mgr Quality/Compliance • PH/Mgr Safety • PH/Mgr Security	• Fleet / Component Serviceability and Reliability Report • AMP Effectivity Review • AMP Significant Findings Report • AMP Interval Escalation Plan • Fleet ETOPs Report • SB / Modification embodiment plan • Maintenance and Engineering Incidents / Events
6 Monthly Task **Accountable Manager / Post Holder, Safety Review Board.** • Accountable Manager • NP/PH Flight Ops • NP/PH Ground Ops • NP/PH Continuing Airworthiness • NP/PH Training • PH/Mgr Quality/Compliance • PH/Mgr Safety **CHAIR** • PH/Mgr Security	• SMS General Report • Safety Culture Review • Safety Audit Review • Safety Findings Review • Significant MOC`s Review • Significant Hazard Review • Safety Incidents / Events / Reports and Reporting Culture Review

(continued)

Table 6.2 Cont.

6 Monthly Task **Accountable Manager / Post Holder, Quality and Compliance Review Board.** • Accountable Manager • NP/PH Flight Ops • NP/PH Ground Ops • NP/PH Continuing Airworthiness • NP/PH Training • PH/Mgr Quality/ Compliance **CHAIR** • PH/Mgr Safety • PH/Mgr Security	• QMS/CMS General Report • Quality / Compliance Culture Review • Quality / Compliance Audit Review • Audit Findings Review • Audit Programme Review • Non Conformity Report Reviews
6 Monthly Task **Accountable Manager / NAA Principle Ops and Airworthiness Inspector, General Review Meeting.**	• Compliance Status—general review of the company. • Safety Status—general review of the company. • Audit Non-Conformities and Findings Review • Financial status general review of the company. • Post Holder / Nominated Person performance general review • Accountable Manager board support review.
6 Monthly Task **Accountable Manager / Post Holder Detailed Support Meeting, One on One (with each individual PH/NP)**	• Do you have any compliance issues in your department? • Do you have any safety issues in your department? • Do you have the need for funding in your department? • Do you have the need for training in your department? • How are you performing with regards to your regulatory duties and responsibilities within your department?
6 Monthly Task **Accountable Manager / Chairman and Board Safety and Compliance Report**	• The status of regulatory compliance within the company? • The status of safety compliance within the company? • Is there a need for further funding for the company? • Is there a need for further training for the company? • How is the Post Holder performing with regards to their regulatory and safety duties and responsibilities within the company?
6 Monthly Task **Emergency Response Programme Drill**	• A simulation of an emergency event such as a bomb threat, an aircraft crash, a facility fire etc. • A chance to review the companies' readiness for an emergency event and to improve where short falls are identified.

knowledge and will struggle to be sure that he or she is compliant with the civil aviation regulations as a safe and compliant operation.

Proper leadership of the post holders is not to delegate to them and to leave them to get on with it; it is to support them and understand that the tasks are being accomplished on time and in accordance with the regulations. For example, how does the AM, who signs the compliance and quality statement, know the company is compliant if he or she does not ask the compliance manager to show them the list of audits accomplished, audit findings, and open non-compliances? So, in this case, how can the AM honestly say he or she is accountable for compliance?

With safety management, the AM is the signatory for the safety statement. If he or she does not ask the safety manager to show him/her the safety reports and the safety findings that remain open, how can he or she know that he or she is running a company that is managing the safety culture as a priority? The AM is the signatory to the aircraft Approved Maintenance Programme (AMP). If he or she does not attend the AMP reliability review or at least be briefed by the PH for continuing airworthiness, how could he or she know whether the AMP is effective and applicable? If there are no "one on one" review meetings with each PH, asking the detailed and difficult questions, how can the AM know whether the PH is receiving the correct funding and support from the AM in meeting the regulatory requirements, or whether the PH is struggling, and in need of development and support. So when to delegate and receive reports, when to oversee and review in detail, and when roll up one's sleeves and get involved is a balance the AM must develop and achieve to ensure he or she is confident in meeting the regulatory accountable responsibilities and in supporting every PH or nominated person in creating a culture of compliance and safety.

Fiduciary accountabilities

Now that we understand the regulatory accountabilities and the fiduciary responsibilities, and we have now an SOP timetable to follow in order to ensure that the AM/CEO is getting correctly briefed and informed so as to meet his or her accountable obligations, let's once again review the detailed function of the AM/CEO from a new point of view (Table 6.3):

1. Leading the organisation in its way forward by communicating to the directors clearly and on a regular basis.
2. Understanding and overseeing the implementation and compliance of the civil aviation regulations by reviewing and asking the PHs on their individual responsibilities.
3. Funding, enabling and empowering the directors and managers that report to the AM and ensuring they have the funding and support they need.
4. Creating a culture of safety and compliance, thereby ensuring that safety is the priority of the company.

Table 6.3 A timetable of fiduciary meetings for the Accountable Manager

Weekly Task **Flight and Aircraft** **Performance Review** • Accountable Manager • Director of Commercial **CHAIR** • Chief Financial Officer • Director NP/PH Flight Ops • Director NP/PH Ground Ops • Director NP/PH Continuing Airworthiness	**Review Time Frame: Last week's flights.** • Operational Fleet Number • Non-Operational Fleet Number • No of Commercial flights flown in last week • No of Commercial flight hours flown in last week • No of idle hours in last week • No of AOGs • No of lost hours due to AOGs • Load Factor of each Flight per route • Yield of each Flight per route • Cost of each flight per route • Route success factor • Customer feedback of each flight • On-time departure of each flight • On-time arrival of each flight • Cancelled flights review
Monthly Task **Commercial Performance Overview** • Accountable Manager • Director of Commercial **Co Chair** • Chief Financial Officer **Co CHAIR** • Director NP/PH Flight Ops • Director NP/PH Ground Ops • Director NP/PH Continuing Airworthiness	• Revenue Per Available Seat KM, RASK • Available Seat KMs, ASK • Revenue YTD vs Budget • Revenue YTD vs Last Year • Revenue Budget vs Actual Variance Review • Next Month Revenue Budget review • Spending & Cost Actual vs Budget review • Spending and Cost Actual vs Budget Variance Review • No of Passengers flown • Ticket Purchase Sources • Top 10 spendings for the month
Quarterly Task **Commercial Performance Detailed Review** • Accountable Manager • Director of Commercial **Co CHAIR** • Chief Financial Officer **Co Chair** • Director NP/PH Flight Ops • Director NP/PH Ground Ops • Director NP/PH Continuing Airworthiness	• Route Performance Revenue Passenger KMs, RPK • Route Performance Available Seat KMs, ASK • Route Performance YTD vs Budget • Route Performance YTD vs Last Year • Route Performance Budget vs Actual Variance Review • Aircraft by fleet financial performance • Maintenance Cost • Top 20 spendings for the quarter • Share Price • Profit and Loss • Cash Flow • Debt vs Equity

5 Ensuring the assets of the company are used to their maximum to bring revenue to the shareholders.
6 Reporting to the board on the state of the company, and informing the board of the status of the financials and the regulatory compliance.
7 Making recommendations to the board on how the company can compete in the current environment and how it should progress in the future.
8 Applying the board's directions and instruction in managing the company.

It can be seen that a significant part of the AM/CEO's role is enabling, supporting, and facilitating their senior staff, nominated persons or PHs to do their work effectively and to ensure the company is meeting the regulatory obligations.

Having established an SOP of oversight meetings, let's see how we can develop a "Dashboard of Metrics", which at a glance gives the AM a clear view of his or her accountabilities, using quick reference symbolic dials and data.

A dashboard of information for the Accountable Manager

To be able to be informed of your regulatory and fiduciary responsibilities, it helps to have big data available at a glance. It is recommended that a good management information software (MIS) is utilised that extracts operational, technical and commercial information from the individual detailed systems. Further, it displays the information in a "dashboard" format for the CEO/AM to be able, at a glance, to see high-level information getting an effective feel for the health and status of the company.

The Operations Dashboard (Figure 6.1) shows the main point of where the fleet is, on-time performance, MEL and ETOPs status, aircraft utilisation, and pilot utilisation. This information helps the AM know easily the status and whereabouts of the fleet he or she is responsible for.

The Technical Dashboard (Figure 6.2) shows the main point of the maintenance and technical status of the fleet, defects that caused delays, next scheduled maintenance, total flight time and landings per aircraft, and serviceability of the fleet. This information assists the AM to know at all times and easily the technical and maintenance highlights of the fleet he or she is responsible for.

The Safety Management Dashboard (Figure 6.3) shows the main point of status of the SMS within the company. This information assists the AM, as the champion of safety, to know at all times his or her safety accountabilities.

The Compliance/Quality Management Dashboard (Figure 6.4) shows the main point of status of the Compliance/Quality Management System within the company. This information assists the Accountable Manager to know at all times easily the safety accountabilities of the safety champion the AM.

108 *A tool kit and SOPs for the AM*

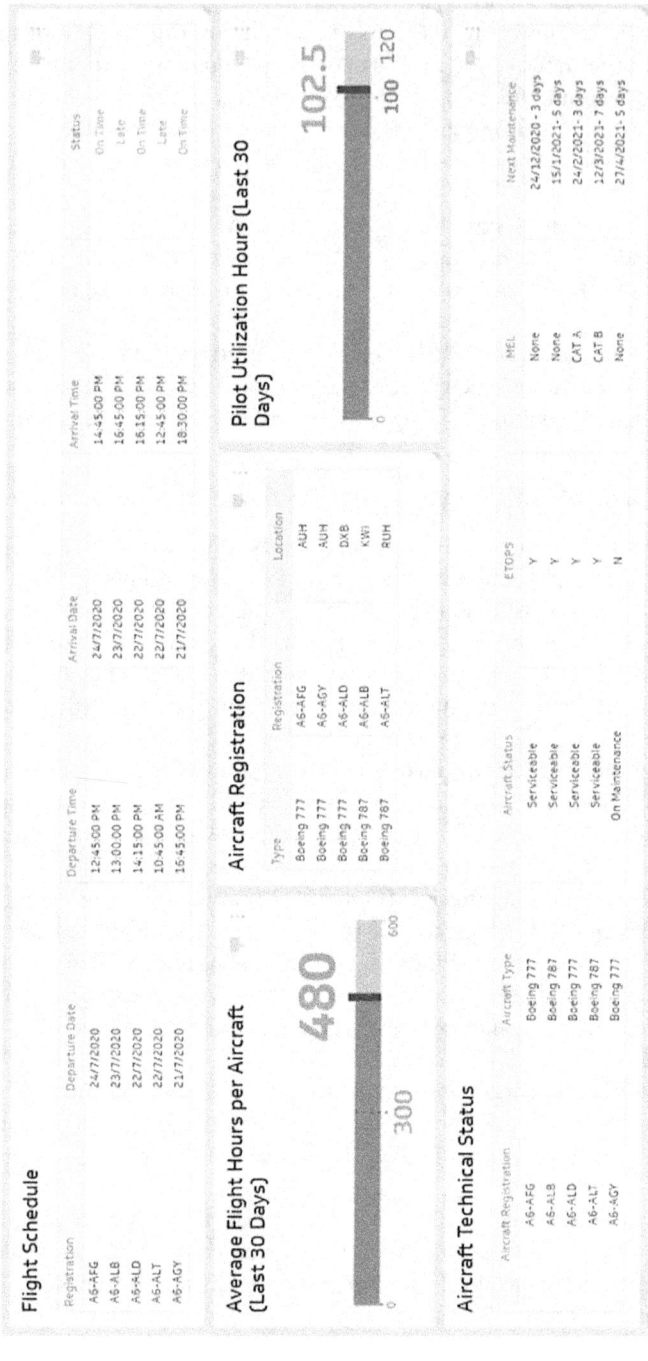

Figure 6.1 An operations dashboard for the Accountable Manager.

Reason for Late Departure

Registration	Delay Time	Reason
A6-AFG	24 Hours	APU Failed
A6-ALB	48 Hours	Engine Change
A6-ALD	4 Hours	Fuel Leak
A6-ALT	12 Hours	Passenger Connection
A6-AGY	2 Hours	Baggage Security

Maintenance Plan

Registration	Short Term	Medium Term
A6-AFG	A Chk 26/1/2021 to 26/...	C Chk 1/12/6021 to 30/...
A6-ALB	A Chk 20/2/2021 to 20/...	C Chk 25/3/2022 to 25/...
A6-ALD	A Chk 30/3/2021 to 30/...	C Chk 24/4/2022 to 29/...
A6-ALT	A Chk 15/4/2021 to 15/...	C Chk 20/2/2023 to 20/...
A6-AGY	A Chk 21/5/2021 to 21/...	C Chk 28/8/2023 to 18/...

Fleet Technical Status

Type	Registration	Age (Years)	Status	Total Flight Time	Total Landings
Boeing 777	A6-AFG	14	On Maintenance	52,122	8,687
Boeing 787	A6-ALB	6	Serviceable	22,338	3,723
Boeing 777	A6-ALD	11	Serviceable	40,953	6,826
Boeing 787	A6-ALT	5	Serviceable	18,615	3,103
Boeing 777	A6-AGY	12	AOG	44,676	7,446

Figure 6.2 A technical dashboard for the Accountable Manager.

110 *A tool kit and SOPs for the AM*

Figure 6.3 A safety dashboard for the Accountable Manager.

Figure 6.4 A quality/compliance dashboard for the Accountable Manager.

The Commercial/Financial Dashboard (Figure 6.5) shows the main points of the state of the company's commercial and financial activity. This information assists the AM, if he or she is also the CEO, to know at all times easily if the company is performing well as a commercial organisation.

Dashboards help the AM to meet his or her regulatory accountabilities by being informed constantly of the highlighted items, while also showing the fiduciary accountabilities of running a sustainable, efficient, and profitable company.

Both responsibilities are essential, and both are the responsibility and accountability of the CEO and AM, and they must be balanced. A wonderfully

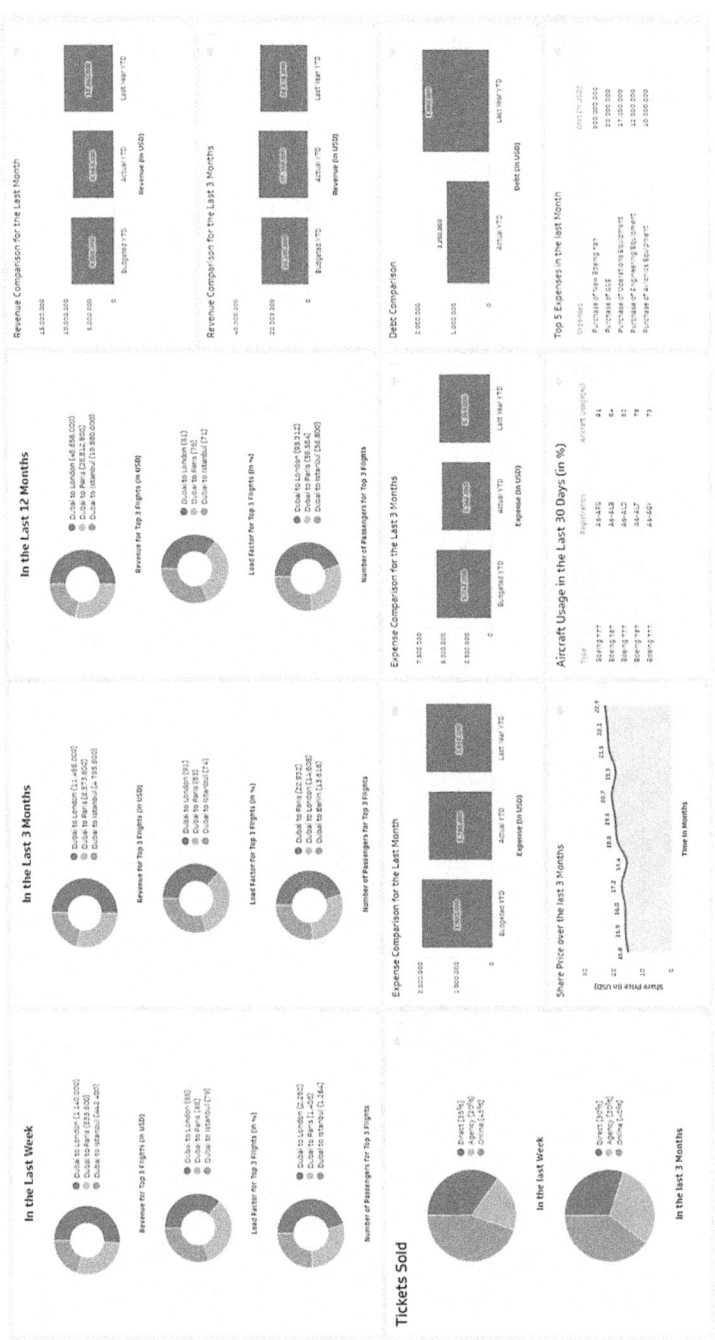

Figure 6.5 A commercial/financial dashboard for the Accountable Manager.

safe and compliant operation that loses millions per year is not a sustainable company. A highly profitable company that cuts corners on such expenditure and maintenance and safety should not last. A safe and compliant company that makes a profit and is a sustainable well-run company, where both the regulator and the shareholders are happy, is what we wish to achieve.

7 How to select an effective Accountable Manager

We saw earlier that the selection of the AM is a task for the chairman and board. Perhaps, the most important task of the chairman and board is the selection of the next CEO. We understand the tasks and challenges of the AM. If the AM is also the CEO, these challenges just increase, balancing the regulatory accountable responsibilities with the fiduciary responsibilities. The chairman and board should understand that the AM and CEO are essential to the company's success, and there are many important skills and attributes that the person taking the position must hold. Selection of that person is a sensitive and very important task.

Studies have been made on the selection of CEOs and their predominant background and qualifications (Russell & Gui, 2019). A CEO could be from a financial, operational or engineering or other background; from an aviation or non-aviation background; and from within the company or brought in from outside the company. Let's first consider whether the candidate is from an aviation or non-aviation background.

In a small to middle size company, the CEO, as the top executive, is often also the AM, but even also the largest operators will allocate the AM position to the CEO, as this is preferred by the NAA. This means the CEO must be acceptable to the NAA and should have a good working knowledge of the civil aviation regulations, aviation safety, and aviation quality/compliance. This is difficult for a non-aviation professional and requires the person to undertake a course or to study preparing for the position and to begin with preparing for the NAA interview. It can take as long as 24 months to prepare a new CEO for the AM role if the appointee is not familiar with aviation management and regulations. If we look today at airline CEOs, we find that many are not from aviation backgrounds but are professional CEOs. This means they must prepare for the position and learn about the aviation business and the accountable responsibilities that come with the position. In the event that the CEO is a newcomer to the aviation industry, very often a second in command, who is an aviation expert or aviation professional with the knowledge and understanding of the civil aviation regulations, not only takes on the role of AM but also to coach the CEO on aviation and regulative matters preparing him or her to be able to take on the AM role at a later stage. It is not unusual for the NAA to allow the second in command, who is an aviation expert, to take on the role of AM

DOI: 10.4324/9781003094685-8

until the new CEO has been trained adequately and has attained the required level of knowledge the NAA expects and requires for the CEO to hold the AM position. It was also seen in the study that as many as half of the CEOs in the top 10 airlines had financial backgrounds. In fact, the larger the airline, the more likely it was that the CEO had a financial background—perhaps a reflection on the complexity of running an airline with regards to financial management. CEOs with an operations background at present account for a quarter of airline CEO positions. This perhaps is also a reflection on the fact that airlines' profits are so thin and at times very hard to achieve that it takes very skilful financial attention.

The selection of the AM is so important, not only for the board but also for the NAA; many NAAs give assistance and advice to the chairman and board in accomplishing the task. This is because, in the past, so many AMs were presented to the NAA who were just not adequately trained or knowledgeable in civil aviation regulations, safety, and quality. The assistance the NAA gives is not so much in the qualification and training of the person but in the person's required authority as the AM or accountable executive (AE). Transport Canada (TC) was so interested in ensuring that chairmen and boards understand who to select and how to empower the AM/AE that it issued an "Advisory Document" (Transport Canada, 2021) on identifying the authority required for TC to accept the proposed candidate, based on their delegated corporate authority. Also, TC requires any newly appointed AE or AM, within 30 days of appointment, to sign the compliance statement. To do so, the AE or AM must have knowledge of what he or she is accountable for. This means briefing, training, educating and coaching the newly appointed person on the civil aviation regulations and the AE/AM's accountable responsibilities (Figures 7.1 and 7.2).

SELECTION OF YOUR ACCOUNTABLE EXECUTIVE

Reference: Canadian Aviation Regulation (CAR) 106.01 and 106.02

Effective in 2005, holders of a flight training unit operating certificate, approved maintenance organization certificate, manufacturer certificate, and air operator certificate, will be required to appoint an accountable executive. The accountable executive will be a single, identifiable person within each organization who will assume full responsibility for the organization's ongoing compliance with the CARs (ref CAR 106). It is imperative that the correct person is identified as the accountable executive, and that the individual understands and accepts the roles and responsibilities associated with that position. This is not intended to be a position title without accountability. To assist organizations with the selection of their accountable executive, Appendices A and B provide a flow chart and series of questions, respectively. Appendix A identifies several organizational structures that will lead to a corresponding accountable executive. Once this person is determined, the questions in Appendix B will confirm the selected person is the correct choice. All questions must receive a " yes"

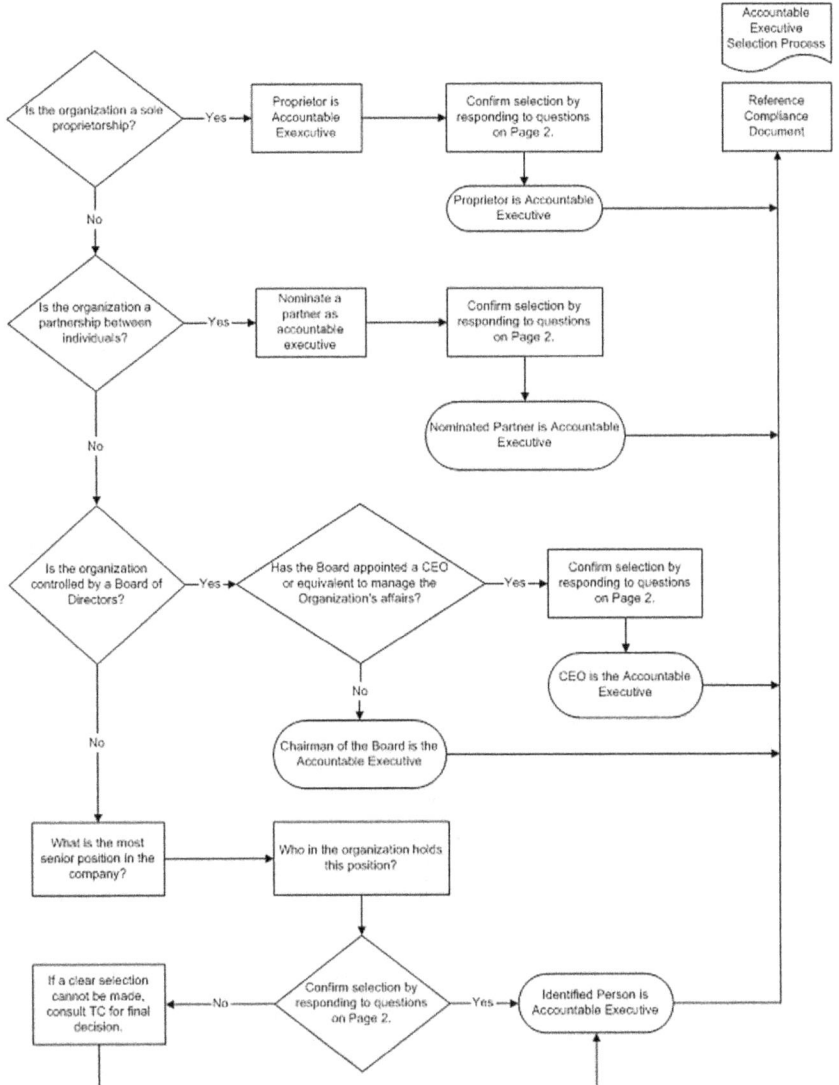

Figure 7.1 An Accountable Manager/executive selection flow chart (Transport Canada, 2021).

answer for the candidate to be acceptable. Should any of the questions result in a " no" answer, the selection process must start again with a new candidate. The organizational structures included in the Appendix are intended to cover the majority of situations that will be encountered. Should there be an organizational structure that does not result in the clear selection of

116 *How to select an effective AM*

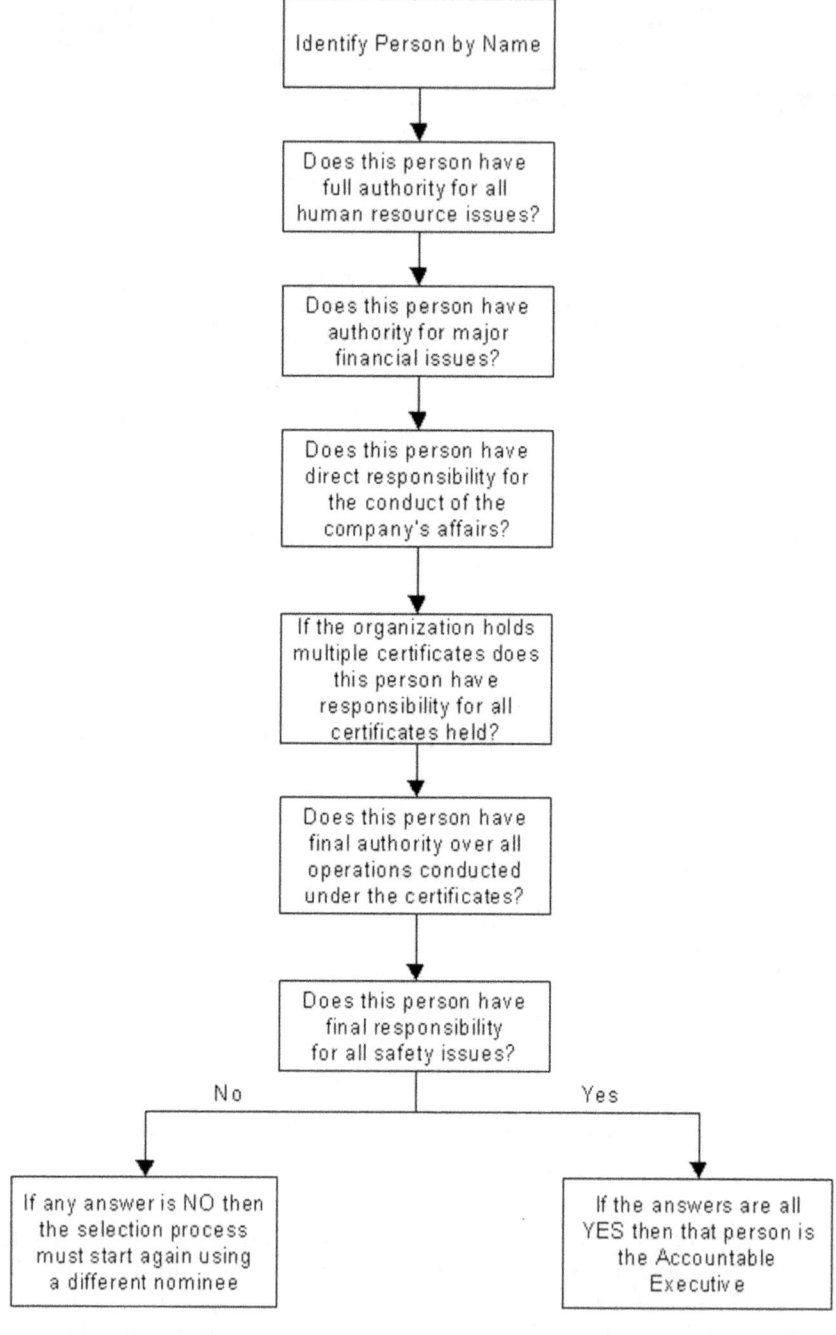

Figure 7.2 An Accountable Manager/executive selection question list (Transport Canada, 2021).

an accountable executive, an appropriate candidate will be selected in consultation with Transport Canada.

Organizations required per the above references, to name an Accountable Executive must, within 30-days of appointing the Accountable Executive:

(a) Complete the attached Compliance Statement or provide a similarly signed statement confirming that the Accountable Executive accepts the responsibilities of the position; and
(b) Submit the document to their principal operations or maintenance inspector as applicable.

Organizations are hereby authorized to amend their Flight Operations Manual, Maintenance Control/Policy Manual, or Quality Program Manual to incorporate the name of the Accountable Executive. This amendment does not require Transport Canada's approval. The nomination of the Accountable Executive will be validated during the next inspection, regulatory audit, or safety management system assessment. Inserting a copy of this document into your approved manual constitutes an acceptable means of compliance with this requirement.

(Transport Canada, 2021)

So

- if the selected and presented CEO, AM or AE is authorised as required by the NAA with the financial authority to finance and fund the company to ensure a safe and compliant operation;
- the NAA interview was carried out successfully; and
- the NAA is satisfied that the proposed person can hold the position;

that person's name can appear in the company's NAA approved documents, approvals and licences. It should be noted that there should not be a period where there is no AM or AE in place. This means the board should have a qualified and acceptable stand-in or a hand over period between the outgoing and the incoming AM. This can be discussed and agreed upon with the NAA prior to removing the incumbent.

References

Russell, W., & Gui, L. (2019). Airline CEOs: Who are they, and what background and skill set are most desirable. *Transportation Research Interdisciplinary Perspectives, Elsevier*.

Transport Canada. (2021). Canadian Aviation Regulation 106.1 & 106.2 Selection of the Accountable Executive. Montreal: Transport Canada.

8 Female Accountable Managers and the added challenges

Dr Laurie Earl, PhD, MSc, BSc (Hons), CNZHFE learnt to fly in New Zealand and is a human factors specialist in both the medical and aviation field. As well as working in the aviation industry with large and small aviation companies, Dr Earl has also worked as a lecturer and as a research specialist at many prestigious universities. Dr Earl has contributed largely to this section to give a female aviator's perspective.

This chapter explores the obstacles females face when taking on leadership roles in the civil aviation industry. The chapter combines research from the literature with interviews with female executives from around the world to offer first-hand accounts of the challenges women face in addition to all the other challenges of the AM. This chapter hopes to deliver informed advice for females—not only those entering the industry but perhaps already leading in the industry. The objective of this chapter is to assist aspiring female AMs to show it is very possible to become an AM and to perhaps encourage them into civil aviation leadership, using the successful role models mentioned in the following paragraphs of this chapter.

Although the number of women in the aviation industry is steadily increasing, there are still significantly fewer women in leadership roles in aviation as compared to other industries. Despite a marked increase in the number of female pilots in the past three decades (less so with female aircraft engineers), women continue to be underrepresented in AM positions, and internationally fewer than 5 percent of airline CEO/COOs are female (Statista, 2020).

Not only do female AMs have to overcome the technical challenges of this complex highly regulated industry but also gender challenges that come with being a leader in a very male dominated industry.

A study by Kaur and Arora (Kaur & Arora, 2020) shows that gender-diverse teams perform 73 percent better than non-diverse teams in terms of measurable results and returns.

> Merren McArthur, CEO of Tiger Airways, said (McArthur, 2020), "diversity drives performance until it becomes a business objective."
>
> Claudia Sender CEO of LATAM Airlines Brazil at APEX 2019 said, "Companies that have women in senior management positions or on

DOI: 10.4324/9781003094685-9

the board tend to perform much better than peer companies that don't. Diversity adds value."

(Sender, 2019)

Some airlines are moving quickly to increase workplace diversity. At Qantas Airways and Air New Zealand, senior management is 40 percent and 44 percent female, respectively. Alan Joyce, CEO of Qantas, said in an interview that such diversity is a "competitive advantage". He went on to say that: "It's the right business thing to do, and it's the right moral thing to do" (Editor, 2018).

Since trailblazer Barbara Cassani, CEO of GoFly in 1997, we can find female aviation leaders and AMs that not only hold or have held the leadership position, but excel at it:

- Carolyn McCall, CEO of Easy Jet UK 2010
- Airleen Omar, CEO of Air Asia Berhad Malaysia 2012
- Merren McArthur, CEO of Virgin Australia Regional Airline 2013
- Rasha Abdulaziz Al-Roumi, MD of Kuwait Airlines 2014
- Mandi Samson, Acting MD of Air Namibia 2015
- Claudia Sender, CEO of LATAM Airlines Brazil 2017
- Christine Ourmieres Widener, CEO of Flybe 2017
- Joanna Geraghty, President & COO of Jet Blue USA 2018
- Anne Rigail, CEO of Air France 2018
- Carrie Hurihanganui, COO of Air New Zealand 2018
- Jayne Hrdlicka, CEO or Virgin Australia 2020
- Harpreet A De Singh, CEO of Air Alliance India 2021.

And, of course, there is Dr Fan Liu (Secretary General of ICAO 2015), who, though not an AM, is a very important civil aviation leader.

What are the challenges facing women in senior management roles? Why do they persist? And what are the barriers preventing women from holding these positions in the first place? These questions were discussed with multiple female AMs and Dr Earl engaged them in dialogue about how women can take on and be supported in these roles.

In a study by Puckett and Hynes (Puckett & Hynes, 2011), women in senior management roles in the aviation industry reported on how they had achieved success, relevant to those entering the workforce and striving to become AMs. The results revealed that a full 80 percent of the study sample felt that it was difficult to become a female leader in commercial aviation, and none of the study participants felt that the process had been "easy".

The authors of the study identified five categories of struggle reported by participants:

1. Workplace climate
2. Mentors
3. Male resistance

4 Leadership traits
5 Fulfilment

Workplace climate/culture

Participants in the Puckett and Hynes (Puckett & Hynes, 2011) study acknowledged that 80 percent of the aviation industry encourages female leadership, and this has a positive effect on women's leadership skills and ambitions within the industry. The downside to this is that positive discrimination—forcing a gender equality outcome—can lead to particular women being promoted into roles they are not adequately prepared to hold. When they fail in those roles, this reinforces negative attitudes toward female leadership. Many of the women spoken to for this book, or whose reports were found published, reported feeling that this was apposite and said they preferred to succeed on their own merits and not because they helped to fulfil a gender quota. Forcing a gender equality outcome was not good for the individual or for the industry. Karen Walker said, "Promoting without merit does everyone a disservice" (Walker, 2018).

It is hypothesised in industry circles that there are still many aviation organisations where there is no place for women in senior management roles. According to Christine Ourmieres-Widener, former CEO of Flybe, improving gender diversity in high-level aviation roles "must involve a cultural change at the highest corporate levels". Ourmieres-Widener emphasises that the boards at airlines and other aviation organisations must advocate for gender diversity and actively pursue avenues for creating workplaces that offer flexibility in terms of how and where work is performed (Szakal, 2020).

Recent comments from a male senior IATA board member underline the sector's problem with gender diversity. Discussing the lack of women in top jobs in the Middle East, a board member suggested that a woman couldn't do his job because "it's challenging". The comment sparked outrage and the board member later apologised, saying his remarks were meant to be a joke. He added: "It will be my pleasure to have a female CEO candidate I could then develop to become CEO after me". Female aviation leaders were very disappointed to hear this from the association that is supposed to support and embrace improvement and change (Editor, 2018).

Mentors and role models

Most Puckett and Hynes (Puckett & Hynes, 2011) study participants agreed that although they experienced great difficulty advancing to senior management levels, they received significant encouragement and support from mentors and role models within the industry. Many of those interviewed reported that their greatest support in their careers came from influential mentors. Merren McArthur said that having opportunities and support from management in the airline industry was of "paramount importance" (McArthur, 2020), to her in her career. She cited John Borghetti (CEO Virgin Australia) as being instrumental in helping her to gain an AM role with Tiger Air.

Other leaders said that "sponsorship advocacy" (Lusty, 2021) was an important key to success. Jeanette Lusty, CEO of Nelson Helicopters, credited her mentors and role models with making the difference between her business being a success and going under (Lusty, 2021).

> Carol Anderson, General Counsel at Gulf Air, saw the "distinct lack of female role models at the highest corporate levels" (Szakal, 2020), as a major challenge for women in the industry.
>
> Claudia Sender of LATAM at APEX 2019 supported these sentiments and encouraged women to:
> "Never give up. We're rare. There are very few role models out there" (Sender, 2019).
>
> Stephanie Weir said that networking is the best strategy for women seeking senior level positions. "Never give up an opportunity to network" (Weir, 2020), she said. In particular, she stated that social events—as opposed to conferences or other industry events — are the "greatest opportunity to network" (Weir, 2020). Carolyn McCall (easyJet, CEO) saw the importance of "Building a personal network of advisers both within and outside of your own organisation" (Prior, 2021). Leona Qi, president of VistaJet US also sees networking as vital:
> "Success doesn't happen overnight. You have to be prepared for your next opportunity, which entails research and networking"
>
> (Robinson, 2020)

Male resistance

Participants in the study by Puckett and Hynes agreed that they met with male resistance when trying to break into leadership positions in the aviation industry. One respondent stated that she faced hardships specifically related to male resistance early on in her career when it was "unheard of" to have women in aviation. Participants reported facing ridicule, harassment, alienation, and malicious comments, having to "prove that they were capable of doing the job". Although attitudes in the industry have evolved over time, inherent gender biases still remain.

An analysis of gender and leadership by Eagly and Carli (Carli & Eagly, 2011), suggests that women may be disadvantaged by cultural beliefs that they are not as effective as men in leadership roles perhaps due to a lack of assertiveness and industrious behaviours.

These cultural beliefs may lead to cognitive dissonance, as unconscious assumptions about women's interests and capabilities conflict with conscious beliefs about the importance of promoting women into top roles. For example, care and empathy are typically considered to be feminine traits, while competition, confidence and assertiveness (aka leadership traits) are often viewed as masculine. These cultural norms make it difficult for women to fit into the parameters expected of them, because when they exhibit traits normally associated with males, they are often seen as aggressive. Gender stereotypes thus have a major impact on women's career progression.

When female leaders do exhibit some of the so called "male traits" they are often criticised or viewed unfavourably. Ourmieres-Widener believes that many old-fashioned perceptions and assumptions relating to women still go unchallenged in the aviation industry. A study in 2016 exploring Schein's "think manager, think male" (Schein, Mueller, Lituchy, & Liu, 1996) experiments in 1973 saw separate groups of participants rate "men in general", "women in general" and "successful middle managers" on a list of 92 traits. Results and analysis suggested an over whelming prejudice towards women leaders, who were seen as "less legitimate". Female participants discussion generally agreed that men are "risk takers" and "put themselves out more" (Weir, 2020). They did concede that as females they found it more difficult to put themselves forward than their male counterparts.

Imposter syndrome

One of the most important steps aspiring leaders can take is to put themselves forward for challenging roles even if they don't feel completely prepared. Ourmieres-Widener advises women, "You don't always have to wait until you are 100% ready for the next role up. You can stretch yourself" (Szakal, 2020).

Many women in the study agreed that confidence can be an inhibitor for women and that they themselves have suffered from "imposter syndrome". Michael Ball said that on average women feel they need to be 90 percent qualified before they can apply for a management role, while men will apply for roles for which they perceive themselves to have only 10% of the necessary qualifications. It would appear that a woman will consider her capability before applying for a role, while a man will seek to develop the necessary capabilities once appointed. As Karen Walker said, "women tend to grow and develop confidence whilst it comes naturally to men" (Walker, 2018).

Merren McArthur's advice to women was to, "grab at any opportunity that presents itself, no matter how scary, and give it your best shot" (McArthur, 2020).

For women wanting to move into leadership roles in aviation, it is critical to have the courage to be bold and forthcoming and to effectively communicate your goals. Speaking up about your interests and long-term aspirations early can prompt others to think about you when relevant opportunities arise.

Leona Qi encouraged women to, "Focus on your strengths. Don't let imposter syndrome paralyse your progress. Let your skillset speak for itself and steer the narrative in your favour" (Robinson, 2020).

Leadership traits

Researchers have found that women tend to have a distinct leadership style, a style that mimics Richard Branson's. Transformational leaders aim to enhance motivation, morale and job performance by working with their teams to identify needed changes, create shared visions and guide through inspiration. They invest time in coaching their teams and demonstrate concern for the personal development of each team member. They emphasise teamwork and authentic communication as keys to success.

In 2019 at an APEX panel discussion on woman leadership in aviation the female participants talked about the qualities of successful leaders and identified "Four Cs"—confidence, competence, collaboration and credibility. Claudia Sender said that successful leadership requires "limitless passion, pushing boundaries and getting comfortable with being uncomfortable" (Lenhoff, 2019).

In the Puckett and Hynes study of 2011 study of female leadership in aviation, the women interviewed identified the most important traits of a successful leader as: "excellent communication skills, integrity, compassion, competence and patience". Of these responses, "compassion" was the least expected by the researchers. The respondents clarified this by saying that leaders needed compassion to effectively mentor and train others, ensuring the comfort of other females in their organisations.

In the same study, participants' leadership activities outside of their work in the aviation industry seemed to have transferred to their workplaces. Many participants said that non-work leadership roles had influenced their career paths and aided their acquisition of leadership skills.

Fulfilment

A Podcast on woman in aviation recognised that both men and women must make sacrifices to hold senior level roles, and that includes loss of time with their family. Stephanie Weir said that women need to become more mobile in order to be competitive with their male counterparts (Weir, 2020). Weir herself gained a promotion when she moved overseas to become the Director of Economics and Aviation at the Tenerife Tourism Corporation.

Senior-level women are under the same pressure to perform as senior-level men—and then some. However, they are often held to higher performance standards than men, and are more likely to take the blame for failure. This means that when the stakes are high, senior-level women could face more criticism and harsher judgement (Coury, et al., 2020).

A Korn Ferry report on females in aviation leadership also identified five key drivers to women's success in the industry (Nasser & Bell, 2020):

1 Publicly recognise and highlight female role models.
2 Senior leadership commitment to diversity and inclusion.

3 Set expectations with individual contributors and management for advancement.
4 Ensure women have a seat at the table—included in senior level decision making.
5 Invest in more inclusive talent management and succession processes.

In 2019, Air New Zealand was appointed the recipient of a new award sponsored by IATA, the inaugural Diversity and Inclusion Team Award at the 2019 International Air Transport Association (IATA) Annual General Meeting held in Seoul, Korea. The award internationally recognises Air New Zealand as leading the way for diversity and inclusion in the aviation industry.

Since 2013, the airline has elevated its gender diversity by increasing the number of females in its 80 strong senior leadership team from 16 percent in 2013 to 43 percent in 2019 with an aim to reach 50 percent, which was achieved in 2021. Among the initiatives Air NZ implemented were a women in leadership programme, unconscious gender bias training and the appointment of passionate diversity and inclusion champions throughout the business.

An Air New Zealand article said (AirNewZealand, 2019) that companies in the top quartile of ethnic and gender diversity are 33 percent and 38 percent respectively more likely to have a higher than average market share and we encourage diversity of thought in our decision-making processes to authentically reflect our customer base.

Some more quotes from woman aviation leaders:

Anne Rigail—Air France
In an industry where executive-level roles are typically filled by men, it's exciting to see a woman earn the opportunity to lead an extraordinary airline.

(Rigail, A. 2019, see Bohmer, 2019)

Mandi Samson—Air Namibia
It has been proven time and again that women can effectively execute jobs that are traditionally known to be for men.

(Samson, M. 2018, see Bohmer, 2019)

Joanna Geraghty—JetBlue
… at this stage in my life, it's the women of JetBlue, hundreds of whom I have come to know well, who inspire me the most.

(Geraghty, J. 2018, see Bohmer, 2019)

Aireen Omar—Air Asia
Helming the organization boils down to being task-driven, not gender-driven. It is all about focus, perseverance and determination.

(Omar, A. 2017, see Bohmer, 2019)

Leona Qi, President of VistaJet US, says:

> Focus on these essential principles:
>
> - Prepare for your next step. Success doesn't happen overnight. You have to be prepared for your next opportunity, which entails research and networking.
> - Find your passion. As you transition to your next position, if it doesn't excite you, it's time for you to look elsewhere. Having a passion keeps you focused and determined to succeed.
> - Focus on your strengths. Don't let imposter syndrome paralyse your progress. Let your skillset speak for itself and steer the narrative in your favour.
>
> (Qi, L 2020; Robinson, 2020)

Captain Jeanette Lusty, CEO and Pilot, of Nelson Helicopters, New Zealand, says:

> to be a successful AM:
>
> - Build a network of knowledgeable and experienced people who can advise and support you.
> - Take responsibility for your staff—these people are relying on you for their livelihoods.
> - Take responsibility for your passengers—these people are relying on you for their safety.
> - Always own mistakes and learn from them.
> - Build as much safety around operations as possible.
> - Never be afraid to ask for help and be honest and open with people.
> - Choose your team well with people that fit the team ethos. One person in the wrong role can collapse the whole team.
> - Face challenges head on, have faith in yourself.
> - Don't underestimate kindness, people will respond to it far more than they do to aggression or domination.
>
> (Lusty, 2021)

It is now obvious that the leadership role of the CEO/COO and Accountable Manager is not exclusive for a particular gender, but it can be seen that perhaps a greater challenge remains for females who have to overcome the gender factor in getting a chance to take on the role of the AM. Whether it is one of the most successful airlines in recent history being led by a female CEO and AM or one of the most historical national flag carriers, female CEOs & AMs can and are taking on the role with great success.

Finally, an important comment to be noted is this:

> Judge us by our success and not by our gender, but title us successful Aviation Leaders not as female Aviation Leaders, so gender becomes unimportant.
>
> (Dedovic, 2021)

References

AirNewZealand. (2019, June 3). *Air New Zealand wins international diversity and inclusion award*. Retrieved from https://www.airnewzealand.co.uk/press-release-2019-airnz-wins-international-diversity-and-inclusion-award.

Bohmer, J. T. (2019, March 8). *Breaking the Cloud Ceiling—Female Leaders in Aviation*. Retrieved from https://medium.com/yieldr/breaking-the-cloud-ceiling-female-leaders-in-aviation-9ddc94af72a1.

Carli, L., and Eagly, A. (2011). Gender and Leadership. *Sage Handbook of Leadership*.

Coury, S., Huang, J., Kumar, A., Prince, S., Krivkovich, A., and Yee., L. (2020, Sept 30). *Mckinsey & Co: Women in the Workplace*. Retrieved from https://www.mckinsey.com/featured-insights/diversity-and-inclusion/women-in-the-workplace.

Dedovic, S. (2021, April 5). Woman Leadership in Aviation. (M. J. Pierotti, Interviewer)

Editor. (2018, June 5). International Air Transport Association, IATA, AGM Press Conference Sydney. *Arabian Business*.

Kaur, N., & Arora, P. (2020). Acknowledging Gender Diversity and Inclusion as Key to Organizational Growth. *Journal of Clinical reviews*.

Lenhoff, I. (2019, Oct 3). *Viasat CFO Shawn Duffy leads panel on women in leadership at aviation conference*. Retrieved from Viasat: https://www.viasat.com/about/newsroom/blog/women-in-leadership/.

Lusty, J. (2021, March 12). Woman Leadership in Aviation; Jeanette Lusty. (L. Earl, Interviewer).

McArthur, M. (2020). Women in aviation: Soaring through the glass ceiling. On Line: Routes on line. Retrieved from Women in aviation: Soaring through the glass ceiling:https://www.routesonline.com/podcasts/women-aviation-soaring-through-the-glass-ceiling/.

Nasser, A., & Bell, M. (2020). *Soaring Through the Glass Ceiling; Taking Global Aviation to New Hights Through Diversity & Inclusion*. Korn Ferry.

Prior, D. (2021, March 1). Woman Leadership in Aviation; Carolyn McCall. (L. Earl, Interviewer).

Puckett, M., & Hynes, G. (2011). Feminine leadership in commercial aviation: Success stories of women pilots and captains. *Journal of Aviation Management and Education*.

Robinson, C. (2020, Dec 17). How VistaJet's Leona Qi Represents The Future Of Female Leadership In The Airline Industry. *Forbes*.

Schein, V. E., Mueller, R., Lituchy, T., and Liu, J. (1996). Think manager—think male: a global phenomenon? *Journal of Organisational Behaviour*.

Sender, C. (2019). Airline Passenger Experience Exhibition. *APEX 2019*. Boston: APEX.

Statista. (2020). *Gender Distribution of Selected Senior Roles in the Aviation Industry*. Retrieved from Gender Distribution of Selected Senior Roles in the Aviation Industry: www.statista.com/statistics/740571/airline-industry-senior-roles-by-gender/.

Szakal, A. (2020, Feb). *Is gender still holding women back in the aviation industry?* Retrieved from https://saiblog.cranfield.ac.uk/blog/is-gender-still-holding-women-back-in-the-aviation-industry.

Walker, K. (2018, May 22). Interview with Karen Walker, Editor-In-Chief at Air Transport World. (BTCRadio, Interviewer).

Weir, S. (2020). Women in aviation: Soaring through the glass ceiling. On Line: Routes On Line. Retrieved from https://www.routesonline.com/podcasts/women-aviation-soaring-through-the-glass-ceiling/.

9 A lawyer's review of the Accountable Manager's responsibilities

Mr D. Anthony Frances BEc, LLB, LLM, AMRAeS is senior counsel at a leading international law firm specialising in aviation and maritime law. Mr Frances has worked in Europe, Australasia and the Middle East acting for airlines, operators, suppliers, OEMs, national governments and civil aviation authorities. Mr Frances contributed largely to this chapter to bring the lawyer's point of view of the AM to the subject. The opinions expressed in this chapter are those of the author only and do not necessarily reflect that those of his firm.

Introduction

This section of the book mentions the relevant laws and treaties that are in place that the AM should be sensitive to and also draws attention to particular accidents and incidents that an AM should be familiar with. From the point of view of a lawyer, it will comment on the most senior of the regulatory civil aviation roles, the AM.

The world of commercial civil aviation is an ever-changing industry with cutting edge technologies and advancements in aircraft design, efficiency and operation. It is also subject to one of the most stringent regulatory and legal regimes of any industry. As a general rule, there are numerous domestic and international rules and regulations for any airline or operator to consider (and irrespective of jurisdiction) that must be followed—these have been put in place to promote and maintain the safety and security of the travelling public and the public below the flight path.

In the last 35 years, aviation has unfortunately drawn significant adverse publicity and criticism due to events such as: (i) the loss of four aircraft during the September 11 attacks on New York and Washington in 2001 (Government of the United States, 2004); (ii) the loss in March 2015 of the German Wings A320 in the Swiss Alps due to deliberate pilot action by a man who was suffering mental issues at the time (BEA the French Civil Aviation Safety Investigation Authority, 2016); and (iii) the loss of a B747 Pam Am PA103 in 1988 over Lockerbie Scotland (Air Accident Investigation Branch of the UK, 1988), due to a systematic failure of the airline and security services to detect explosives. It is rather unfortunate that these matters detract from the good work and

DOI: 10.4324/9781003094685-10

progress that the airline industry has made in aviation governance and oversight in the last 40–50 years. The recent figures of aircraft losses and significant incidents do show a progressive improvement in safety and that is due, in part, to the changes in management and operational culture. The importance of being the AM is reflective of this trend.

In the light of the above, the purpose of this section is for the AM to (i) understand the legal regime for airlines and operators which they operate (and in conjunction with the PHs or nominated persons); (ii) consider the international laws and regulation that an AM must consider and apply; (iii) consider the regulatory regime (on a State level) that the carrier or airline operates under and (iv) consider any other matters that the AM should take into consideration for his or her work to promote safety and security.

We have seen earlier in the book the reason and method for appointing the AM along with their nominated PHs or nominated persons.

The importance of the AM in aviation cannot be understated as the safety and security of the industry is at stake. Organisational behaviour has become a relevant issue now for any operator—particularly transport where a potential safety breach could lead to death or personal injury. Therefore, poor organisational behaviour and bad management (which includes a poor AM) often result in accident and incidents. A recent article sets this out:

> The very basis for the principle used to explain accidents as failures at anyone of these stages is that management decisions propagate downwards and progressively turn into productive activity; Bad management decisions propagate downwards and progressively turn into unsafe activity, and possibly accidents.
>
> (World Press, 2016)

This section now shall review further the relevant legal framework.

Legal framework

Aviation contains both domestic and international aspects. An operator who flies domestically within the same state will have to follow the domestic laws and to international regulations to the extent that they apply. This is particularly relevant where domestic carriers operate in conjunction with an international carrier. An AM must therefore consider all contractual and liability aspects and standards between the two carriers.

International

Airlines and operators who fly internationally are subject to various international laws, rules and regulations.

There are rules and regulations for liability (such as the Montreal Convention 1999 (IATA, 1999), the Warsaw Convention 1929 (IATA, 1929) and the Hague

Protocol 1955 (IATA, 1959)) are all applicable to an operator where the flights involve contracting States, but an analysis needs to be made of the state of departure and arrival for a flight to determine which Convention applies. Other regulations such as state liability regulations—for example, the EU Law Regulation (EC) No 889/2002 (European Union, 2002)—set out minimum limits on carrier liability above other Conventions.

We have already seen earlier in this book that, with respect to the European Union, all 27 states forming part of EASA utilise and adopt the EASA regulation and guidance and incorporate them into their state laws. As a member of the EU, each state is required to follows such rules and regulations subject to any "local" amendments which each state is entitled to have. For example, the Hellenic Republic restricts night flights for private and some commercial operations while other states have certain pilot language requirements for domestic services.

Domestic

Where operators do not fly internationally (often due to the size of the country that they operate)—they are subject to two main legal regimes. The first legal regime consists of the domestic laws that specify the regulatory and liability laws for domestic carriage. These laws are mostly technical and operational. The second legal regime is where the domestic carrier is in partnership or in a interline agreement with another entity (who does international carriage), where the carrier liability may be far more due to the special legal rules that apply for international carriage.

From a legal perspective, the operator must adhere to the local regulations only insofar as operation, maintenance and oversight but may for the purposes of being the "interline" partner, are required to follow some of the international regulations. This may include the number of PHs (and the experience requirements for the AM) who must be appointed and also follow the local requirements for the certain types of operations—for example, small turboprop and seaplane operators.

From the above, it is clear that any operator (and AM) must have a full appreciation and knowledge of the domestic and international laws and regulations for the operation they conduct.

A manager's corporate responsibility

As stated above, the regulatory requirements will depend upon the size of the operation, number of aircraft and the complexity of the operation. In the UAE, the GCAA sets out this analysis:

> The qualifications and level of experience of post holders and key operational staff will vary according to the scope and size of the proposed operations. Post holders and key operational staff shall have an understanding with

Human Factors and Human Performance limitation besides the following specific requirements.

(UAE GCAA, 2021)

An AM must satisfy not only the regulatory authorities but also its corporate responsibilities, especially where the AM is also a director of the owning or operating company.

Furthermore, airlines have unique corporate structures as between ownership and management of its operating assets. Aircraft that are acquired with a form of finance are often set up in offshore jurisdictions for liability and finance operating reasons. Aircraft management companies or operators are usually incorporated in the same country as their main operational base and for the purposes of their Air Operators Certificate ("AOC")—as this is a regulatory requirement for operation of aircraft. The situation within the EU bloc is slightly different, where the aircraft management company can be located in one EU state and the main base for the aircraft operation is in another state.

The AM (if also a director of the company as is often the case—generally the AM is the CEO of the company) must also take into account the responsibility as a director of a company and to the company shareholders (to operate fiducially efficiently and issue dividends). The AM must fulfil his or her obligations to always act in the best interests of the company and ensure that he or she regularly attends the required meetings and conducts other required duties and obligations. In addition, he or she must also ensure compliance with the regulations of the applicable aviation authority. In other jurisdictions, a trust structure for ownership of aircraft is often used but the AM will still be required to fulfil the company's obligations to the owner or trustee. Therefore, as the AM is usually a senior manager or director of the airline or operator, he or she have two roles to fulfil, which at times may conflict. It is important that the AM ensures that he or she prioritises the regulatory aviation safety and security role as the primary role, and may be asked to prove that he or she has done so.

An AM's responsibility in aviation (where he or she is the CEO or a director) is very distinct to those of other directors for non-transport businesses—for example, those that produce goods and services. The AM in an aviation company has a higher responsibility and must act to a higher standard in the operation and for oversight. By way of example, the safety manager and compliance manager of any operator are required, as part of their responsibilities, to audit and oversee staff closely and ensure that the pilots, engineers and ground staff are following procedures. Further, they are required to report any flight safety and non-compliance findings straight to the CEO and AM, in order to avoid any potential failure by intermediate staff to advise the board of directors, the AM or senior management of any immediate compliance, safety and security issues—such as funding, training and maintenance of aircraft and staff.

An AM must also be aware of the standards that he or she must maintain as part of his or her role.

In addition to the above, any operator who flies aircraft commercially (i.e. passengers or freight for reward) must do so in accordance with their AOC. This document sets out the type of aircraft that can be operated, from which jurisdiction and on what terms. An AM must be fully informed and aware of the restrictions (if any) of the AOC and must ensure that all requirements under the AOC (as set out in the State's regulations) are followed.

Airline or operator liability

An AM must understand and appreciate that aviation is a high valued industry with extensive high value liabilities for when loss and damage is caused by aircraft and through its operations.

An airline or operator's liability falls into three main categories which the AM must consider in making operational decisions. They are:

i   Passenger, baggage and cargo liability for flights;
ii Liability of flight crew, management and maintenance and the operation of the aircraft; and
iii General liability for loss and damage.

This section deals with each one in turn.

Passenger, baggage and cargo liability

An airline or operator under the various international liability conventions (as set out above) will be liable and responsible to passengers and/or cargo interests for death, personal injury, loss and damage to cargo and baggage. Unlike general negligence claims for example, motor accident or industrial accidents (where the claimant must prove "fault" or "negligence" for loss and damage), in aviation, the liability falls automatically on the airline or operator and for a specific minimal amount (in the EU, its 100,000 SDRs, Special Drawing Rights) unless the carrier can show that it took all necessary action to avoid the incident or accident which caused the death, personal injury and/or loss/damage or that the carrier was not negligent (or was due to the acts of a third party). Therefore, it is a "reverse" burden on the airline or operator for any sum above the "limit". The airline or operator will need to show (on the balance of probabilities) that it took the necessary steps or took all reasonable measures to avoid the loss and damage or that it was not negligent. This is not an easy burden to shift and the relevant laws are not specific as to how to disprove negligence in order to exceed the strict liability limits. Normal industry standards are therefore often relied upon when this assessment is made by a judge or arbitrator. For example, an operator would need to show that it followed the industry standards or procedures where an accident or incident occurred. This of course is a question of fact to be considered by the trial judge or arbitrator. Proof of damage (and quantum) is also required.

An AM must therefore be up to speed with industry practices and ensure that they are followed and enforced in the company and operationally. He or she cannot simply assert that he or she "*did not know*" as the AM is required to be aware of all major issues affecting the operation and aircraft.

Liability of flight crew, management and maintenance for the operation of the aircraft

An airline or operator's management is ultimately responsible under its AOC obligations to operate and manage the aircraft and the company to follow the best standards and practices to ensure safety and security. This is the overriding duty and its falls on the AM to ensure that this overall principle is followed.

With respect to flight crew, the AM must ensure that the operator's procedures are in place for training, medical and mandatory reporting systems for the flight crew. This also entails that the company has the financial resources to undertake this task.

As for maintenance, the AM is also overall responsible for ensuring that (i) proper maintenance is undertaken on each aircraft, (ii) that such maintenance is properly done and in the correct intervals in accordance with the OEM's maintenance manual, the aircraft maintenance schedule and the State of registry of the aircraft, (iii) the aircraft is monitored by properly qualified engineers or LAMEs (including CAMO), and (iv) that the operator has the finances to pay its creditors for maintenance and overhauling—as well as spare parts, etc.

Any liabilities that arise from the above will fall on the managers (or "nominated persons") and ultimately on the AM. The way in which these matters are dealt with on a practical level is for weekly meeting of divisional heads, nominated persons and senior staff to deal with any impending issues. Checklists and updates should form part of the regular schedules and follow up and cross monitoring techniques should also be applied.

General liability for loss and damage

An AM and the PHs (or nominated persons) must also take account of its other liabilities—such as employment, health and safety, finances and environmental liabilities. Each of these areas has potential ramifications for an operator and the AM must therefore ensure that they are updated on the various areas regularly—in particular by their "regulatory team" and general legal counsel. By way of example, health and safety laws (from that state of operation) will govern any workplace injury as well as for any aircraft that is registered in that state or jurisdiction.

Regulatory considerations

Aside from the company obligations as a director or chief executive officer, the AM must also be aware of the regulatory legal regime in place and accordingly adopt practices and policies that take these legal issues into consideration. Gone are the days that senior managers or directors could adopt a *laissez-faire* attitude to aircraft operations.

The main regulatory legal regime for the AM to consider is set out below:

> First, there is the Chicago Convention (The Chicago Conference, 1944) on international aviation which deals with all aspects of regulation of civil aviation (i.e. Aircraft registration, flight operations, airworthiness, passenger details, etc.) and also includes 19 Annexes (ICAO, 2021 a–c) (including "Safety Management"—Annex 19 (ICAO, 2021 a–c); "Air Accident & Incident Investigation"—Annex 13 (ICAO, 2021 a–c)), which are "Standards and Recommended Practices" "SARPs". SARPs provide guidance to the selected area for AMs especially with respect to Annex 6 ("Operation of Aircraft") and Annex 8 ("Airworthiness of Aircraft"). The above matters are all incorporated into national law with some variations. Therefore an AM needs to regularly consult and consider the above to discharge their obligations as an AM.

The Chicago Convention also addresses mutual recognition of registered commercial aircraft from other countries. Although there is mutual recognition by States, civil aviation authorities in many States have banned other States' registered aircraft due to poor oversight, poor regulation and monitoring of their civil aviation activities and the standards of the operators. For example, the member states of the European Union have been very strict and "blacklisted" many operators on the basis of the above. Such states have included Indonesia, DRC and Sudan. It can be observed that sometimes the ban is a blanket one on all aircraft registered in a particular country. Sometimes it may be aimed at a specific operator and sometimes there may be a ban with partial exemptions, such as the ban by the EU on Angolan aircraft, but TAAG is allowed to fly to Portugal.

Further while the Chicago Convention provides a broad outline of civil aviation regulations, many States create their own rules and regulations taking into account local conditions. Many countries, such as the UAE, whilst they have their own regulatory authority and rule making abilities, closely follow the EASA rules and regulations, save for certain exceptions. Other states such as the PRC (China) closely follow the FAA standards. There is no right or wrong, but ensuring that the aircraft flown by the operator must comply with the State of Registry (which often follows either FAA or EASA) and the OEM requirements. It is important that an AM becomes familiar with these two standards, as well as those of the State of registry.

Second, there is the Rome Convention (ICAO, 1952) which has not been universally adopted by States. This deals with carriers' liability for loss or damage to persons or objects on the ground arising from an aircraft. A carrier would therefore be liable for loss and damage caused by an aircraft or any part thereof falling and causing loss and damage on the ground. Of course, this is a usual insurance risk but again the standards adopted by the operator are crucial to any assessment of negligence.

Third, and one of the most important issues for any AM, is that relating to the operator's AOC and general regulatory compliance. There are two aspects for an AM to consider.

The first is that pertaining to the operator's AOC. The State of registry requirements for the aircraft itself (i.e. type and operating restrictions) and their operations must be strictly followed. There may be conditions attached to the AOC which must also be strictly followed (for example, the AOC being temporary, conditional or being subject to regular review) which an AM must be aware of.

The second relates to the State of registry (or civil aviation authority itself) which also will have strict requirements for the aircraft and flights. Often these are related to the competency and the training requirements of flight crew, engineers, and management. For example, in the European Union, there are minimum educational and experience levels for different types of operations—helicopter, seaplane, and commercial aircraft. In any event it is important for the AM to regularly review and ensure compliance with both regulatory regimes (which overlap). This is further developed below.

Operational matters

The next question relating to the above is what does an AM need to do on a day to day basis to comply with (i) his or her obligations to the aviation authority or state of registry of the aircraft and (ii) to comply the laws that apply to the aircraft and its operations?

This section now deals with these in turn.

An AM is obliged to act in the best interests of the company by which he or she is employed and to ensure that the company and its directors (including the board of directors) are sufficiently advised of all material and major issues with respect to which the AM (and the nominated persons) must also take into account. For example, and on a practical basis, the AM must consider the maintenance requirements and planning for each aircraft (and through use of the CAMO department), which will also require that any maintenance and repairs are done properly and in accordance with the regulatory requirements. The AM must also ensure payments of staff, flight crew and third party invoices to ensure that the operator is not working on "credit". This is becoming a large problem currently due to the Covid-19 pandemic which has severely affected the cash flows of many airlines, both large and small. The AM must therefore ensure that, as an ongoing business, the operator can pay its salaries and suppliers and maintain it operation (or has the available finance to do so). Safety is the primary concern.

Further, the theory behind the financial wellness of the company as part of its AOC, is its obligation to retain sufficient funds to pay for its staff, maintenance and is not operated without sufficient reserves—this is a policy requirement and it is reflected in the UK, the European Union, the USA, the UAE and many other countries. Many operators have had their licences and AOCs revoked due to their dire financial position. By way of example, in the UAE the applicable regulations state as follows:

> All applicants for AOC initial and renewal must undergo a financial fitness/competence by the relevant Department of Civil Aviation (DCA). In the event, the relevant DCA is unable to do so, the GCAA will conduct the assessment.
>
> (UAE GCAA, 2021)

As is apparent from the above, the AM has an ongoing duty and responsibility to ensure compliance.

One other matter which an AM must consider is that pertaining to criminal liability—both the company and as individuals. As part of the Annex 13 process for accident and incident investigation, many countries appoint a judge or local prosecutor to investigate whether any criminal behaviour led to the accident or incident. In the UK, for example, they passed the Corporate Manslaughter and Corporate Homicide Act 2007 (Ministry of Justice UK, 2007) which deals with corporate criminal responsibility in the UK. Although it permits prosecutions of companies, it does not deal with individual director's criminal responsibility—a matter dealt with in the Health & Safety Act 1974 (Ministry of Justice UK, 1974) (as amended). In other countries, such as Italy, the Hellenic Republic and the Eastern bloc states usually have dual investigations open when there is a transport accident.

As a result, it is important that the AM bears the above in mind particularly where the countries to which the operator may operate may have more stringent rules and regulations regarding criminal liability, especially for individual directors and the AM.

Instances of Accountable Manager issues

As stated above, this section provides a general outline of the laws and regulations that regulate aviation and flights and to provide the AM (and PHs or nominated persons) with the types of legal and regulatory issues that they need to consider.

In order to provide further guidance on responsibilities and potential pitfalls, set out below are examples of where AM issues (and corporate failures) have arisen and the catastrophic effects on the relevant operator.

The first deals with the loss of Pam Am 103 in Lockerbie, Scotland, in December 1988. The aircraft was destroyed mid-flight due to an explosive bomb having been placed on board the aircraft from a flight from London to New York. All 288 passengers and 13 people on the ground perished.

One of the main issues in the US litigation that is relevant to the current consideration relates to the "acts and omissions" of the Pam Am management with respect to aviation security and the way that their subsidiary "alert systems" failed to take adequate precautions to protect the aircraft and its passengers. The acts of the agents' "alert systems" were held to be referable back to the Pam Am management as well as their negligence in their management of the risk. The Court of Appeals (NY, USA) in the litigation that followed addressed the airline's procedure failures which were relevant and indicative to what an AM must consider to discharge his duties:

> The most wilful disregard of passenger safety, bordering on the outrageous, was in December 1988 when Pan Am received an FAA Security Bulletin advising that the United States Embassy in Helsinki had received a telephone warning that a Pan Am flight from Frankfurt to London and on to New York would be bombed. (Helsinki Warning). The Helsinki warning came just 14 days before the instant tragedy and specifically referred to the Toshiba Warning. Despite these warnings, Pan Am failed to conduct searches of unaccompanied interline luggage, and instead inspected such bags only by x-ray. Pan Am did not even alert x-ray technicians to watch for Toshiba radios. It violated FAA regulations by failing to match the bags with particular tickets without advising the FAA in writing that interline bag match had been discontinued. And it violated other FAA regulations by failing to warn pilots about the unaccompanied bags on board for fear that the crews might become "jittery." Additionally, Pan Am did not replace several members of its security team who were woefully undertrained given their responsibility for thwarting terrorist attacks.
> (US District Court for the Eastern District of New York, 1993)

As is apparent from the above, the Court of Appeal was very critical of the organisational failures of the Pan Am management and the way that they conducted themselves. In summary, Pan Am's management fell well short of applying proper safety and management standards which led to the loss and damage. This resulted in large pay-outs to a number of the passengers' families.

The second example dealt with aircraft maintenance and management failure that was referable again to organisational failure and senior management decisions that proved fatal. In 1997, Alaska Airlines flight 261 crashed into the Pacific Ocean while flying from Mexico to Seattle.

The final accident report concluded that probable cause of the loss of the aircraft was as follows:

> The National Transportation Safety Board determines that the probable cause of this accident was a loss of airplane pitch control resulting from the in-flight failure of the horizontal stabilizer trim system jackscrew assembly's acme nut threads. The thread failure was caused by excessive wear resulting from Alaska Airlines insufficient lubrication of the jackscrew assembly. Contributing to the accident were Alaska Airlines extended lubrication interval and the Federal Aviation Administration's (FAA) approval of

that extension, which increased the likelihood that a missed or inadequate lubrication would result in excessive wear of the acme nut threads, and Alaska Airlines extended end play check interval and the FAA's approval of that extension, which allowed the excessive wear of the acme nut threads to progress to failure without the opportunity for detection. Also contributing to the accident was the absence on the McDonnell Douglas MD-80 of a fail-safe mechanism to prevent the catastrophic effects of total acme nut thread loss.

(NTSB, 2000)

Further there were allegations of poor maintenance and incorrect paperwork were also flagged and referenced in the report. In particular, Alaskan Airlines' maintenance program it was concluded had widespread systemic deficiencies. Alaskan was also fined nearly US$1m in 2000 for these failures.

The third example was with respect to Helios Airways HCY522 flying from Cyprus to Athens, Greece, in 2004. The aircraft crashed due to fuel starvation but the contributing factors were that the flight crew and passengers were overcome by hypoxia and the crew lost control of the aircraft. The accident report concluded that the airline's management was poor and reviews were deficient. It stated as follows:

> There were organizational safety deficiencies within the Operator's management structure and safety culture as evidenced by diachronic findings in the audits prior to the accident, including: a) Inadequate Quality System; b) Inadequate Operational Management control …
> (Hellenic Republic Ministry of Transport, 2006)

As is apparent from the Helios Airways case, there was systematic failures in the management which contributed to the loss of the aircraft.

The final case that is of interest is that pertaining to the loss of the Germanwings Airbus A320 flight from Spain to Germany in 2015. The first officer, Andreas Lubitz, deliberately sent the aircraft into an unrecoverable dive into the Swiss Alps and killed all the crew and passengers. It later transpired that he had been suffering from mental health issues for some time and this was known to his personal doctors and, to a limited extent, the airline knew of his history of mental health issues. This accident had a profound effect on management oversight and health of its staff. It also raised a number of issues for operators about the mental health of their flight crews and staff.

The above are just demonstrative examples of where organisational failures have led to loss and damage, as well as large reputational damage. In the case of Pan Am and Helios Airways, they went in liquidation not long after the accidents. For German Wings, the company changed its name to "Eurowings". An AM must therefore take into consideration that such failures can lead to catastrophic outcomes.

Conclusion

Aviation combines the best of modern technologies and skill sets for all those involved in the day to day running of an airline and aircraft—including pilots, engineers, managers, support staff, environmental specialists and flight safety staff.

The Covid-19 pandemic has certainly affected the ability of people to travel and the potential liabilities that airlines may now have with the spread of the virus between countries. The airline industry has been aggressive in their assessment of the potential spread of Covid-19 on board an aircraft and through the air-conditioning systems. It is of course a new potential threat to aviation and airlines especially since there appears to be some legal uncertainty as to the potential liabilities of airlines and operators. An AM must therefore consider the risk and adopt best practices.

Furthermore, it is clear that any AM (including PHs or Nominated Persons) and board of directors must adhere to strict procedures for the day-to-day operations of the aircraft and the operator and be aware of potential safety and environmental factors. This does not mean that other factors such as aircraft security and terrorism are not real and current threats, but rather that states are again locking up their borders during 2021 with a reduced exposure to criminal acts.

As for the liability of the AM, whilst there are a number of rules and regulations governing aircraft operations and the AOC, many are general guidelines and points. Therefore an AM has to take into account not only his or her responsibilities to the company but also the aviation authority/State of Registry to whom he or she is also responsible.

Therefore the AM must adopt and follow best practices from an industry and organisational behaviour point of view and ensure that any decision (material or not) must be rationalised against the operational requirements, flight safety, State of registry requirements and environmental risks. To this end, it is important that any AM clearly identify his or her role in the risk management matrix and put into place procedures which the AM and his or her department can follow and enforce. It is clear now, whether it is regulatory, legally or morally, the AM must take his or her accountability seriously and not with a "I'll learn on the job attitude" or with a "I'll delegate that task" strategy. You can maybe delegate a task but you cannot delegate accountability.

References

Air Accident Investigation Branch of the UK, 1988. *Report on the accident to Boeing 747-121, N739PA*. [Online] Available at: http://libraryonline.erau.edu/online-full-text/ntsb/miscellaneous-reports/MR-02-90.pdf [Accessed 26 April 2021].

BEA the French Civil Aviation Safety Investigation Authority, 2016. *German Wings Accident Final Report*. [Online] Available at: https://www.bea.aero/uploads/tx_elyextendttnews/BEA2015-0125.en-LR_08.pdf [Accessed 26 April 2021].

European Union, 2002. *Regulation No 2027/97 on air carrier liability in the event of accidents*. [Online] Available at: https://eur-lex.europa.eu/legal-content/EN/TXT/PDF/?uri=CELEX:32002R0889&from=EN [Accessed 26 April 2021].

Government of the United States, 2004. *The 9/11 Commission Report*. [Online] Available at: https://fas.org/irp/offdocs/911commission.pdf [Accessed 26 April 2021].

Hellenic Republic Ministry of Transport, 2006. *Aircraft Accident Report; Helios Airways Flight HCY522*, Athens: Hellenic Republic Ministry of Transport & Communications.

IATA, 1929. *The Warsaw Convention for the Unification of certain rules relating to international Carriage by Air*. Warsaw: https://www.iata.org/contentassets/fb1137ff561a4819a2d38f3db7308758/mc99-full-text.pdf.

IATA, 1959. *The Hague Protocol to Amend the Convention for the Unification of Certain Rules Relating to International Carriage by Air*. The Hague: https://www.iata.org/contentassets/fb1137ff561a4819a2d38f3db7308758/mc99-full-text.pdf.

IATA, 1999. *The Montreal Convention for the Unification of certain rules relating to international Carriage by Air*. Montreal: International Air Transport Association.

ICAO, 1952. *The Rome Convention on Damage Caused by Foreign Aircraft to Third Parties on the Surface*. [Online] Available at: https://www.icao.int/secretariat/legal/List%20of%20Parties/Rome1952_EN.pdf [Accessed 26 April 2021].

ICAO, 2021a. *Annex 13 Air Accident Investigation*. Montreal: International Civil Aviation Organisation.

ICAO, 2021b. *Annex 19, Safety Management*. Montreal: International Civil Aviation Organisation.

ICAO, 2021c. *ICAO Annexes & SARP`s*. Montreal: International Civil Aviation Organisation.

Ministry of Justice UK, 1974. *Health and Safety at Work Act (HSE)*. [Online] Available at: https://www.hse.gov.uk/legislation/hswa.htm [Accessed 1 May 2021].

Ministry of Justice UK, 2007. *The Corporate Manslaughter and Corporate Homicide Act (HSE)*. [Online] Available at: https://www.hse.gov.uk/corpmanslaughter/about.htm#:~:text=The%20Corporate%20Manslaughter%20and%20Corporate%20Homicide%20Act%202007%20is%20a,of%20a%20duty%20of%20care [Accessed 14 May 2021].

NTSB, 2000. *Loss of Control and Impact with Pacific Ocean Alaska Airlines Flight 261*, Washington DC: National Transport Safety Board.

The Chicago Conference, 1944. *The Chicago Conference of Civil Aviation Minutes & Articles*. Chicago, PICAO.

UAE GCAA, 2021. *Acceptable Means of Compliance 08, Issuance or Renewal of an AOC or POC*, Abu Dhabi: General Civil Aviation Authority.

US District Court for the Eastern District of New York, 1993. *In Re Air Disaster at Lockerbie, Scotland, 811 F. Supp. 89 (E.D.N.Y. 1993)*. [Online] Available at: https://law.justia.com/cases/federal/district-courts/FSupp/811/89/2006132/ [Accessed 14 May 2021].

World Press, 2016. *Living Safely with Human Error in Human Factors in Aviation*. [Online] Available at: https://livingsafelywithhumanerror.wordpress.com/ [Accessed 21 April 2021].

10 Case studies of Accountable Manager challenges

Now we understand the fiduciary and regulatory accountable responsibilities of the AM, let's review scenarios of challenging situations and decisions that AMs have faced.

Case study 1: Funding safety training or a marketing campaign

A small airline with an AOC, operating narrow body European built jets on a combination of commercial scheduled flights and commercial charter flights, was facing hard times with reduced revenues due to competition. The revenues for Q1 fell short of the targeted budget for the same period by around US$3 million. As Q2 was entered, the board called an extraordinary board meeting to express their displeasure with the position the company was in and with the CEO for not achieving budget revenues for Q1 and directed the CEO, who was also the AM, to stop all training in Q2 and Q3 and to divert up to 50 percent of the funds budgeted for the training to an aggressive marketing campaign. This was done to improve ticket sales, increasing revenue, and saving the balance of the 50 percent not spent. The CEO had not achieved the budgeted revenue and profit for the last year and was under pressure to cut costs and to improve revenue and profit. So, the CEO took this action item from the board and started to develop an aggressive marketing plan with his director of commercial with 50 percent of the training funds to be used. In aviation, there are two main types of training, mandatory training, and non-mandatory training. Mandatory training is regulated and must be accomplished, such as pilot recurrent training, crew safety and emergency procedure training and many others. In order to develop a safety culture within the company, training is a very important pillar of establishing and maintaining a good level of safety knowledge and, therefore a good corporate safety culture. Some of that training is mandatory, but most of it is not. Still, it does go a very long way to supporting a safety culture. The CEO, the safety manager, and the compliance manager knew that the company's safety and compliance culture was nurtured by continuous and active training for all staff.

The CEO did as he was asked and stopped all non-mandatory training such as customer relationship training, computer skills training, silver service training, and others. Also, the CEO stopped all non-mandatory safety training that used to be conducted, such as human factors for check-in crew and an introduction to safety management systems for ground staff, as well as many other employees free training on civil aviation regulations, quality management systems, and more. By cutting this training, the company safety culture was affected. The CEO saved US$1 million on the training budget and diverted US$500,000 of that into a marketing campaign. The other US$500,000 was reported as savings. The result was, as the board wanted, the marketing campaign helped increase the ticket sales, and therefore, so did the revenue. But the absence of six months of safety training resulted in a compromised safety culture where employees followed the CEO's example and prioritised tasks other than the safety and compliance-related tasks. The CEO pleased the board, but his strategy had a direct effect on the safety focus and safety culture of the company as well as the compliance culture.

What could the CEO and AM have done differently? How could the CEO have dealt better with balancing this fiduciary shareholder demand and their regulatory accountability? The CEO could have negotiated with the board and agreed to accept a stop on all non-mandatory training except safety-related training. Also, perhaps the CEO could have agreed to reduce the spending on non-mandatory safety training by developing in house trainers rather than using the expensive contracted external training companies. He could have requested computer-based training. CBT would be made readily available to all staff, eliminating the cost of lecturers and maintaining access to safety training material. A CEO who is also the AM with good knowledge of his or her responsible accountabilities and their importance of being the safety and compliance champion enables such fast thinking when confronted by a profit-hungry board. There is a possibility that a CEO with limited knowledge of his or her civil aviation accountabilities but a stronger focus or emphasis on his or her fiduciary responsibilities would often be biased towards taking actions that cut the cost or develop additional revenue at the expense of the safety compliance and regulatory compliance culture. Though the CEO and AM did not break any regulation in their action, they acted in a way that was not conducive to safety and compliance. This action was noticed by the NAA, so in some ways, it damaged the relationship between the CEO/AM and the NAA.

Case study 2: Conducting commercial operations on a private category aircraft

Private jet or turboprop owners sometimes place their aircraft with air operators to manage the operations and maintain their very expensive asset. These AOC holders offer a full service of private jet management and offer to place the aircraft on the charter market to make revenue to offset the cost of ownership when the owner does not need the aircraft for their own use. This action can generate up to US$12,000 per hour of additional and welcome revenue. The owner of the private aircraft may also offer the management company a percentage of the charter revenue their sales team generate. But many private jets are registered with their NAA as non-commercial category aircraft. This means they are for the private use of the owner only and not to be presented to the market for commercial charter and not to take commercial revenue in any form or kind. If a private aircraft owner wishes to use aircraft for revenue generation, he or she must register the aircraft in the commercial or public transport category and have the aircraft placed on a commercial air transport operator's AOC.

A very wealthy and powerful man who owned a private jet under the management of a very well-established AOC operator was based in Dubai for a six-month period to conduct some important business. He instructed his pilot team to coordinate with the management company AOC and offer the aircraft for commercial charters from Dubai to generate revenue. The AOC that was managing his aircraft was under financial pressure and finding it difficult to generate enough revenue to pay the monthly salaries. So the CEO of the AOC operator, who was also the AM, agreed with the private jet owner to share any commercial charter revenue generated 50:50 after direct operating costs were paid. The captain was also incentivised to cooperate by getting paid a bonus for each flight conducted. This is acceptable only if the correct licences, permissions, and CAT approvals are in place. The CEO and the private jet owner knew they did not have the correct commercial licences in place, and the aircraft was a non-commercial category registered private jet. Nonetheless, the CEO decided to avoid asking the board to supplement the shortfall in salaries for six months but went ahead in attempting to generate supplementary income through chartering the private jet.

The CEO prioritised revenue generation over compliance with the civil aviation regulations that forbade commercial operations on non-commercial private aircraft. Also, by doing so, he would have, knowingly or otherwise, invalidated the aircraft's insurance, which was not for commercial air transport, a very serious non-compliance that in itself has grave implications of a derogation of fiduciary and regulatory accountable duties. Importantly, by agreeing to do this, the CEO and AM encouraged a disregard by his captain for the culture for regulatory compliance. This disregard for compliance results in a company culture that was not safety or compliance-focused, but open to cut corners and turn blind eyes to violations. Safety management and compliance management are two of the most important tasks and accountabilities of the AM. The illegal action went unnoticed by the regulator and was never reported by any of the crew. The CEO generated an income of just short of US$1 million in a two-month period; a nice additional amount shared, after direct operation costs deductions, with the owner of the jet.

What could have the CEO and AM done differently? There is no doubt the CEO should have rejected the jet's owner's request to conduct commercial activities by simply saying "we are not licensed to do so". By agreeing to do so, the AM infected the captain of the jet with a lack of compliance culture, by suggesting no harm was done. A confident and knowledgeable AM who took his or her accountabilities seriously would have coaxed the jet's owner to have registered the aircraft as a CAT operation if he desired to generate extra revenue. Otherwise, he should have advised him against the commercial charter, especially as it violated the aircraft insurance that was for private operations only.

Case study 3: Adjusting pilot duty time to allow for the arrival of a VIP

A private jet, managed by an operator who did have the correct licences and approvals as an AOC holder for the jet to conduct commercial air transport operations, was taking a very important person to a meeting in London. The departure time for the flight home from Singapore was 20:00 local time. This was a departure time that enabled the crew to make the return home flight with their rest period regulatory compliant with flight duty periods and flight time limitations. The crew used 19:00 local time as their reporting time of start of their duty, one hour before the ETD. 20:00 came, and the VIP did not appear, 21:00 came, and the VIP still did not appear. Now the crew FDPs were being used waiting for the VIP, risking the crew running out of duty time and being unable to execute the flight back to Singapore. The captain called the CEO, who was also the AM, and informed him that the VIP had not appeared, they were two hours into their duty and that if they did not depart by 22:30, they could not execute the flight due to the expiry of their available duty time when in flight. The CEO, knowing the VIP was a very powerful man and a very good friend of the chairman who appointed the CEO, instructed the captain to wait for the VIP and to adjust his reporting time to one that allowed the FDPs to be compliant if he had to. This was an egregious request by the CEO and AM, as FDP and FTLs are civil aviation regulations and are there to ensure that the flight crew are rested and not so fatigued that their ability to fly safely is compromised. The CEO disregarded this, as he knew the crew members were staying in a wonderful five-star hotel with luxury amenities. For the CEO and AM to ask for this blatant disregard of the regulations and safety was a grave error on his part.

To assume that because the crew stayed in a comfortable hotel, the crew were rested was a grave misunderstanding and disregard of safety management systems and pilot fatigue. Under pressure from the CEO, the captain complied with the CEO's request. The VIP turned up, and the flight took place. One week later, the CAA was informed through anonymous voluntary reporting of what had happened. After investigation, the captain and the first officer were suspended for breaking FDPs and FTLs. The CEO was also removed by the CAA as an AM and was not permitted again to be an AM in that country. This is an example of a CEO preferring to please a VIP and board chairman to keep his job, rather than comply with the regulations and be a real responsible AM and safety champion.

What could the CEO have done differently? Firstly, the CEO should have supported the captain and sent the crew back to the hotel for rest and to comply with the FDPs and FTLs. He should have made it clear to the VIP and chairman that it was essential for the VIP to be on time or no later than one hour; otherwise, the flight could not take place unless a second substitute crew was available on standby. Instead, he enabled a culture of disregard and an actual violation of the regulations, but the captain pilot himself should have informed the PH Flight Operations of the situation, and the PH would have hopefully supported the captain in not undertaking the flight.

Case study 4: Imposing on the PH Continuing Airworthiness not to report an AD overrun

An Airworthiness Directive (AD) was issued to inspect the aileron attachments of the B737-NG; it was to be accomplished every 4,500 flight hours. The task was linked to the C Check that was accomplished every 4,500 flight hours or three years, whatever was sooner. This meant the AD task was always issued with the C Check and always done on or before when it was due. The C Check was escalated to 5,000 flight hours or three years due to reliability studies suggesting more flight hour life could be achieved safely. The airline started flying more and on one C Check it was found that 4,800 flight hours were achieved in the three year period. It was noticed that the 4,500 flight hour interval aileron inspection AD had not been called for accomplishment on time and had been accomplished only at the C Check down time at 4,800 flight hours. That meant a 300 flight hour overrun. ADs are mandatory inspections and are not allowed to be escalated without the regulator's acceptance, which is very unlikely. This meant the aircraft flew out of compliance for 300 flight hours, violating the certificate of airworthiness. The PH CAMO brought this to the attention of the CEO and AM and recommended that the CAA be informed immediately through the CAA reporting system. The CEO asked the PH whether the task was accomplished. He replied yes. The CEO asked, "Was the aileron bearing found in good condition?" The PH replied "yes". The CEO said no harm was done with the overrun of the AD and convinced the PH CAMO not to report the overrun and learn from the incident and not to let it happen again.

The PH CAMO found that his professional consciousness could not allow compliance with the CEOs request and he anonymously reported the overrun to the CAA. Upon investigation, the CAA discovered that the board had given the CEO a bonus-related KPI to reduce CAA reportable incidents by 20 percent on last year, and to have reported this overrun would have spoiled the CEO from meeting that KPI and would have affected his annual bonus. This meant the board KPI encouraged the CEO and AM to act as he did, but this was not an excuse as the AM failed in his accountabilities to create a compliance and safety culture by asking the PH to neglect to report the overrun. The CAA confronted the AM on the overrun and gave him a written warning that to neglect to report incidents, accidents, and violations through the CAA reporting system was a neglect of his accountable duties. The AM was served a final warning, and if it was found again that he was negligent in his regulatory duties, he would be blacklisted from being an AM ever again in the CAA's territory.

What could the AM have done differently? The AD overrun was an accident, resulting from the CAMO PH's mistake in "bucketing" an AD into a C Check package rather than it standing alone. A culture that encourages compliance and continuous improvement, including reporting discoveries of such an incident, would have helped create an open culture, where finding faults and correcting them was encouraged. Instead of forcing the PH to hide the incident, the AM should have received the report from the CAMO PH and instructed him or the quality manager to report it to the CAA immediately upon finding, followed by an investigation of the root cause and subsequent recertification action to ensure it does not happen again.

Case study 5: Maximising airline crew utilisation without affecting the safety or compromising compliance

For the last three years, the airline's share price had moved up and down equally, resulting in a 1% positive increase in the final share price. At the AGM of the board this was brought to the attention of the CEO, who was also the AM. The board then gave the CEO a few action items to help to try to increase the share price. These were: (1) to reduce operational costs; (2) to increase operational efficiency; and (3) to increase the utilisation of operational resources. The CEO started to look at restructuring the operation to meet his new board appointed targets. He looked closely at operating costs. While reviewing these costs, he noticed that very often the flight crews were not getting utilised to their full 120 duty hours per month. In fact, at times, as much as 50 percent of crew possible duty time was being lost each month. This inefficient use of crew costs the company millions of dollars per year. So the CEO had a careful review of the FDPs and FTLs with his PH Flight Operations and decided to look at a better way of managing his flight crew duty times and rosters. The PH Flight Operations went to the IT market and found a professional aviation roster management software that could manage crew duty times and crew rostering. The software was a small investment compared to the saving it brought by maximizing the crew duty time at no cost to compliance or safety. This was a great example of the CEO/AM working with his PH and working within the regulations to make a more efficient and cost-effective operation. The board was very pleased with this improved use of the most expensive human assets, the flight crew. The NAA was pleased that an efficient and transparent crew rostering software was being employed at the airline.

Case study 6: The CEO attempts to impose a Post Holder appointment on the Accountable Manager

One of the most important tasks of the AM is to appoint and manage the PHs and nominated persons. The AM is responsible to the regulator for the correct selection and employment of qualified PHs and nominating them to the NAA for the position. Then, if the nomination is accepted, the AM should continually assess each PH for effectiveness and success in the role of a PH. At times in some AOC operators the AM is not the CEO. This is a sensitive subject that the NAA is cautious about, but do accept provided the delegated financial authority is granted to the AM to run a safe and compliant operation as well as the authority to hire and manage the PH team. On this occasion, the CEO, who was not the AM, favoured the replacement of the current PH Flight Operations with an operational captain whom he knew personally. The AM was nervous about this suggestion, feeling that his ability to manage this new possible PH would be compromised due to his relationship with the CEO. The AM felt the incumbent PH was doing an acceptable job and there was no need to make this change. The CEO was a larger than life character and took the AM and presented to him a completed PH nomination form for the NAA that detailed the captain he preferred. All the AM had to sign the form and submit it to the NAA. The AM, with full authority to hire, fire, and manage all PHs, declined to sign the nomination form and insisted on keeping the incumbent in his position but agreed to manage the situation by closer leadership of the incumbent, thereby increasing the responsibility and training of the CEO's preferred captain to develop his ability and experiences in flight operation management. The CEO was satisfied.

In this case, the AM, who was not the CEO, managed the situation well and satisfied the requirement of his boss, the CEO, while exercising his AM responsible accountabilities. But the sensitive situation that can be noticed here is, the AM, who is not the CEO, was forced to manage a possible situation that violated his authority as AM. Also, the company culture that comes from the top could have been damaged, as it could have been seen that the driving champion of culture in the company was not the AM but the CEO. This is another reason why the NAA prefers the most senior leadership being both CEO and AM.

Case study 7: When a board member imposes a pilot's selection on the Accountable Manager

Airlines recruit pilots regularly. Each airline has its own process for selecting pilots and for assessing their ability and suitability for the type of operations they conduct. Selection and interview of any staff members can be a sensitive task and is certainly a very important task to ensure you select the right person with the right skills and qualifications for the job. Pilot selection and recruitment are no different. This airline uses a variety of selection techniques for pilot recruitment.

Paper assessment, interview, reference checking, logbook reviewing and, finally, simulator testing are some of the selection techniques. In the simulator, you have a chance to really see a pilot at work and to assess their skill as a pilot. Many pilots pass all assessment tests and reviews with flying colours, but occasionally they fail when it comes to the simulator assessment.

The CEO and AM was approached after a board meeting by a board member who started to tell him about his son and how he applied for a position in the airline as a pilot, first officer. He made it to the interview and assessment, but was not selected. The CEO and AM said he would take his name and look into why he was not selected and give the board member feedback for his son to consider. The board member's son was a young but qualified pilot, having worked on small aircraft. He had a few thousand flight hours in his logbook and felt ready to join an airline to start on the larger jets. The CEO asked the HR manager to find the file of the young man and to review why he was not selected, and to brief him on the reasons. The HR manager found the file and also reviewed it with the PH training and PH flight operations, both very qualified and experienced captains with tens of thousands of flight hours between them. The PH training remembered the young man and remembered his awkward ability and lack of flying skills. In fact, the PH training was surprised that the young man chose a career as a pilot as he struggled with flying in the simulator. So this is why he was not selected even though he did well on the other parts of the interview and assessment. The HR manager and the PH training briefed the CEO that the airline could not afford to take on such pilots with poor skills that needed extensive re-training and coaching. The CEO promised the board member he would call him and brief him once he found out why the young man was not selected, so he did carefully and sensitively suggesting that the young man continued training to improve his skills. The board member was very upset as he had spent thousands of dollars on his son's training to obtain his commercial pilot's license. The board member demanded that the CEO recruit the young man and induct him into the airline as a first officer. The CEO knew the board member was a powerful and active board member of the airline, and the CEO respected the contribution the board member brought to the airline in its oversight and governance. But he was not prepared to overrule his two senior PHs who made flight crew selection decision and who were responsible for the company's flight standards. So he declined to recruit the board member's son and instead offered a coaching session in his office with the PH training and the HR manager to improve his flying skills and get selected for airlines. He also offered that the young man should try again in a year's time.

On this occasion, the CEO and AM dealt with this delicate matter very well. He managed to maintain flight deck standards by avoiding the recruitment of substandard pilots while being sensitive to a board member's personal situation.

Case study 8: When the CAA told the new AM that the PH Quality was just not competent enough

The new CEO and AM was one month into her new job, and the date for the CAA inspector interview was set. So, to prepare, she attended a course on civil aviation regulations, aviation safety management, and aviation compliance and quality management. She also spent one week with the PHs, talking with them and listening to them on their challenges in accomplishing their roles.

The CAA interview took place, and she was very well prepared. All the preparation tasks she had done set her in good standing with the CAA inspector and helped raise her knowledge on civil aviation and her accountable responsibilities. During the interview, the CAA inspector told her that he had concerns about the Compliance and Quality PH and his ability to do the job effectively. This was a very sensitive subject as the PH Quality and Compliance is the key link to the CAA and, in many ways, is the CAA's representative in the company. In her preparation for the interview, she became aware of this from other PHs' comments, so she was prepared for this subject. She informed the CAA Inspector that as the AM (hopeful), she was well aware that she was responsibly accountable for the quality and compliance management system, and she was responsible for the hiring, firing, and development of PHs. She told the CAA inspector that it was her intention to get to know each PH intimately, assess them regularly, and identify development needs for each of them. If, after that, she believes any PH to be unable or incompetent, she would take action to replace that PH as her accountable duty required her to do. She assured the CAA inspector she would take all his comments into consideration and would get on with the job and task of managing a competent PH team. The CAA inspector was pleased to hear this and told her they would talk again in six months' time on the same subject, by when she would have a much better picture of the situation.

On this occasion, the AM was very well prepared and educated on her new position. She went into the CAA inspector meeting with a good level of knowledge of what was required of her and of specific issues that the airline currently had as well as having an action plan to address them. This eased the CAA inspector's decision to allow the appointment of the new AM without objection.

Case study 9: A board instructed the CEO/AM to incentivise maximum utilisation by minimum turnaround time, with a company target turnaround time of 30 minutes

The board of the low-cost carrier was interested in maximising the utilisation of the aircraft each day. An aircraft on the ground is an aircraft not making revenue. The board was supportive of having a fleet of a reasonably young average age. With this in mind, the board wanted the CEO to ensure that the aircraft were being utilised to their very maximum out of the 24 hours per day. This meant careful route planning, tight operational control, and fast Formula 1 style turn arounds. In fact, the board was so much in support of this that it gave the CEO, who was also the AM, a KPI of minimising turnaround times and maximum aircraft daily utilisation times. By minimising turnaround times, it promoted and encouraged efficient planning, preparation, and action, making the airline very efficient and maximising the use of their very expensive assets, thereby allowing the airline to get more flights per day, meaning more ticket paying passengers. This formula 1 pit style encouragement did make the airline's line maintenance department very efficient and did contribute to great preparation for the arrival of an aircraft and fast and efficient turnaround times.

This being an important KPI for the CEO, he passed it down to his directors and managers to also have minimal turnaround times. Each director, to meet their new KPI, did their best to manage the arrival and departure as efficiently as possible.

Achieving a KPI in this airline meant a significant contribution to the bonuses paid out every six months. This airline was very supportive of profit sharing and bonus distribution, if KPIs were met and they resulted in more profit or less cost. Those that achieved their KPI were rewarded. Three months into the new financial year, with the new KPI set, and cascaded down from the CEO to the directors, the director of maintenance noticed that there were trends in base maintenance where overtime had increased regularly from the previous year's overtime expenditure. Upon careful review, it appeared that the aircraft coming into the hanger for base maintenance had more defects than they were used to and resulted in needing more attention to rectify the defects. Upon further review, it was noticed that the line engineers responsible for meeting the aircraft, reviewing the technical log, and discussing any defects with the flight crew were supportive of a fast turnaround time. This motivation was to meet tighter ETDs to maximise the utilisation of the aircraft. This meant allowing aircraft to fly with defects that they would have had more time to repair in the past. Instead, with the intention to minimise turnaround time, they would not address the defects and would wait till the end of the day when the aircraft would be scheduled to go to the hanger for base maintenance to address the defects. This could be understood as allowing the aircraft to fly with defects that previously before the new KPI would have been addressed there and then when found. The Director of Maintenance was convinced that the new KPI to minimise turnaround time was assisting efficiency in his department, but was rewarding and encouraging the avoidance of reporting and rectifying findings during the turnaround time. With this opinion, the director of maintenance decided to inform the CEO and AM. The director of maintenance presented a finding that on a few occasions showed tire wear being unaddressed and tires that would normally be changed on a turnaround were being allowed to dispatch and be replaced later when the aircraft would go into the hangar for its base maintenance. While the CEO was very pleased that an extra flight per day was achieved due to the quick turnaround times and was pleased that he and his team were meeting the KPI set by the board, after careful consultation with his PH director team, he decided to document and present to the board the worrying implications of the KPI set at the start of the year. He suggested that the KPI encouraged behaviour that could be overlooking defects. He recommended to the board that the KPI be removed and that the airline revert back to the previous turnaround times, which meant that the utilisation of the aircraft went back to the previous number. The board was not pleased that the CEO had achieved a KPI establishing a greater utilisation of the fleet, then presented to them a case that required they removed the KPI.

150   Case studies of AM challenges

They would have preferred the CEO to have achieved the KPI and kept the previous level of maintenance quality. The CEO explained it was not possible to have both and could not support a KPI on his directors that encouraged overlooking safety items.

This showed good judgment and a balanced decision on account of the CEO and AM, putting safety before revenue. The board correctly took the advice of the AM as they should on safety matters, avoiding a situation where the AM would have felt compromised between a decision of higher profit and reduced safety. When accepting a KPI, the AM must decide whether the KPI is in accordance with the company's safety and compliance culture or could be misinterpreted and could encourage behaviour, not in line with the safety and compliance culture the AM is trying to promote. Being both CEO and AM, he helped the board understand this and in turn can execute the correct action.

Case study 10: A CEO/AM of an MRO reduces certifying LAE head count to cut salary costs

The MRO was a large facility with the capability for large and medium jet overhaul and maintenance. Each audit from the CAA went well, and the AM, who was also the CEO, ran a tight and compliant operation. The board gave the CEO and AM a target for the coming summer period to cut costs because the summer was a quiet time for the MRO as most operations wanted their aircraft flying at this time and not on maintenance. To do so, the CEO and the CFO reviewed the highest ten costs in the company and saw the salary of the highest position and noticed Licensed Aircraft Engineers (LAEs) as the highest salary group cost. The MRO operated a bay system where the aircraft in each bay was split into four work zones, with a LAE for each work zone and with three unlicensed technicians working under the LAE`s lead. This ratio of one licensed person to every three unlicensed people was accepted by the CAA, and the qualified manpower numbers were never an issue and satisfied the CAA inspectors who conducted the audits. It was understood that the Part 145 regulations require a manpower plan to be produced that showed an adequate qualified workforce to conduct the work that the MRO would undertake. The CEO decided as the LAEs were the highest cost salary group to increase the ratio of LAEs to Technicians to 1:6, so that each bay had two LAEs attending rather than in the past four, and each bay was split into four zones with an LAE covering two work zones each. The nominated person maintenance and the AM reflected this new adjustment in their newly revised manpower plan. This nearly halved the certifying capability and cut headcount salary costs significantly. The restructuring was favoured by the CFO, and HR was instructed to start to select those that should be released and to work with the nominated person director of maintenance. The quality manager insisted that, along with the newly revised manpower plan, a management of change process should be followed, and a risk analysis was to take place to document the change and to identify the risks associated with the change and how to mitigate those associated risks. At this time, SMS was not mandated for Part 145 AMO MROs. The quality manager voiced his concern as to the risks this brought, putting added stress on the remaining two LAEs in each bay and requiring them to certify twice as many tasks and inspections for each maintenance input as they did previously. The CFO supported the cost-cutting action, so the CEO, who was the AM and the nominated person maintenance, had to assess whether he could accept the risks as shown by the risk assessment and explained to him by the nominated person director of maintenance and the quality manager were manageable and acceptable. The quality manager warned him that such a change should be reported to the CAA and if not, he should be prepared to do so, as he was sure it would be expected that an anonymous report would be sent to the CAA from the MRO staff and the CEO should be prepared to explain the action and to prove that safety had not been compromised at all.

Reporting to the board that he had saved as much as 10 percent on headcount salary went down well, and the CEO, along with his CFO, was given credit for achieving this. But the CAA, having received a VORSY anonymous report that the LAEs' workload had doubled, meaning less time to fully inspect all tasks, they were displeased to find this out in a VORSY. It was the CAA's opinion that this reduction in certifying staff created an unsafe condition. The CEO and AM with the nominated person maintenance argued with the CAA that this was not the case since the summer workload was lighter than other times. Their action to reduce the LAE numbers was accompanied by a revised manpower plan and management of change study that supported the action. The CEO/AM explained this action was a balance between him his fiduciary responsibilities to the board and meeting his responsible accountabilities for regulatory compliance and a safe operation. The risk assessment which the Maintenance Director had filled out supported this claim. The CAA inspector accepted the change with the condition that the manpower plan was visited regularly, and any adverse results after the change were reported to the CAA inspector. This was a case of the AM, along with the nominated person maintenance, working together using the management of change process and the manpower plan with a risk assessment to make their company efficient and sustainable within the bounds of the regulations.

In hindsight, the CEO should have reported to the CAA of his intended actions along with the supporting management of change and risk assessment and mitigation report. It is important to inform the CAA of significant changes to ensure any VORSY that goes into the CAA is met with prior knowledge.

Case study 11: Serving plastic bottles of water on board

A medium-size airline was flying around 100 narrow-body flights per day. This meant serving more than 10,000 meals and snacks per day. This included over 10,000 plastic bottles of water as well as other plastic service utensils. The CEO understood that the plastic bottle took between 400 to 900 years to degrade. Also, the CEO understood from a customer survey that the passengers preferred a handy water bottle to a filled cup. She was also aware that attempts to replace the bottle with a refillable paper cup in the past were met with disapproval and continuous negative feedback from the passengers. So the CEO had her cabin service director search for a biodegradable water bottle. The search found a bottle that was made of biodegradable material that reduced its life from 400 years to 10 years. This bottle cost was three times greater than the regularly used product. The CEO now had a dilemma, whether to accept the environmental impact of the normally used bottle and incur no additional cost on the operation or absorb the cost and use the new biodegradable bottle or use a paper cup with refills from an attendant. After consideration and discussion with her team and the board, the CEO directed the cabin service director to start to procure and use the biodegradable water bottle and to stop using the normal bottle. She also instructed the marketing director to start a campaign to inform the public of the airline's decision to prioritise environmental considerations in this case, and hopefully, the campaign would result in employee pride in the ethical culture of the company and in increased ticket sales attracting new customers as a result of the company's environmentally aware policies.

This initiative was based on ethical leadership and was an example of the CEO trying to make the company environmentally responsible in the reduction of non-biodegradable plastics while understanding there might be a financial impact on the company, so trying to offset that impact by a marketing campaign.

Summary

The intention of this book was to compile and explain the role and responsibilities of the most senior leadership position in a civil aviation company with regards to accountable responsibility to the regulator, the National Aviation Authority. This position, as we have learned in the book, is called the Accountable Manager or Accountable Executive.

The book intends to document the main areas of knowledge that the leadership role must initially acquire to take on the position and to continue to hold the position successfully. In addition, the author hopes for this to be a handbook or a guide of accountable responsibilities that will assist the Accountable Manager as the senior leader in executing their responsibilities and in meeting the challenges of the fiduciary and regulatory responsibility in an efficient and complete manner.

We have seen the very important and responsible position of the AM and we tried to convey the very seriousness of the role and why the selection of the person to hold this position is a very important decision that carries severe implications. It is not a simple role that any talented senior executive can take on easily. It is a professional position that a leader either needs to evolve into from within the industry or, if external to the industry, needs to undertake serious training and careful induction into the position, which could take time. However, it can be seen that if the management system in place is safe, compliant and robust with expert management personnel, this can greatly assist the AM on taking on the role.

We looked at the origins of modern civil aviation standards and practices and how they cascade into each member and signatory state of the Chicago Convention and the International Civil Aviation Organisation as regulations. This is important as the AM must understand why aviation is regulated and understand the main standards that exist, especially for the company that they lead. We then looked at the National Aviation Authority, the regulator and their responsibilities under the Chicago Convention and how they enforce and oversee the regulations within their territory. We studied the important civil aviation regulations for operations of civil aircraft, and then looked at the NAA's approach to aviation leadership, starting with the Accountable Manager, and then the Nominated Persons. We looked at the relationships between

DOI: 10.4324/9781003094685-12

the Accountable Manager and their Nominated Persons or Nominated Post Holders, and especially the very important particular relationship with the Post Holders or named persons, the Compliance Manager and the Safety Manager.

We reviewed the leading aviation authorities of the FAA and EASA, and looked closely at a new coming leading regulator, the GCAA, and how, in a short time, they have developed a very effective and supportive set of regulations harmonised to a large extent and supportive of their national civil aviation industry. We now understand that the regulations are there to support civil aviation and protect citizens, ensuring that they board a safe and compliant operation. We looked at the aviation leadership and their role with safety management and compliance management, and we now understand the accountable responsibilities, the undertakings and the declarations of compliance that the Accountable Manager assumes and takes by accepting the role, making them accountable by law as the executive leader.

We went on to look at the CEO role of a civil aviation company and the fiduciary responsibilities they assume, and if the CEO is also the Accountable Manager, the challenges of balancing the regulatory accountabilities with the fiduciary accountabilities. We saw that the regulator prefers the CEO to also assume the AM role but does not insist on it. We looked at civil aviation company organisational structures and the differences between the main territories of the USA, the EU and the UAE. Having previously reviewed the very important leadership relationships the AM has with the NAA and also with the post holders, we then added another important relationships of the AM, who is also the CEO—the relationship with their boss, the chairman of the board. We reviewed the sensitivity of that relationship and how the Accountable Manager balances their fiduciary responsibility that the Board is very interested in with the regulatory responsibility that the NAA is very interested in.

After establishing the theory of the Accountable Manager, we then went on to review the daily practical responsibilities and work activities of the Accountable Manager. We developed a job description for the Accountable Manager and assisted the Chairman and the Board in their selection of the right person with the right delegated authority. We then developed a practical "tool kit" for the AM to refer to, starting with an interview preparation guide for the proposed selected person to become the next AM in order to help prepare them for the position and the NAA interview. Then a very practical Timetable of meetings and oversight activities that, if followed, should give the AM confidence that they are knowledgeable of all that they are accountable for. We then designed a dashboard of critical information for their daily oversight, further giving the confidence they need for the operational status as well as financial status on a daily basis. This tool kit is intended to assist the AM in successfully accomplishing their job and being able to focus on the very complex function of being both CEO and AM of a civil aviation company.

We finished with a series of scenarios and examples of challenges and case studies that CEOs and AMs have been faced with. All are examples that occur regularly and often. Hopefully, they will support the AM in ensuring that they are prepared enough.

The glossary in this book details essential aviation words and phrases that the AM should be familiar with and will learn to use over time if they are not from within the industry. If they are from within the industry all should be already familiar.

The other intention of this book was to address a much-undocumented subject and profession of the civil aviation AM. It is hoped that this book will assist those selecting the AM to understand the seriousness of the position and, more so, to assist those taking on the role to help them understand the essential accountabilities that come with the position and that they must be prepared for the serious legal responsibilities that lie ahead. Further, the book is to help prepare the new AMs for the management of the expert aviation management team of Nominated Persons and Post Holders that they shall rely on heavily for their tenure in the role. Hopefully, this book assists those involved in civil aviation and perhaps improves safety and compliance in the civil aviation industry.

Finally, civil aviation leadership is a pleasure and a privilege that comes with enormous moral obligations as well as significant legal obligations. We owe it to every single employee that we lead, as well as to every single person that gets on our aircraft and to every single person that invests in the company, that we do our very best to ensure a safe, airworthy, secure, compliant, ethical and financially sustainable civil aviation operation. If we cannot take on those obligations, we should not take on that role.

Remember, you can maybe delegate the task, but you cannot delegate the accountability.

Glossary

Acceptable Means of Compliance, AMC: a method of complying with a regulation or mandatory instruction that is not the original method described.

Accountable Executive, AE: the person who is accountable and responsible by law for a civil aviation company to comply with the civil aviation regulations. Usually the most senior leadership position of the company such as the CEO. This term is used in the Canadian and US civil aviation regulations.

Accountable Manager, AM: the person who is accountable and responsible by law for a civil aviation company to comply with the civil aviation regulations. Usually the most senior leadership position of the company such as the CEO. This term is used in most of the civil aviation regulations of the world except Canada and the USA.

Accident: a negative event that occurred that resulted in damage to people or assets.

Aeronautics: the science and art of flight and associated subjects.

Aeroplane: a vehicle that uses aeronautical science to fly in the air. Usually using fixed aerofoils called wings to generate lift.

Air Carriers Certificate, ACC: the certificate issued by the US FAA for a certified Part 121 commercial aircraft operator.

Aircraft: a vehicle that uses aeronautical science to fly in the air.

Airplane: a vehicle that uses aeronautical science to fly in the air. Usually using fixed aerofoils/wings to generate lift.

Air Operating Certificate, AOC: the certificate issued by the EASA, the GCAA and many other civil aviation authorities for a certified commercial aircraft operator.

Air Training Academies for Maintenance Technician: a training school that trains technicians/maintenance engineers, if an EASA or GCAA certified it shall be a Part 147 certified centre, training in accordance with Part 66.

Air Training Organization for Pilots: a training school that trains pilots, if an EASA or GCAA certified it shall an ATO certified centre, training in accordance with Part FCL.

Glossary 157

Air Transport: a mean of transport for people or cargo in a vehicle that flies.

Aircraft Accident Investigation Branch, AAIB: the branch of the UK department of Transport that investigate accidents in the civil air transport industry.

Aircraft Design Organisation: a civil aviation company that designs aircraft.

Aircraft Manufacturer: a civil aviation company that manufactures aircraft. Also referred to as an OEM.

Aircraft Engine Manufacturer: a civil aviation company that manufactures aircraft power plants. Also referred to as an OEM.

Aircraft Maintenance Engineer: a qualified technical person that holds an Aircraft Maintenance Engineering License. In some jurisdictions, this person is also referred to as an Aircraft Maintenance Technician or Aircraft Mechanic.

Aircraft Maintenance Engineer License: a license that is issued by a CAA/NAA to a person that is qualified and certified in aircraft maintenance.

Aircraft Maintenance Facility: a facility that conducts aircraft maintenance utilising Aircraft Maintenance Engineers. This facility is usually certified and regulated by the CAA/NAA under Part 145 of the civil aviation regulations.

Aircraft Maintenance License: a license that is issued by a CAA/NAA to a person that is qualified and certified in aircraft maintenance.

Aircraft on Ground, AOG's: a term used to describe an aircraft that is not airworthy to fly due to a defective status. Could also be referred to as unserviceable U/S.

Aircraft Parts and Components Manufacturer: a civil aviation company that manufactures aircraft parts and components. Also referred to as an OEM.

Air Safety Report, ASR: an internal company method to report a safety event, incident or accident to the safety department for further consideration. ASR's can go on to become ROSI's.

Aircraft Type: the official name given to a CAA/NAA certified aircraft that appears on the Type Certificate of the aircraft. Such as B737 NG or A320.

Airline: a civil aviation company that operates aircraft usually as a commercial enterprise.

Airline Transport Pilots Licence, ATPL: the professional certified qualification of a commanding pilot operating in an airline.

Air Training Organisation, ATO: a NAA /CAA certified pilot training organisation for Ab Initio or for Type training.

Airworthiness Directive, AD's: a mandatory instruction requiring specific action to correct or detect an unsafe condition with in a defined time frame issued by the CAA/NAA. Often AD's are issued to mandate SB's from the OEM.

Apprenticeship Programme: a training programme for young people that results in some form of qualification or certification. Usually in a technical subject such as aircraft maintenance.

Approved Maintenance Organisation, AMO: a CAA/NAA (EASA, GCAA and others) Certification status under Part 145 civil aviation regulations for an aircraft or aircraft component maintenance facility. The AMO certificate shall state the types of aircraft or part numbers of components the facility is certified to maintain.

Approved Maintenance Programme, AMP: a CAA/NAA approved document for an air operator that contains the aircraft maintenance tasks required to be accomplished to ensure the continuing airworthiness of the aircraft. The tasks in that document must be proven to be effective and applicable in maintaining the airworthiness of the aircraft.

Articles of the Convention: the Articles of the Chicago Convention that took place in Chicago USA in 1944 that give the details of the attending states agreement on establishing different civil aviation rules and regulations in an attempt to standardise and regulate civil aviation worldwide.

Audit: the action to study and review a defined written process taking place, then giving details where it was found that the actual implementation of the process deviated from the actual defined written process. The deviations are identified are referred to as findings or non-conformities.

Audit Plan: a calendar plan of when an audit of particular processes shall take place.

Audit Reports: a report of findings and non-conformities from a conducted audit.

Available Seat Kilometres, ASK: is a measure of passenger carrying capacity. It is equal to the number of seats available multiplied by the number of miles or kilometres flown.

Aviation: a general subject title for flight, aircraft, aeroplanes or air transport and other items pertaining to such a subject.

Aviation Security, AvSec: a general title for the security issues associated with aviation.

Aviator: a person involved in aviation usually a pilot.

Avionic: aviation-related electronic items and systems.

Balance Sheet: a collection of financial data that reflects assets and liabilities of a subject such as a person or company.

Block Hours: the number of hours an aircraft has undergone from engine start to engine shut down. This is not the same as aircraft flight hours.

Board of Directors, BoD: a group of senior elected persons that oversee or govern a company or organisation.

Bucketing: grouping aircraft maintenance tasks in to a common collection, intended for accomplishment at the same time.

Budget: a defined value of funds that are allocated to be expended for a particular task.

Budget Variance: the difference between the budget allocated amount and the actually expended amount.

Business plan: a detailed report on a business concept or business strategy detailing the main idea and the associated financial data usually showing if it is a profitable concept.

C Check: a collection or bucket of maintenance tasks due to be accomplished together at a particular time.

C Suit Team: the senior executive management team that run the day-to-day operations of a company such as the CEO, CFO, COO and CCO.

Captain: a pilot who holds an ATPL and is in charge of a flight.

Cargo Manifest: the report detailing the exact cargo items loaded on a particular aircraft.

Cascade: to pass on down through a reporting line or organisation. This can be conceptually or physically.

Certificate of Airworthiness, CofA: a certificate issued by the regulating NAA/CAA that details that a particular aircraft that bears their national registration mark is airworthy in accordance with the civil aviation regulations issued by that NAA/CAA.

Certificate of Registration, CofR: a certificate issued by the regulating NAA/CAA that details that a particular aircraft is registered on that regulators civil aircraft register. The certificate details the actual registration mark allocated to that particular aircraft. The aircraft is then subject to the aviation regulations of the state of register.

Certifications Specifications, CS: a civil aviation regulation that is required to be complied with for an aircraft or component to be certified for civil aviation use.

Chairman: the leadership position of a board of directors.

Chicago Convention: the convention on civil aviation that took place in 1944 in Chicago USA.

Chicago Convention Annexes and SARP's: the basis for developing standard acceptable and recommended procedures that signatory states of the 1944 Convention are required to develop into civil aviation regulations.

Chief Commercial Officer, CCO: the senior executive responsible for commercial activities in a company.

Chief Executive Officer, CEO: the most senior executive responsible for leading all activities in a company.

Chief Financial Officer, CFO: the senior executive responsible for financial activities in a company.

Chief Information Officer, CIO: the senior executive responsible for information technology activities in a company.

Chief People Officer, CPO: the senior executive responsible for human resource activities in a company.

Chief Pilot: the most senior active pilot in an aircraft operating company.

Civil Aviation Advisory Publications, CAAP's: publications issued by a civil aviation authority aimed to give advice and guidance on civil aviation matters.

Civil Aviation Authority, CAA: another term for a National Aviation Authority responsible for regulating civil aviation in a particular territory.

Civil Aviation Industry: a collective name for the civil aviation business and for civil aviation companies that exist for commercial or private reasons. The civil aviation industry is subject to the civil aviation regulations.

Civil Aviation Law: mandatory legal codes issued by a legal authority pertaining to civil aviation.

Civil Aviation Regulations, CAR`s: the mandatory rules that are developed by a civil aviation authority regulator based on civil aviation law designed to regulate civil aviation activity in a territory.

Civil Aviation Standards: defined processes and procedures designed to be followed in the civil aviation industry.

Coaching Session: an activity where a person with knowledge advices and instructs a particular person wishing to gain knowledge.

Code of Federal Regulations, CFR: the laws of the USA.

Commercial Air Transport, CAT: where aircraft are used to generate commercial gain.

Commercial Operators: an operator of civil aircraft that uses aircraft to generate commercial gain.

Commercial Pilots License, CPL: a licence to be held by any pilot who generates commercial gain by piloting civil aircraft.

Common Carriage: offering and operating civil aircraft for commercial air transport.

Competent Authority: a NAA or CAA that have the capability to regulate and oversee particular civil aviation industry activities.

Compliance: accomplishing a task in accordance with the civil aviation regulations.

Compliance Culture: where the spirit and intention of a civil aviation company and its employees is to always comply with the civil aviation regulations.

Compliance Management: the oversight and management of a company's compliance with civil aviation regulations.

Compliance Statement: a physical documented statement from the companies Leader and Accountable Manager of how a company approaches the discipline of compliance.

Compliance Undertaking: a legal obligation where a person or company commit to comply with that obligation.

Components: a part of an aircraft such as an electric generator or a hydraulic actuator etc.

Continuing Airworthiness: the process of managing an aircraft's technical status to ensure that is continues to comply with the initial type certificate design specification and also continues to comply the civil aviation regulations of where it is registered.

Continuing Airworthiness Management Organization, CAMO: an approved civil aviation company that is certified by an NAA/CAA to manage the continuing airworthiness of an aircraft type.

Continuous Improvement: an ISO 9001 Quality Management System concept that through audit, correction of findings, training and clear procedures, a company shall continuously improve its service and processes.

Contracting Member State: a state or country that signed the Chicago Convention on Civil Aviation and in doing so became a member of the International Civil Aviation Organisation, ICAO.

Controlling Mind: the person in a company who is directing and driving corporate strategy. Normally is the most senior Leadership position of the company.

Corporate Culture: the spirit, attitude and behavioural norms of a company.

Crew: those members on board an aircraft that have duties and responsibilities to ensure the aircraft operates correctly. Usually pilots, flight engineers and flight attendants but can also be aero medics and other operators in complex aircraft.

Crew Training: mandatory and other training that aircraft crew members should undertake to stay current with their aviation license requirements.

Culture of Compliance: where the corporate spirit, attitude and behavioural norms include obedience and conformity to the companies procedures and the civil aviation regulations.

Culture of Safety: where the corporate spirit, attitude and behavioural norms include observing safe practices.

Dangerous Goods: loose equipment or parts that when carried on an aircraft can present safety threat if not packed and managed carefully. Such as chemicals and pyrotechnics.

Dark Traits: part of a leaders personality behaviours that can be considered as damaging or destructive.

Dashboards: the gathering and presenting of information in a single display.

Defects: a deviation from the approved design or original intention that should be corrected.

Delegated Authority: a documented passing of decision-making ability from one person or position to another.

Department of Transport, DoT: a government department with governance responsibility for industry and vehicles that carry people or goods.

Design Organisation Approval, DOA: a civil aviation company that is certified by the NAA/CAA to design aircraft and air transport vehicles, systems or components.

Direct Operating Costs, DOC: the financial costs that are attributed to the direct operation of the aircraft. Such as fuel, landing, over fly, catering and so on.

Director General, DG: the most senior leadership position of a NAA/CAA or Organisation.

Director of Maintenance, DoM: the position responsible for aircraft maintenance, usually also holding the Post Holder/Nominated Person position.

Director of Operations, DoOps: the position responsible for aircraft operations, usually also holding the Post Holder/Nominated Person position.

Director of Safety, DoS: the position responsible for aviation safety, usually also holding the Post Holder position.

Domestic Airline Operations: flights originating and terminating within a countries territorial boarder.

EASA Basic Reg's: the civil aviation regulations of the European Union regulated and overseen by the European Aviation Safety Authority.

Emergency Response Plan, ERP: a defined and practiced process to address an emergency situation, part of a safety management system.

Empathy: a desirable leadership trait, the ability to listen, understand and share the feelings of another.

Environmental Impact: an effect on nature or the environment as a result of operations. The effect is usually a negative effect.

Escalate: to increase the interval of a maintenance task as a result of reliability studies.

Ethical Leadership: leadership decision-making and action that takes into consideration fare and conscientious behaviour.

EU Member States: counties that are part of the European Union hence signing to comply with all EU laws and regulations.

European Aviation Safety Agency, EASA: the civil aviation regulator for the EU and all its member states.

European Civil Aviation Conference, ECAC: a membership of European countries that includes non-EU member countries, which have committed to harmonise civil aviation regulations between them to promote cooperation with in the civil aviation industry.

Events: the occurrence of an incident or accident that should be recorded or reported and learned from in an attempt to prevent it from occurring again.

Executive Authority: a leadership ability to direct or mandate through decision-making.

Extended Twin Engine Operations, ETOPs: also referred to as Extended Diversion Time Operations EDTO. ETOPs/EDTO procedures describe standards to be practiced and complied with for the safe operations of twin engine aircraft to fly more than 60 minutes diversion time from an alternate airfield, and now also for 3 and 4 engine aircraft to operate with a high diversion time from an alternate airfield.

External Audit: an activity where a civil aviation company conducts a compliance audit of another company external to them that supplies or is about to supply services or do business with. As opposed to an internal audit.

Federal Aviation Administration, FAA: the civil aviation regulator for the USA.

Federal Aviation Regulations, FAR's: the civil aviation regulations of the USA, regulated and overseen by the Federal Aviation Administration.

Fiduciary: a person with authority to manage a company in a financially compliant and responsible manner.

Fiduciary Responsibilities: the delegated authority and responsibility to a person or position to ensure a company is managed in a financially compliant and responsible manner, which could also mean ensuring a return on investment is achieved for the investors and shareholders.

Findings: a discovery that during a civil aviation regulatory audit a non-compliant situation is found. The findings are rated 1 to be corrected immediately, 2 to be corrected with in a defined time frame or 3 an observation to be considered.

First Officer: a pilot that reports to and takes direction from to a Captain during a flight. Can be the second in command after the Captain.

Fleet: a group of aircraft operated by a specific operator or airline.

Flight Attendants: licensed cabin crew that operate on a flight.

Flight Crew License: the license or certification that is issued to an aircraft crew member to identify that they are qualified to operate. Issued by the regulator of the aircraft or the regulator of the operation.

Flight Data Monitoring, FDM: the action of monitoring actual flight parameters of an aircraft operation to ensure compliance with the operating standards and the recording of exceedances. Part of the safety management system.

Flight Duty Period, FDP: the civil aviation regulation that states how consecutive days and how many total days per month a crew member can be on duty.

Flight Hours: the number of hours an aircraft has flown from aircraft take off to aircraft landing. This is not the same as aircraft block hours.

Flight Operations Department: the department of an air operator led by the Director of Flight Operations that manages the flight, the flight crew and all associated operational issues.

Flight Operations Quality Assurance, FOQA: that activity of monitoring the quality of flight performance of each flight by using FDM to monitor for compliance with SOP`s and to monitor exceedances.

Flight Time Limitations, FTL: the civil aviation regulation that states how many hours per day and how many hours per month a crew member can operate.

Form 4: the EASA form for the application of the Accountable Manager and the nomination of the Nominated Persons for an approved civil aviation organisation such as an ATO, AOC, AMO or DOA.

France DGAC: the regulator of civil aviation in France. Note that the French are EU members of EASA so adhere to EASA regulations.

General Civil Aviation Authority, GCAA: the regulator of civil aviation in the UAE.

Guidance Material, GM: information documentation on civil aviation used by ICAO, IATA and regulators to give advice and general information on civil aviation issues, procedures, practices and standards.

Harmonization: when NAA`s/CAA`s of different ICAO member states work together in the spirit of Article 37 to make their civil aviation regulations in each state as aligned as possible.

Hazard Identification: the action of identifying hazardous issues in advance of them appearing. Part of a management of change process.

Hazards: a possible risk that could result in an event, incident or accident if not identified and mitigated prior to its appearance.

Human Factors: how people interact with tasks and the possible negative out comes from that interaction.

Implementing Rules, IR`s: the detailed EU civil aviation regulations issued and over seen by EASA.

In Accordance With, i.a.w.: a term implying that the task was carried out i.a.w a defined process or procedure.

Incidents: a negative event that occurred that could have but did not resulted in damage to people or assets.

Income Statement: a financial report on revenue coming into the company.

Initial Airworthiness: the initial engineering and operational safety standard that a Type Certificated aircraft, component or system is designed and certified to at its initial design. For example, i.a.w. FAA FAR 23, 25 or EASA CS 23 or 25.

Inspectors: sheriffs of the NAA`s/CAA`s responsible for regulating and over sight of civil aviation regulation.

Internal Audit: an activity where a civil aviation company conducts a compliance audit of their own company. As opposed to an external audit.

Internal Evaluation Programme, IEP: the US FAA recommended quality management system and quality assurance programme recommended for Part 121 Air Carriers that includes internal audit activities.

International Airline Operations: flights originating in one national territory and terminating in another national territory or over flying in another national air space.

International Air Transport Association, IATA: a trade association for airlines and air carriers with the intention for inter airline cooperation, formed in 1945 in Havana just after the Chicago Convention of 1944 that formed ICAO.

International Civil Aviation Organization, ICAO: a department of the United Nations with member states. ICAO over sees international civil aviation standards and practices formed out of the Chicago Convention of 1944.

IOSA: IATA Operational Safety Audit, is an evaluation system carried out by IATA auditors designed to evaluate the operational management and control systems in place for an airline or aviation operator. All IATA members must be IOSA qualified passing the IOSA. Many insurers or lessors require airlines to be IOSA qualified.

ISO 9001: the international organisation for standards that defines quality management systems, QMS.

Job Description: a document that details the reporting lines, the function, the tasks, the required skills, the required qualifications and the KPI`s for a particular job.

Joint Aviation Authorities, JAA: the predecessor of EASA, but did not have the legal authority as EASA has.

Joint Aviation Requirements, JAR: the predecessor to EU basic regulations on civil aviation and implementing rules, but were not mandated by all EU states as legal regulations.

Just Culture: a corporate system that believes that mistakes are inevitable and those that perpetrate mistakes or errors are not to be blamed or punished, unless it is intentional neglect or wilful carelessness.

Key Performance Indicators, KPI's: important targets that are given to an individual to achieve. Achievement of these targets reflect good performance.

Lean Management: a management technique or method to ensure a minimal head count exists in the company.

Legal Accountabilities: an individual's responsibilities that are legally binding.

Legal Obligation: an individual or company's accepted responsibility that legally must be achieved, such as an undertaking.

Licence: a certification showing that the holder is qualified to operate a vehicle or machine or to accomplish a task.

Machiavellianism: a personality trait that is a self-serving and manipulative to another's.

Maintenance Department: the department of an air operator or MRO, led by the Director of Maintenance that manages the maintenance of aircraft and all associated technical issues.

Maintenance Plan: a calendar plan that shows when maintenance is planned to be accomplished and planned to be completed to support the continuing airworthiness of a fleet.

Maintenance, Repair and Overhaul, MRO: the maintenance engineering action carried out by a Part 145 AMO that is accomplished to ensure an aircraft or fleet remain airworthy. Also referred to as the MRO industry.

Maintenance, Repair and Overhaul Organization: an Approved Maintenance Organisation, AMO, under Part 145, qualified and certified to carry out maintenance on aircraft.

Management of Change, MoC: a management method used to manage changes in an organization. The method includes risk analysis and risk mitigation.

Management Personnel: the FAA term for the senior executives responsible for the management of a civil aviation company such as a Part 121 ACC, the most senior member is referred to as the Accountable Executive. Similar to the EASA Nominated Persons and GCAA Nominated Post Holders.

Management System: the EASA term for the management methods employed for managing the compliance in an approved civil aviation company. Sometimes referred to as the QMS or CMS.

Managing Director, MD: a term used often in the UK meaning the most senior executive responsible for leading all activities in a company. Also referred to as the CEO or GM in some territories.

Mandatory Training: the civil aviation training that is mandatory as per the civil aviation regulations. Such as re currency training for pilots and SEP training for crew.

Manufacturing Facility: a civil aviation company that is certified to manufacture aircraft. Such as Boeing Field in Seattle.

Minimum Equipment List, MEL: one of the mandated aircraft documents for the issuance of a Type Certificate. The MEL details the equipment that must be serviceable for the aircraft to be airworthy and therefore to operate.

Modification: a change to the original Type Certificate Design. Such a change is only permitted in civil aviation when approved by the OEM or a Part 21 approved organisation or through an STC approved by a DER.

Moral Obligation: a duty that is more than a regulated responsibility but has societal or humane importance.

Narcissistic: a personality trait that is a self-serving with disregard to others.

National Aviation Authority, NAA: another term for a Civil Aviation Authority responsible for regulating civil aviation in a particular territory.

National Register: the national register of civil aircraft overseen and regulated by a particular NAA/CAA. The preceding letter or letters is an indicator of which NAA/CAA register the aircraft exists on. For example N is the US FAA, G is the UK CAA, I is the Italian ANAC, A6 is the UAE GCAA.

National Transport Safety Board, NTSB: the branch of the US department of Transport that investigate accidents in the civil air transport industry.

Nominated Person: the person Nominated to EASA by the Accountable Manager in an approved or certified civil aviation company responsible for compliance with the regulations in a particular civil aviation discipline. For example, Flight Operations, Continuing Airworthiness, Ground Operations and so on.

Nominated Post Holder: the person Nominated to the GCAA by the Accountable Manager in an approved or certified civil aviation company responsible for compliance with the regulations in a particular civil aviation discipline. For example, Flight Operations, Continuing Airworthiness, Ground Operations and so on.

Non-conformities: findings discovered during an audit or any other time that shows deviation from a defined or regulated procedure.

Non-regulatory Audit: an audit of procedures and policies that is not related to civil aviation regulations. Such as an inflight service audit.

Occupational Health and Safety, OHS: the discipline of health and safety of staff, employees and customers that are related to regulations and law other than civil aviation regulations often regulated by the DoT. Such as the wearing of protective foot wear.

Original Equipment Manufacturer, OEM: the approved or certified civil aviation company that was responsible for the manufacture of the aircraft or its equipment. Such as Boeing, Airbus, Rolls Royce and so on.

Open Reporting: a corporate culture that encourages and facilitates staff and employees reporting events, incidents, accidents or hazards without the fear of being reprimanded.

OPS SPEC: Operations Specification, issued by the NAA/CAA as part of the Air Operators Certificate, AOC, that details the names of the executive management team as well as the AOC's aircraft type qualifications for operations.

OMA: Operations Manual A, the first of the many manuals required to be in place to apply for an AOC. OMA details the methods, policies and procedures on how the AOC is managed as a safe and compliant operation. It includes the names of the executive management team.

Organisational Structure: the corporate reporting structure of a company.

Oversight: the action and responsibility of overseeing or auditing to ensure continued compliance with procedures or civil aviation regulations.

Package: a group of aircraft maintenance task placed together to be accomplished at the same time. For example, C Chk package, Major Package, 3 year Check package and so on.

Pillars of Quality: a concept in Aviation Quality Management Systems that are Quality Policy, Quality Assurance through audit, Quality Promotion and Continuous Improvement.

Pillars of Safety: a concept in Aviation Safety Management Systems that are Safety Policy, Risk Management, Safety Assurance and Safety Promotion.

Pilot: a person that operates an aircraft.

Power Plant: the part of an aircraft that generates the mechanical force to drive a shaft or to drive a propeller or to generate thrust with the purpose to generate aircraft movement also called an engine.

Private Aircraft Operations: aircraft operations that are for an individual person or group, not for the general paying public. Private Aircraft Operations can be non-commercial or commercial air transport.

Private Category Aircraft: aircraft that are certified for non-commercial operations.

Private Jet: an aircraft that undertakes private aircraft operations for an individual person or group, not for the general paying public. Private Aircraft can be non-commercial or commercial air transport.

Proactive: to take an action in advance of an event or occasion. Such as risk analysis or hazard identification.

Provisional International Civil Aviation Organization (PICAO): the name given to ICAO prior to their ratification in 1947.

Psychopathic: a personality trait that shows anti-social behaviour, egotistical behaviour and a lack of empathy for others.

Q1, Q2, Q3, Q4: calendar quarters of the year.

Quality Assurance: a management system that includes audit, detecting non-conformities and continuous improvement. Not to be confused with quality inspection or quality control.

Quality Management: the use of quality assurance principles and methods to implement a quality management system.

Quality Policy Statement: a statement signed by the Accountable Leader that explains the companies approach to quality assurance and a quality management system.

Ratified: when something is made law.

Reactive: to take an action after an event or occasion. Such as correcting a non-conformity found during an audit.

Regulator: the competent NAA or CAA.

Regulatory Responsibilities: responsibilities or accountabilities to be complied with regarding the civil aviation regulations.

Reliability: the probability that a system or process shall perform as designed, as intended and as certified repeatedly.

Report of a Safety Incident, ROSI: a civil aviation system for mandatory reporting of events, incidents and accidents to the NAA/CAA.

Revenue per Available Seat Kilometre, RASK: a commercial metric used in the airline business to compare airlines with.

Risk Management: a proactive method of assessing an action prior to accomplishing it with the intention to identify risks and hazards associated with that action and then implementing tasks or further actions to mitigate the identified risk or hazard.

Risk Mitigation Actions: a proactive action taken to reduce the impact or severity of an identified risk or hazard.

Root Cause: the core factor that caused a non-conformity, incident, event or defect and should be identified then permanently eliminated to ensure it does not reoccur.

Russia FAVT: the NAA/CAA of Russia.

Safety and Emergency Procedures, SEP: crew procedures to be accomplished to support a safe flight including crew procedures to be accomplished in an event of an incident or accident.

Safety Assurance: part of the safety management system that includes safety audit, detecting non-conformities and continuous improvement.

Safety Champion: the Leadership position that promotes safety and is a good example of a supporter of safety management systems.

Safety Culture: where the spirit and intention of a civil aviation company and its employees is to always practice, support and promote aviation safety.

Safety Management: the use of aviation safety principles and methods to implement a safety management system.

Safety Policy Statement: a statement signed by the Accountable Leader that explains the companies approach to aviation safety and a safety management system.

Safety Promotion: the action of always through broadcasting, actions, training and announcement supporting a safety culture.

Safety Reports: reports of safety-related conditions, incidents or events.

Service Bulletin, SB: a maintenance inspection or modification task to address a design defect or design improvement issued by the aircraft OEM type certificate holder such as Boeing or component manufacturer such as Hamilton Standard. SB`s can be categorised as Alert if safety related and can also be mandated by AD`s.

Serviceability: when an aircraft or its components are airworthy and compliant with the Type Certificate and all systems are working as required by the MEL.

Glossary 169

Simulator: a training devise used by pilots to train on.

Standard Operating Procedures, SOP`s: the procedures and processes that the company, operator or OEM recommend are followed to operate the aircraft or system correctly i.a.w. its designed intentions.

**Standards and Recommended Procedures, SARP`s:** civil aviation procedural guidance documentation issued by ICAO that NAA`s/CAA`s should take to develop civil aviation relations.

Supplemental Type Certificate, STC: an FAA term for a change or modification to the original OEM type certificate, approved by an FAA DER as per FAR 21 subpart e.

Sustainable Company: a company that generates enough revenue to cover all their expenses and financial commitments.

Three Wicked Behaviours: the damaging and destructive personality traits of narcissism, Machiavellianism and psychopathy, occasionally seen in people in leadership roles.

Tool Kit: a collection of strategies or methods to accomplish a task or to take on a challenge.

Toxic Culture: a company spirit that is damaging and destructive or where destructive inter personal behaviours are common place and encouraged.

Toxic Work Environment: a work place that is psychologically damaging and destructive or where destructive inter personal behaviours are common place and encouraged.

Transport Canada, TC: the NAA/CAA of Canada.

Turnaround Time: the time for an aircraft between arriving on stand then departing from stand.

Type Certificate, TC: the certificate issued by the NAA/CAA of country of manufacturer for an aircraft type to show its compliance with the civil aviation regulations for design and manufacturer such as FAA FAR 23 or 25 or EASA CS 23 or 25.

Type Rating: a qualification issued by a NAA/CAA to a pilot or maintenance engineer to show they are qualified on a particular type of aircraft.

Type Rating Examiner, TRE: a pilot qualification issued by the NAA/CAA that certifies them to examine other pilots for a particular aircraft Type Rating.

Type Rating Instructor, TRI: a pilot qualification issued by the NAA/CAA that certifies them to train other pilots for a particular aircraft Type Rating.

UK CAA: the NAA/CAA of the United Kingdom of Great Britain.

Undertaking: a legal promise or commitment.

United Nations, UN: an international organisation formed in 1945 to align countries in different areas of political and economic cooperation to promote peace, security and unity.

Voluntary Report of a Safety Incident, VORSI: a civil aviation system for voluntary reporting of events, incidents and accidents to the NAA/CAA.

World Health Organization, WHO: a part of the United Nations with the intention to align countries in the subject of health to promote common international standards of health and well-being.

Yesterday Today and Tomorrow, YTD: a window in time used as a management technic to review current aviation operations.

Yield: the return on investment generated on a particular airline route.

Index

Note: Page numbers in *italics* indicate figures and in **bold** indicate tables on the corresponding pages.

accountability: civil aviation regulatory 96–97; fiduciary 97; preparation guide for NAA interview 97–99
accountable, definitions of 25
Accountable Managers (AM) 1–2, 24–26, 153–155; budget for 28–29; dashboard of information for 107–112; ethical leadership and 90–95; executive leadership and 54–63; female 118–125; funding safety training or a marketing campaign case study 140–141; job description of 84–89; lawyer's review of responsibilities of 127–138; Nominated Persons, Nominated Post Holders and management personnel and 66–73; occupational and environmental safety and health (OHS) programme and 45–46; Quality Monitoring System (QMS) and 36–40; regulatory responsibilities of 26–36; relationship between Post Holders and 73–78; relationship with the NAA 46–53; safety management system (SMS) and 40–45; selecting effective 113–117; seniority of 28; standards applicable to 29–36; timetable of meetings for 99–107; tool kit for 97
airline crew utilisation maximisation 145
Airworthiness Directive (AD) 144–145
Annexes and Standards and Recommended Procedures (SARPs), Chicago Convention 5–8
aviation regulation: Accountable Managers (AM) and Post Holders (PH) and 1–2; Chicago Convention and the International Civil Aviation Organization and 3–8; civil 26–36; national and civil aviation authorities and 8–13; safety management and 20–22; US federal 13–18

board of directors (BoD) 54–55, 59–63

Canadian Civil Aviation Authority, Transport Canada (TC) 30, 31–32
case studies: adjusting pilot duty time to allow for the arrival of a VIP 143–144; board instructed the CEO/AM to incentivise maximum utilisation by minimum turnaround time, with company target turnaround time of 30 minutes 148–150; CEO/AM of MRO reduces certifying LAE head count to cut salary costs 150–151; CEO attempts to impose a Post Holder appointment on the Accountable Manager 145–146; conducting commercial operations on a private category aircraft 141–143; funding safety training or a marketing campaign 140–141; imposing on the PH continuing airworthiness not to report an AD overrun 144–145; maximising airline crew utilisation without affecting the safety or compromising compliance 145; serving plastic bottles of water on board 151–152; when a board member imposes a pilot's selection on the Accountable Manager 146–147; when the CAA told the new AM that the PH quality was just not competent enough 147–148
Chicago Convention 3–5, 96; on airworthiness of aircraft 16, **16–17**;

172 Index

Articles, Annexes and Standards and Recommended Procedures of 5–8; National Aviation Authorities (NAAs) and 8–13; on operations of aircraft 17–18

chief executive officer (CEO) 54–56; as Accountable Manager 113–114; attempts to impose a Post Holder appointment on the Accountable Manager 145–146; board of directors (BoD) and 59–63; compared to chief financial officer (CFO) 56–59

chief financial officer (CFO) 56–59

chief operating officer (COO) 56

civil aviation organisational structure: correct 79–82; job description of Accountable Manager (AM) in 84–89; wrong 82–84

civil aviation regulatory accountability 96–97, 99–105

civil aviation regulatory responsibilities 26–36; Accountable Managers (AMs) and 26–36; corporation leadership 54–56; fiduciary corporate responsibilities 53–54; financial leadership 56–59

Code of Federal Regulation (CFR), United States 15–16

commercial/financial dashboard 110, *111*

commercial operations conducted on private category aircraft case study 141–143

Compliance Management System (CMS) 37–40; dashboard 107, *110*

corporate leadership 54–56

Covid-19 pandemic 138

dashboards 107–112; commercial/financial 110, *111*; compliance/quality management 107, *110*; operations 107, *108*; safety management 107, *110*; technical 107, *109*

empathy 94–95

ethical leadership: empathy in 94–95; employees and 90–91; environment and 91–93; passengers and 90; values in 93–94

European Aviation Safety Agency (EASA), European Union 12; Accountable Manager role in 26–27, 67; establishment of 14; Nominated Person/Nominated Post Holder continuing airworthiness 68; Nominated Person/Nominated Post Holder-crew training 68; Nominated Person/Nominated Post Holder flight operations department 67–68; Nominated Person/Nominated Post Holder-ground operations 68–69; Nominated Person/Nominated Post Holder-maintenance 69; Nominated Persons/Post Holders and management positions 67–69, **72**; Quality Monitoring System (QMS) 36–40; safety management and 22, 41–45; standards applicable to Accountable Managers in 30–31, 36; structure of regulations under 18, *18*, **19**

Federal Aviation Administration (FAA), United States: on airworthiness of aircraft 16, **16–17**; establishment of 13–14; Nominated Persons/Post Holders and management positions **72**, 72–73; on operations of aircraft 17–18; safety management and 22, 41–45; standards applicable to Accountable Managers in 32–36; structure of regulations under 15–16

female Accountable Managers 118–125; fulfilment and success of 123–125; imposter syndrome and 122; leadership traits of 123; male resistance to 121–122; mentors and role models for 120–121; workplace climate/culture and 120

fiduciary accountability 97, 105–107

fiduciary corporate responsibilities 53–54

financial leadership 56–59

Frances, D. A. 127–138

General Civil Aviation Authority (GCAA), United Arab Emirates 12; Accountable Manager role in 27–28; establishment of 14; Management/Post Holders Qualification Resumes 49–50; Manager/Nominated Post Holder quality and compliance 69–70; Manager/Nominated Post Holder Safety Management Systems 70–71; Manager/Nominated Post Holder Security 71; Nominated Persons/Post Holders and management positions 69–71, **72**; Quality Monitoring System (QMS) 36–40; safety management and 22, 41–45; standards applicable to Accountable Managers in 29–30, 36; structure of regulations under 19–20

Index 173

imposter syndrome 122
International Civil Aviation Organization (ICAO) 3–5, 96; safety management and 20–22, 40–45; safety management system (SMS) and 40–45

job description, Accountable Manager (AM) 84–89
Joint Aviation Authorities (JAA) 14–15
Joint Aviation Requirements (JARs) 14–15

leadership: c-level 54–63, 97; empathy in 94–95; ethical 90–95; values in 93–94; women and 123
legal issues: airline or operator liability 131–132; instances of Accountable Manager issues 135–137; introduction to 127–128; legal framework 128–129; manager's corporate responsibility and 129–131; operational matters 134–135; regulatory considerations 132–134

marketing campaign funding case study 140–141
meeting timetable 99–107; fiduciary accountabilities 105–107; regulatory accountabilities 99–105

National Aviation Authorities (NAAs) 8–13; on Accountable Managers (AMs) 24–26; Accountable Managers (AMs) relationship with 46–53; fiduciary corporate responsibilities and 53–54; occupational and environmental safety and health (OHS) programme and 45–46; preparation guide for Accountable Manager interview with 97–99
Nominated Persons (NP) 1, 153–155; appointment and leadership of 96–97; introduction to 66–73
Nominated Persons (NP) continuing airworthiness 76
Nominated Persons (NP) crew training 75
Nominated Persons (NP) flight operations 75

Nominated Persons (NP) ground operations 75–76
Nominated Post Holders 66–73

occupational and environmental safety and health (OHS) programme 45–46
operations dashboard 107, *108*
organisational structures, civil aviation company *see* civil aviation organisational structure

pilot duty time adjusted for arrival of VIP 143–144
pilot selection 146–147
plastic bottles served on board 151–152
Post Holders (PH) 1–2, 48, 49–50, 153–155; imposing on the PH continuing airworthiness not to report an AD overrun 144–145; introduction to 66–73; relationship between Accountable Manager and 73–78
private aircraft, commercial operations conducted on 141–143

Quality/Compliance Manager 76–77
Quality Management Systems (QMS) 36–40, 74, 96; dashboard 107, *110*

Roper, A. J. F. 4

Safety Management Systems (SMS) 20–22, 40–45, 70–71, 74, 96; dashboard 107, *110*; funding safety training or a marketing campaign case study 140–141
Safety Manager 77–78
salary cost cuts 150–151
selection of effective Accountable Managers (AMs) 113–117

technical dashboard 107, *109*
tool kit, Accountable Manager (AM) 97

VIP arrivals, adjusting pilot duty time to allow for 143–144

For Product Safety Concerns and Information please contact our EU
representative GPSR@taylorandfrancis.com
Taylor & Francis Verlag GmbH, Kaufingerstraße 24, 80331 München, Germany

www.ingramcontent.com/pod-product-compliance
Lightning Source LLC
Chambersburg PA
CBHW052123300426
44116CB00010B/1774